Insuring National Health Care

Insuring National Health Care

The Canadian Experience

Malcolm G. Taylor

The University of North Carolina Press

Chapel Hill and London

Library of Congress Cataloging-in-Publication Data

Taylor, Malcolm G. (Malcolm Gordon)
Insuring national health care : the Canadian experience / by
Malcolm G. Taylor.
p.   cm.
Includes bibliographical references.
ISBN 0-8078-1934-4 (alk. paper).—ISBN 0-8078-4295-8
(alk. paper : pbk.)
1. Insurance, Health—Canada—History.   2. Insurance, Health—
Government policy—Canada.   I. Title.
HD7102.C2T34   1990
368.4'2'00971—dc20   90-50014   CIP

This book is an abridgment and revision of Malcolm G. Taylor's *Health Insurance and Canadian Public Policy: The Seven Decisions That Created the Canadian Health Insurance System* © 1978 The Institute of Public Administration of Canada/L'Institut d'administration publique du Canada (Canadian public administration series/Collection Administration publique canadienne), copublished with McGill-Queen's University Press; and *Health Insurance and Canadian Public Policy: The Seven Decisions That Created the Canadian Health Insurance System and Their Outcomes* (2d ed.), © 1987 The Institute of Public Administration of Canada/L'Institut d'administration publique du Canada (Canadian public administration series/Collection Administration publique canadienne), copublished with McGill-Queen's University Press.

Design by Julianne Mertz Whitling

The paper in this book meets the guidelines for permanence and durability of the Committee on Production Guidelines for Book Longevity of the Council on Library Resources.

Manufactured in the United States of America
94   93   92   91   90   5   4   3   2   1

For

Helen, Deanne, Diana, and Burke

Contents

Tables

Preface

There are four essential criteria on which to evaluate a health services system: the quality and availability of its health care facilities and professional services; the comprehensiveness of the range of insured benefits; the equity of its system of financing, including taxes or premiums and the amounts of deductibles and coinsurance; and, not least, the proportion of the gross national product (GNP) that a comprehensive health services system requires to be allocated to it. Canada's health services system may be excelled by other countries on any one of these criteria, but taking all four together, Canada's system ranks at or near the top.

Such, at least, was the conclusion of Spyros Andreopoulos, editor of the proceedings of the Sun Valley Forum on National Health, which met in Sun Valley, Idaho, in the summer of 1974 to focus on the Canadian health services and insurance system.[1] In the concluding chapter, Professor Theodore Marmor noted that Canada "is enough like the United States to make the effects of Canadian health policies rather like a large natural demonstration or experiment" and concluded that the United States could indeed "learn from Canada."[2] In Chapter 10 below, I also conclude that Canada has much to learn from the United States, particularly in improving its forms of health services delivery.

Since Canada is a federal system, with most health matters falling within the jurisdiction of the constituent provinces, and since professional interest groups exert strong political influence, it was not to be expected that the ultimate objective of a nationwide system would be achieved without extraordinary political battles. And so there were, with warfare along three fronts: among the political parties, between the federal government and the provincial governments, and between the provincial governments and their respective medical associations.

This book is the chronicle of that stormy evolution of the Canadian health insurance system over a half-century. In 1919—when there was also a good deal of interest in health insurance in the United States—the newly elected leader of the national Liberal party, Mackenzie King, had persuaded the delegates to the leadership convention to commit the party to a national health insurance program. It was not until 1940, however, that the federal government began to study the issue in earnest. That exercise culminated in the 1945 offer by the federal government to contribute to a comprehensive range of health services to be administered by the provinces. Because of the financial conditions attached by the federal government, the offer was rejected by several of the larger provinces. It would take another eleven years for the federal government to make (most reluctantly, as we shall see) its second, and more limited, offer of the first stage—national hospital care insurance—which took until 1960 to be accepted by all the provinces. In 1965 the second stage—Medicare—was offered, and by 1971 that program was in effect nationwide. (I am aware of the possible confusion of American readers over the use of this term by Canadians, since it refers to two quite different kinds of programs in the two countries. Throughout, my reference to Medicare is to the Canadian program, which covers the entire population and refers only to medical services.)

As a consequence, all residents of Canada are now entitled to a full range of medical and hospital services without deductibles or coinsurance, supplemented in most provinces by nursing home and home care benefits. During the 1970s total health spending (of which approximately 75 percent is public spending) hovered around 7.0 percent of the GNP and rose in the 1980s to 8.6 percent.

This volume is an abridgment of a larger work, now in a second edition, entitled *Health Insurance and Canadian Public Policy: The Seven Decisions That Created the Canadian Health Insurance System and Their Outcomes* (Montreal: McGill-Queen's University Press, 1988, 563 pp.), which not only traces the history but provides policy analyses of why and how the decisions were made in the complex Canadian federal political system. Readers interested in a fuller account and more detailed analyses of major episodes may wish to consult that edition.

This book is divided into three parts. Part 1 contains two chapters: the first, an introduction to the Canadian political process for readers unfamiliar with the wide differences between the political decision making systems in the United States and Canada; the second, a brief overview of the two programs as they now operate. Part 2 describes the major political events in the turbulent struggle to achieve a universal system and the changes introduced since the programs began. Part 3 examines some major problems and opportunities now confronting both the federal and provincial governments, many of them similar to problems and opportunities in the United States.

Canada's population is relatively small—less than that of California. In order to make statistics on facilities, personnel, and expenditures more meaningful in comparison with U.S. data, readers may wish simply to multiply the Canadian figures by ten.

It is hoped that this short history of the Canadian experience, updating by fifteen years the Sun Valley Forum examination and conclusions, may be helpful in some ways to those concerned with the U.S. health care system. It is Canada's foremost and most solidly supported social program. Politicians would now tamper with or reduce its benefits at their peril.

I am grateful to The Institute of Public Administration of Canada/ L'Institut d'administration publique du Canada and to McGill-Queen's University Press for granting copyright permission to publish this present edition.

Toronto, January 1, 1990   M. G. T.

Abbreviations

AALL	American Association for Labor Legislation
AIP	Association of Independent Physicians
AMA	Alberta Medical Association
AMHP	Alberta Municipal Hospital Plan
BCHIS	British Columbia Hospital Insurance Service
BCMA	British Columbia Medical Association
BCMP	British Columbia Medical Plan
BCMSA	British Columbia Medical Services Associated
CAP	Canada Assistance Plan
CCF	Cooperative Commonwealth Federation
CHA	Canadian Hospital Association
CHC	Community Health Center
CHIA	Canadian Health Insurance Association
CLIA	Canadian Life Insurance Association
CMA	Canadian Medical Association
CPI	Consumer Price Index
CPP	Canada Pension Plan
EPF	Established Programs Financing
FA	Family Allowances
FTA	Free Trade Agreement
GNP	Gross National Product
HIDS	Hospital Insurance and Diagnostic Services
HMO	Health Maintenance Organization
HSO	Health Service Organization
HSPC	Health Services Planning Commission

KODC	Keep Our Doctors Committee
MCIC	Medical Care Insurance Commission
MHSC	Manitoba Health Services Commission
MMA	Manitoba Medical Association
NDP	New Democratic Party
OAS	Old Age Security
OHIP	Ontario Health Insurance Plan
OMA	Ontario Medical Association
OMSIP	Ontario Medical Services Insurance Plan
QPP	Quebec Pension Plan
RCHS	Royal Commission on Health Services
SARM	Saskatchewan Association of Rural Municipalities
SHSP	Saskatchewan Hospital Services Plan
SMA	Saskatchewan Medical Association
TCMP	Trans-Canada Medical Plans
UFA	United Farmers of Alberta
UI	Unemployment Insurance
WHO	World Health Organization

Part One

*The Canadian
Governmental and
Health Care Systems*

Chapter One

The Canadian Political Process

If one were to ask why, when Canadian and U.S. societies appear to be so much alike, Canada has a nationwide, universal program of health insurance but the United States does not, the answers would be both numerous and complex—and inevitably incomplete. Many of the explanations, however, would focus on the differences in the political systems: in the allocation of powers between the national and the state or provincial governments, in the respective legislative bodies and their relationship to the executive, in the systems of political parties and their objectives, in the influence of relevant interest groups, and, not least, on the differences in citizens' views on what the role of government in society should be.

One would also have to delve deeply into the collective social attitudes of the two societies, asking, for example, what the shared feeling of responsibility is among the citizenry for low-income earners, the unemployed, the elderly, and the sick and disabled. It is probably easier in a smaller country of only 26 million persons to be more aware of the disparities of living standards among people because they are seen firsthand every day. To use Michael Harrington's term, in Canada the poor are not invisible. Those living below the poverty line are among the reasons for a wide range of universal income-support programs, including family allowances (FA), a federal program that contributes a monthly payment to mothers on behalf of every child; a comprehensive unemployment insurance program; a universal old-age security program providing monthly payments to everyone sixty-five years of age and older, supplemented for most Canadians by a contributory Canada Pension Plan (CPP) and, for those not having CPP, a guaranteed income supplement;

and welfare payments administered by the provinces and their municipalities, subsidized 50 percent by contributions from the federal government through an omnibus program known as the Canada Assistance Plan (CAP). (For a summary of the various federal programs, see appendix A.) Moreover, in Canada there are exceptionally strong voices in political parties and a host of special-interest groups constantly reminding citizens of human needs and of the obligation to achieve a more secure and equitable society, all the while advocating measures toward those ends.

In contrast to the United States, where the roles of chief of state and head of government are combined in the office of the president, in Canada the prime minister is the head of government, and the chief of state is Elizabeth II, queen of Canada. Except when the queen, on her occasional visits to Canada, may open Parliament by reading the Speech from the Throne, the duties of chief of state are performed by her personal representative, the governor-general, appointed by her on the advice of the Canadian cabinet for a five-year term. The incumbent, until January 26, 1990, was Canada's first woman governor-general, Madame Jeanne Sauve. She was succeeded by the Honorable Ramon Hnatyshyn, a former cabinet minister. The queen's representative in the provincial governments is the lieutenant governor, also appointed by the queen on the advice of the federal cabinet.

Like the United States, Canada is a federal system. It comprises ten provinces and two territories, and its central government is based in the capital district of Ottawa-Hull.

The national Parliament is bicameral with an elected House of Commons (295 members in 1989) and a Senate of 104 members appointed by the prime minister. Ontario (which has 36.2 percent of the population) and Quebec (25.7 percent) are entitled to 24 members each, the four western provinces 6 each, the four Atlantic provinces a total of 30, and the two territories, one each. As an appointed body the Senate has little influence, and therefore the advocacy role within the inner circles on behalf of provinces falls primarily on ministers from the respective provinces in the cabinet. If a province elects no members of the governing party—as often has happened in Alberta, which elected a full slate of Social Credit or Conservative members when the Liberals were in power in Ottawa—a senator from that province may be appointed to a cabinet portfolio.

In contrast to the separation of powers concept that shaped the American constitution, Canada adopted the British "unity of powers" model. The cabinet ministers in charge of the executive departments are members of Parliament, with normally only two or three from the Senate.[1] The cabinet— referred to as the government—remains in power only as long as it can command a majority in the House of Commons. Occasionally the government survives with the support of a third party, as was the case when Medicare was passed in 1966. While a government may stay in power for a maximum of five years, most majority governments seek the most propitious time to call an election around the four-year mark. Minority governments often have no choice, as for example the Conservative government of Prime Minister Joe Clark in 1980, which resigned on the defeat of its budget after only nine months in office.

Ministers have a dual responsibility: each is directly responsible and accountable to the House of Commons for the policies and administration of his or her department, and all have a collective responsibility to support the government's policies, a practice known as cabinet solidarity. Should a minister be unable to support the government on a specific policy, he or she must either be silent or resign. In April 1989, for example, three English-speaking members of the Quebec government resigned when the Quebec National Assembly passed Bill 178 prohibiting the use of English-language signs on outdoor business signs but permitting dual-language signs inside business establishments.

The same strict discipline applies to party caucus members, although occasionally a member may vote against his or her party's position or, more likely, may abstain. On such controversial issues as capital punishment and abortion, House leaders may permit a free vote in which each member votes according to his or her conscience. Recent votes on these two issues are of special interest. Despite majority support for capital punishment in the public opinion polls, Parliament has continued to reject the death penalty. In 1988 the Supreme Court ruled that the sections of the criminal code permitting abortions only in hospitals and only on the recommendation of a committee of three doctors violated the Charter of Rights and Freedoms and were therefore unconstitutional. The government thereupon introduced three alternative resolutions ranging from pro-life to pro-choice, hoping in a free vote to achieve a majority on at least one of the resolutions without itself having to declare a government policy on which its caucus and cabinet were divided. All three resolutions were defeated, so that as of the beginning of 1990 Canada had no abortion law whatever, although a proposed new law has passed second reading in the Commons.

Despite these rare exceptions, the whole process is referred to as responsible government, with the cabinet responsible to the House of Commons, and the members of Parliament responsible to the electorate. Obviously, in such a system there are fewer "veto points" than in the U.S. congressional system. Politics in Canada is not thereby any less conflict ridden; it simply means that broad policy platforms must be promulgated by the political parties and that specific policy stances must be determined by the cabinet and the respective party caucuses. Just as the government claims credit for its achievements, so it is directly accountable for major foul-ups, although it is recognized, of course, that as in any democratic election, national issues may be overshadowed by purely regional concerns or obscured by persuasive political personalities.

Because of majority control in the House of Commons and strict party discipline, the Canadian system provides the elements for strong government. If public opinion is clear, as it has been, for example, in the case of Medicare, with generally at least 80 percent approval ratings in the public opinion polls from 1944 to the mid-1960s, and the governing party can maintain its majority or, in a minority position, be assured of support by a third party, it is certain to get its mandate through the legislative process, with occasional delay by the Senate. The government thus dominates and controls the parliamentary agenda, and almost all legislation is the result of government-sponsored bills. (Specified times are allocated for the introduction of private members' bills; occasionally, one passes.) The party discipline also means that most bills will emerge as statutes in substantially the form in which they were introduced. It is the duty of the loyal opposition to criticize, to oppose, to introduce amendments, and to offer alternative policies in order to present itself as a preferable government in the next election.

Whether a government is indeed strong depends, as in any democracy, on its ability to rally public opinion and on its political will and skills. In terms of the political and management capabilities of individual ministers placed in charge of large bureaucracies, it should be emphasized that the pool of talent from which the prime minister can select his cabinet is restricted to members of Parliament. His choices are further limited by the need to balance a variety of interests: regional, linguistic, ethnic, religious, and, more recently, gender. He only rarely has the freedom, as does a U.S. president, of seeking appointees of known political and managerial competence from outside Parliament.[2] It is well known that not all the political skills essential in winning an election are necessarily synonymous with managerial ability. Opposition demands for a minister's resignation are thus not infrequent but are rarely acceded to.

The daily question period in the House of Commons, in which the opposition requests information and explanations and also attempts to discredit the government's actions, is a severe test of a minister's mettle—enhancing some political reputations and damaging others. It is a reasonably effective device for keeping both politicians and civil servants accountable, although there are numerous critics who believe that the advent of television in the House of

Commons has reduced the effectiveness of the question period by placing more emphasis on the histrionics performed in anticipation of the thirty-second TV news clip than on the substance of the interrogation or of the reply.

The civil service is selected and promoted on the basis of the merit principle and is both impartial and largely anonymous. The senior permanent official in a department (or ministry, as they are now called) is the deputy minister, who is formally appointed by the prime minister. Depending on the size of the ministry, he or she will be served by associate deputy ministers, assistant deputy ministers, and directors general, all organized in a formal hierarchy but with effective informal networks. (Deputy ministers may become better known because they can be called before parliamentary committees to *explain* but not to *justify* a departmental policy; the latter function is the responsibility of the minister.) Following the election of a previous opposition party, there is no wholesale change in senior civil service ranks. Occasionally, a new government may decide to change a key official, such as the deputy minister of finance or the secretary to the cabinet, but there is a remarkable tradition of continuity of senior officials, of nonpartisan advice to ministers of whatever political stripe, and of faithful execution of their policies. Since the beginning of Prime Minister Pierre Trudeau's administration in 1968, the practice of rotating deputy ministers among the various departments has developed, with the result that they have become generalists rather than, as in the pre-Trudeau period, specialists in their respective departments. This practice was seen as a means of reducing the perceived excessive power of the "mandarinate" and of bringing the authority of government more directly under the control of elected ministers.

The provincial legislatures are unicameral, and their governments must also command a majority of votes in the legislature to remain in office. In 1989, among all the provinces, only the Conservative government of Manitoba is in a minority position, having achieved a plurality of seats in the elections of May 1988. The opposite situation occurred in New Brunswick, where, in the elections of 1987, the Liberals defeated the incumbent Conservative government by winning all fifty-eight seats, thus creating the anomalous and unique situation of the legislature's including no official opposition party members. The two opposition party leaders are thus limited to viewing the proceedings from the balcony, submitting written questions to ministers which are then read by the clerk, and airing their criticisms in the media.

The political-party configuration in Canada is complicated by the presence of a third and, occasionally, a fourth party at the national level. The dominant party this century has been the Liberals, with the Conservatives governing from 1911 to 1917 (when a wartime Union government was elected), five years from 1930 to 1935, six years from 1957 to 1963, nine months in 1979–80, and four years from 1984 to 1988, when they held the largest majority ever attained by any political party in Canadian history. On November 21, 1988, the Mulroney government was reelected with a reduced majority nationwide but with an increased majority of seats from Quebec, a situation that does not augur well for a Liberal comeback for some time to their traditional dominance in Quebec. Without substantial support in Quebec, no party has been able to form a majority government in Ottawa.

Two other parties have been active on the political scene in Ottawa, both offshoots of the depression and long-standing populist movements in the western provinces. As is to be expected in a federal system, third parties in the House of Commons have tended to originate in provincial political movements, as was the case of the western Progressive party in the 1920s. In the midst of the depression, a Calgary, Alberta, high school principal, William Aberhart, founded the Social Credit movement, based on the economic theories of Major C. H. Douglas. In May 1935 the network of Social Credit "study groups" was organized into a political party. In the ensuing election in August, every member of the governing party, the United Farmers of Alberta (UFA), was defeated. Social Credit dominated Alberta politics for thirty-six years until 1971 and invariably also sent a Social Credit contingent to Parliament in Ottawa. They were joined in the House of Commons for a time by an indigenous Quebec "social credit" party known as the Creditistes. Both Social Credit wings—Alberta and Quebec—have since faded from the scene.[3]

In 1971 Social Credit was replaced in Alberta by a resurgent Conservative party, which continued to win large majorities in the provincial legislature and to send large Conservative delegations to Ottawa. In the November 1988 elections, Alberta elected twenty-five Conservatives, one New Democrat, and no Liberals.

In British Columbia in 1952 a hastily brokered Social Credit party was formed by disgruntled members of a Liberal-Conservative coalition government which had disintegrated. Under the leadership of W. A. C. Bennett, who was succeeded by his son, William, and later by William van der Zalm, the Social Credit party has dominated British Columbia politics for all but three years, 1972–75, when the New Democratic party (NDP) briefly held office. The British Columbia Social Credit party is "social credit" in name only, never having espoused the economic theories of Major Douglas that provided the original raison d'être of the Alberta Social Credit party, which gradually metamorphosed into a traditional right-wing party, its social-credit ideology left behind.

The other party arising out of depression protest was the Cooperative Commonwealth Federation (CCF), which, unlike the Progressive and Social Credit parties, was organized first as a national party, with formation of provincial affiliates (and the electoral success of three of them) coming later. A coalition of farmers, unionists, and a group of intellectuals who had formed the League for Social Reconstruction met in Regina in 1933 to hold the founding convention of the CCF and issued their avowedly socialist Regina Manifesto. In the national elections of 1935, which saw the Liberals under Mackenzie King returned to office, eight CCF members were elected, under the leadership of J. S. Woodsworth. All eight were reelected in 1940, and two by-elections in 1943 brought the number of CCF members of Parliament to ten. But it was in Ontario in 1943 that the party had its first early success, electing thirty-four members and becoming the official opposition. However, in the following election the party was reduced to third place, where it continued to remain until a brief period 1975–77, when it again became the official opposition.

In the meantime, in June 1942, one of the CCF members of Parliament from Saskatchewan, Tommy Douglas, was elected leader of the CCF in Saskatchewan and resigned his seat in the Commons in time to lead the CCF campaign for the provincial election announced for June 15, 1944. The result was a stunning victory for the CCF, which captured forty-seven of fifty-two seats—a gain of forty. It was the first social-democratic government in Canada. It was the government that introduced the first provincial hospital insurance program in Canada in 1947 and the first Medicare program in 1962.

Following the passage of Medicare legislation in November 1961, Tommy Douglas left the premiership in Saskatchewan to become leader of the recently created national NDP, formed through a formal alliance of the former CCF party and the Canadian Labor Congress. The new party's support would be crucial to the minority Liberal government of Lester Pearson in passing the national Medicare Act in 1966. In the 1988 national elections the NDP elected forty-three members.

The NDP's fortunes in other provinces have been less than encouraging. It has been unable to gain a foothold in Quebec and has garnered only a handful of seats at various times in the Atlantic provinces. As noted, it governed for three years in British Columbia and in 1989 was riding high in the polls. It governed Manitoba for fifteen of the nineteen years between 1970 and 1988 but was reduced to third place in the provincial elections in May 1988.

In Ontario, the Conservatives, under a succession of middle-of-the-road leaders, held sway from 1943 to 1985, the longest tenure of any party in

Canadian history. Following a Conservative leadership convention in April 1985, however, the new premier, Frank Miller, called an election for June 2, 1985. The result was an unforeseen disaster for the Conservatives, with the party standings as follows: Conservatives, 52 seats; Liberals, 48; and NDP, 25. During the next two weeks Liberal leader David Peterson and NDP leader Robert Rae negotiated an accord, whereby the NDP would support the Liberals for a minimum of two years, and the Liberals would initiate legislation outlined in their joint Agenda for Reform, signed on May 28. The Agenda contained the highest-priority items of the NDP platform with which the Liberals could agree.

On June 18 the two parties defeated the Conservatives in a vote of non-confidence, and on July 2, the Liberals formed a new minority government. Over the next two years, most of the objectives of the Agenda for Reform were achieved.

As the NDP was aware, shoring up a minority government can be risky for a third party, even if the goal of progressive legislation, which the NDP had been espousing for years, is achieved. The governing party garners the credit. Following the end of the two-year bargain, the Liberals called an election, which they won by an overwhelming majority of 94 of 130 seats. The Conservatives received even further damage by being reduced from 52 seats to 17, and the NDP, reduced to 19, has survived as the official opposition.

Quebec politics is dominated, of course, by the French Canadian majority. From 1944 to 1960, the authoritarian, patronage-ridden Union Nationale party under Premier Maurice Duplessis was dominant. But a new mood was rising in *la belle province*, and in July 1960 the Liberals, under Jean Lesage, were victorious. The government introduced new, enlightened policies that were dubbed "the Quiet Revolution." The educational system was secularized, a new system of junior colleges was created, and new universities were built. An expanded drive for more autonomy within the federal system was launched. But it was not enough for some, and under the dynamic leadership of René Levesque, who rallied the *indépendantiste* forces, the Parti Quebecois came to power in 1976, dedicated to separation from Canada. Legislation was passed requiring French as the language of the workplace, including management levels, and forbidding English signs on business establishments and highways. By using a variety of instruments of government, such as crown corporations, a vast array of entrepreneurial projects was undertaken to which many of the growing number of university graduates were drawn in a bold campaign to overcome the Anglophones' traditional domination of commerce and industry.

Buoyed by the growing Francophone strength in the public sector and by the expanding self-confidence arising out of its enhanced reputation as an

efficient and honest government, in 1980 the government conducted a refer-
endum on separation from Canada, with the objective of forming a new,
vaguely defined relationship called sovereignty-association. Fortunately for
Canada, the referendum failed, but not without massive intervention by
French-speaking federal cabinet ministers led by Prime Minister Pierre
Trudeau and a Liberal government commitment to add amendments to the
Constitution that would recognize Quebec as a "distinct society"—a commit-
ment not yet fully consummated in 1989. In 1985 the Parti Quebecois was
defeated and succeeded by the Liberal party, once again headed by Robert
Bourassa.

In the accompanying turmoil of the 1976–80 period, approximately
100,000 Anglophones and the head offices of a number of major corporations left the province. Interestingly, the young entrepreneurial executives
who had powered the provincial government's forays in the economy began to
fill the vacuum in the private sector created by the departure of the
Anglophones, and there is now an enterprising cadre of Francophone business leaders who are sparking a renaissance of commercial and industrial
activity in Quebec. It was this new entrepreneurial confidence that led Quebec to support vigorously the Free Trade Agreement (FTA) with the United
States, while the government of Ontario opposed it.

In the 1988 federal elections, the most significant national issue was that of
ratification of the FTA with the United States, the issue that had defeated the
Laurier Liberal party in 1911. The treaty was strongly supported by the
Conservative party and was opposed by the Liberals and the NDP. One of the
major reasons for opposition was fear that Canada's social programs, and
especially health insurance, might be placed in jeopardy as constituting
"unfair subsidies," prohibited by the treaty. The campaign became a virtual
plebiscite on the single issue of the agreement. Although the opposition
parties obtained a majority of the popular vote (53 percent to 47 percent), the
Conservatives won 169 seats, the Liberals 83, and the New Democrats 43.
The FTA was approved by Parliament on December 30 and went into effect
on January 1, 1989.

To the American observer, firmly rooted in a two-party system, the Canadian political-party mosaic must appear to be extraordinarily complex and
volatile. Although the Social Credit party has come and gone, the NDP
remains. It has long been described as the conscience of the nation, never
achieving a majority in the House of Commons but always pushing public
opinion and the government agenda toward a more tolerant, supportive,
egalitarian, and socially conscious society, thus forcing other parties to adopt
(some would say, "steal") much of its social platform.

Another major difference between the governmental systems of the United

States and Canada is the nature of the financial relations between the two levels of government. In a federal constitution, once the division of powers and responsibilities between the federal and the local levels has been settled,[4] the fundamental problem is that of so-called fiscal balance, or ensuring that each order of government has the requisite revenue resources to fulfill those responsibilities. This is an ongoing challenge as the needs of society change. For example, when the constitution—the British North America Act, which united the former colonies of Upper Canada (Ontario), Lower Canada (Quebec), New Brunswick, and Nova Scotia in the "Dominion of Canada"— was established in 1867, no one envisaged that three areas assigned to the provinces—health, education, and welfare—would become growth industries, eventually requiring massive reallocations of revenue sources.

Moreover, once the basic division of tax sources has been determined, the second problem is the unequal fiscal capacities of the respective provinces to finance the same responsibilities; that is, the system must deal with the fact that there are low-income provinces and higher-income provinces—the perennial and ubiquitous problem of the haves and the have-nots.

Canadian governments have dealt with this problem in two ways: (1) through a system of equalization grants from the federal government to the low-income provinces to enable each province to provide an adequate level of public services without resort to rates of taxation substantially higher than those of other provinces; and (2) through the exercise of what is known as the federal spending power, whereby the federal government introduces "shared-cost," or grant-in-aid, programs in fields of provincial jurisdiction that are considered to have a national interest.

Federal equalization grants to low-income provinces have now been in effect in Canada for over a third of a century, and the principle was enshrined in the 1982 Amendments to the Constitution. Unconditional equalization payments to seven of the provinces are substantial, totaling $6.3 billion in fiscal year 1987–88, allocated as follows:

Province	$ Millions
Newfoundland	798.8
Prince Edward Island	154.9
Nova Scotia	715.7
New Brunswick	730.9
Quebec	3,083.4
Ontario	—
Manitoba	575.0

Saskatchewan	244.9
Alberta	—
British Columbia	—
Total	6,303.6

The second strategy, shared-cost programs, also involves massive federal contributions. The four major grant-in-aid programs are hospital insurance, medical care insurance, postsecondary education, and the CAP. Federal payments to the provinces in respect of each of these programs in fiscal year 1987–88 were as follows:

Program	$ Millions
Hospital insurance	8,508
Medical care insurance	3,081
Postsecondary education	5,053
CAP	4,192
Total	20,834

The two approaches—equalization payments and broad-scale, shared-cost programs—have clearly created a different, but more equal, Canada than existed prior to World War II. While disparities among provinces still prevail, they are much smaller than before. Indeed, the equalization payments have been called the glue that holds the nation together.

One other arrangement, respecting income taxation, also differs from U.S. practice. After lengthy negotiations it was agreed by the federal government and all the provincial governments except Quebec that the federal government would collect provincially levied income taxes on their behalf. The federal government establishes a "basic tax" on incomes with certain exemptions and three progressive rate-categories. The provinces accept the same exemptions, and their levies, expressed as a percentage of the basic tax, are added to the basic tax. The federal government collects both taxes and remits the provincial revenues to the provincial governments at no cost for their collection. An advantage of the system is that, except in Quebec, taxpayers are required to submit only one income tax return.

Canada created its governmental structure by borrowing from two great examples: the federal system of the United States and the cabinet system of Great Britain. It did not faithfully replicate the U.S. federal system in that the provinces do not have equal representation in the Senate, and the Senate has little power other than that of minor delay. In that respect it resembles the House of Lords in Britain.

During 1980–84, the period of the last Liberal government in Ottawa, only one Liberal member was elected in the four western provinces, leading to an unprecedented sense of alienation and of exclusion from the corridors of power. One result has been a spate of splinter parties.[5] Another has been a vigorous campaign for a constitutional amendment to create an elected—and more powerful—Senate with equal representation from each province. The objective is captured in the slogan "A Triple-E Senate—Equal, Elected, and Effective." The main thrust for Senate reform was triggered by Alberta and is gaining in support in the West. It will undoubtedly be a continuing item on the agenda of federal-provincial conferences for some time to come.

Finally, it is essential to emphasize the shifting balance of power between the provinces and the federal government. During the Second World War there was, necessarily, an enormous concentration of power in Ottawa and the main theme dominating Canadian politics in the postwar period has been the efforts of the provinces to redress the balance. So successful have the provinces been in this endeavor that the new relationship requires negotiations between near-equals which, in Professor Donald Smiley's apt description, are "akin to those of effective international diplomacy."[6]

The institutional vehicle which has emerged to harmonize and reconcile the often divergent—indeed, frequently conflicting—views of the federal and provincial governments is the federal-provincial conference. Ministers and their officials from federal departments meet with their provincial counterparts—some of them annually, others on an ad hoc basis—to achieve agreement in some area of mutual concern. There are as many as five hundred of these conferences of federal and provincial officials annually. The most important of these are, of course, the Federal-Provincial Conferences of First Ministers (the prime minister and the ten premiers), which deal with issues of the highest order, including proposed amendments to the Constitution and the negotiations to conclude the five-year Tax Agreements that provide for the equalization grants noted above.

Because of the need to coordinate the broad range of negotiations constantly underway, both orders of government have established offices which serve an external affairs or embassy function. At the federal level it is the Federal-Provincial Relations Office, and each provincial government has a ministry of intergovernmental relations. So, over time, an extraconstitutional institution has emerged to lubricate the relationship between the federal and provincial governments. So important has it become that it was formally recognized in the Amendments to the Constitution in 1982.

Governing Canada is not easy. The interests of the five regions are diverse and difficult to reconcile, as are the linguistic rights of the English minority in

Quebec and the French minorities in other provinces. Despite the inherent difficulties, however, Canada is a vigorous democracy. (In the national election in November 1988, fully 75 percent of those eligible voted.) With well-conceived health and social security programs, it is now struggling to find its place in a rapidly changing global economy and confronting new and unpredictable trading and other relationships with its neighbor to the south.

Chapter Two

The Canadian Health Care System

Although it is common practice to speak of Canada's national health insurance program, in reality there are twelve programs, administered by the ten provinces and the two territories, each of them subsidized by contributions from the federal treasury.

In 1942, when the federal government established the first Interdepartmental Advisory Committee on Health Insurance (known as the Heagerty Committee, for its chairman, Dr. J. J. Heagerty),[1] consideration was first given to the options on how a national health insurance program should be structured. In 1940 a constitutional amendment had been unanimously approved by the provinces to create a federally administered, national unemployment insurance program. Moreover, there were increasing demands to replace the means-tested old-age pension, administered by the provinces and subsidized by the federal government, with a national contributory social security program. There were strong views at the federal level, especially in the powerful Department of Finance, that all three programs should be administered and financed in the same way—by the federal government—a strategy that would require two more constitutional amendments.

The alternative was conditional grants-in-aid from the federal government, but on this proposal the Royal Commission on Dominion-Provincial Relations, which had reported in 1940, had sent up conflicting signals. First, it had concluded that "two types of Social Insurance—Unemployment Insurance and contributory Old Age Pensions—are inherently of a national character, but Health Insurance and Workmen's Compensation are not, and that in view of Canadian conditions, these can be financed and efficiently administered by the provinces." The commission also took strong exception to the device of conditional grants. "The experience with conditional grants leads us to doubt whether joint administration of activities by the Dominion and a province is ever a practical way of surmounting constitutional difficulties."[2] But it was obvious that many of the provinces could not independently finance a health insurance program, and therefore federal financial contributions would be essential. The critical question thus became, What form should the federal contributions take?

As the Heagerty Committee examined the alternatives in the light of the political realities, it became clear that there was no possibility of achieving unanimous agreement of the provinces to a constitutional amendment transferring health services administration and financing to the federal government. Relieving the provinces of financial responsibility for the unemployed in 1940 (a plus for the provinces) and for old-age pensions some time in the future (another boon) was one thing, but to give up responsibility for health services was quite another, and so the Heagerty Committee rejected the idea of a nationally financed and administered health insurance program. But it also discounted the objections of the royal commission to conditional grants-in-aid and recommended that method of federal contributions.

As all the provinces had anticipated, the federal government invited the provinces to a Dominion-Provincial Conference on Post-War Reconstruction on August 6, 1945, at which it presented a wide-ranging series of policy and program proposals, including social security and health insurance.[3] The financing formula for health insurance was to be grants-in-aid for medical, hospital, dental, pharmaceutical, and nursing benefits, to be introduced in two stages. But the conference collapsed because of the linking of federal financing to transfers of major tax fields from the provincial governments to the federal government, and the health insurance proposals were, for a decade, thrust into limbo.

In 1957, when the Hospital Insurance Act was passed, and in 1966, when the Medical Care Insurance Act became law, the conditional grant-in-aid became the foundation of federal contributions to the two provincially administered health services programs. For more detailed accounts, see chapters 6 and 8.

The Current Programs

As one would expect, the government programs were shaped by then existing structures and practices in the Blue Cross and Blue Shield plans. Indeed, when the Saskatchewan Hospital Services Plan (SHSP) was being planned, a Blue Cross consultant was retained by the Health Services Planning Commission (HSPC). There were differences, of course, for the government programs were required to insure the total population at one stroke, whereas the voluntary plans could grow incrementally. Moreover, although most health matters fall exclusively within provincial jurisdiction, the federal government would necessarily attach conditions to its grants in order to ensure accountability for the expenditure of federal tax revenues.

Five conditions were imposed by the federal government with respect to its contributions. These are now enshrined in the Canada Health Act (1984), which consolidated the Hospital Insurance Act of 1957 and the Medical Care Insurance Act of 1966 and added a number of amendments.

Comprehensive Benefits

The Hospital Insurance and Diagnostic Services (HIDS) Act specified the services to be provided. In general, they were all the "medically necessary" inpatient services a hospital was equipped and staffed to provide at the standard ward level, including professional radiological and laboratory services. Federal cost-sharing also applied to such outpatient services as a provincial plan determined. In the eastern provinces these included radiological and laboratory services, but in Ontario and the western provinces these two services were not included as insured outpatient benefits because of the provinces' inability to negotiate satisfactory agreements with the radiologists and pathologists until the advent of Medicare in the late 1960s.

It should be noted that the Hospital Insurance Act did not include mental hospitals, since these were already largely financed by provincial governments. Larger general hospitals then began adding psychiatric wards where the costs would be shareable. Consequently, a serendipitous effect of the exclusion of mental hospitals was the incorporation of a major portion of psychiatric services into the mainstream of health care.

The Medicare Act also required comprehensive "medically necessary" benefits including the services of both general practitioners and specialists. Some services, such as elective cosmetic surgery, could be excluded, but even these are usually paid for if certified as medically necessary. The services of dental surgeons are also insured benefits when inpatient dental surgery is required. Provinces have added other benefits; Appendix D lists the insured benefits available in Ontario.

Universality

The original legislation had required the provinces to achieve entitlement to benefits of a minimum of 95 percent of their population. However, with the consolidation of the two acts in the Canada Health Act, the requirement was raised to 100 percent. This created no problems for the seven provinces financing their programs from general revenues (they had already achieved universal coverage for all bona fide residents) but did create problems for the three (Ontario, Alberta, and British Columbia) continuing to use premiums when uninsured patients seek medical services. In Ontario, for example, if a doctor submits a bill to the Ontario Health Insurance Plan (OHIP) on behalf of a patient who is in arrears in payment of his or her premiums, the account will be paid by OHIP, which will then endeavor to collect the past-due premiums.[4]

Accessibility

The Medical Care Insurance Act endeavored to limit financial barriers to accessibility by specifying that to receive federal contributions,

the plan provide(s) for the furnishing of insured services upon uniform terms and conditions . . . by the payment of the cost of insured services in accordance with a tariff of authorized payment established pursuant to provincial law . . . on a basis that provides for reasonable compensation for insured services rendered by medical practitioners and *that does not impede or preclude, either directly or indirectly, whether by charges made to insured persons or otherwise, reasonable access to insured services by insured persons.* (emphasis added)

Quebec had outlawed extra-billing by physicians from the beginning of its program in 1970. But the practice was prevalent in Alberta, Ontario, and Nova Scotia, and of lesser consequence in several other provinces. Aggregate additional charges by doctors' extra-billings across Canada were estimated at approximately $100 million in 1983. Two federal public inquiries had criticized the practice, one of them recommending that provinces permitting it be penalized by the withholding of part of the federal payments. Extra-billing, or "the erosion of Medicare," as it was called, was a major issue in the 1979 and 1980 elections. Consequently, on the return of the Liberals to power, Parliament unanimously passed the Canada Health Act, which included provisions authorizing the federal government to deduct from its payments one dollar for every dollar extra-billed by physicians or collected in "user fees" that governments had authorized hospitals to charge. If these charges were abolished within three years, the withheld amounts would be paid retroactively.[5]

By 1987 all provinces were in compliance, so that the insured benefits are, indeed, financially accessible even to those with the lowest incomes, with no extra-billing by physicians and no user fees for hospital services, although extra charges for semiprivate and private hospital room accommodation and for telephone and television services are authorized. For details, see chapter 9.

Portability

It was imperative, if the concept of a nationwide system was to be achieved, that benefits be available to a highly mobile population, everywhere in the country. There were three dimensions to the problem: (1) residents of one province moving permanently to another province; (2) travelers to another province, including students attending university outside their home province; and (3) travelers to other countries, requiring either emergency services or services unavailable in their home province. The first was resolved by establishing a uniform waiting period of three months before the new residents became eligible for services (and liable for payment of premiums, if applicable) in the new province, during which time the province of previous residence would be responsible for any expenses incurred. The second and third aspects were complicated by the fact of different benefit schedules among the various provinces. These arise in two ways.

First, differences exist among the provincial medical association fee schedules. Although, in general, the fee schedules are similar, those in British Columbia, Ontario, and Nova Scotia are considerably higher than those in the other provinces. Moreover, in the annual negotiations between the government agencies and the respective medical associations, different settlements are arrived at, so that, for example, the same surgical procedure may command a different fee in several provinces. The health insurance agencies in nine provinces reimburse out-of-province patients according to the fee schedule of the host-province. As yet, however, Quebec does not, paying only in accordance with its own, uniformly lower fee schedule. This exception has caused a good deal of acrimony, particularly among doctors in the Ottawa, Ontario, area, where a substantial number of Quebec patients receive services. Negotiations are underway to improve the situation.

Second, although hospitals are paid on the basis of an annual total budget, per diem rates are calculated for charges to or on behalf of nonresident patients; these rates vary, of course, among different sized hospitals and between teaching and nonteaching hospitals. Extensive negotiations have taken place over the years among provincial and federal representatives to smooth out the variations, although total success has not been achieved.

On the third aspect, of patients receiving services in a foreign country (mainly the United States), a variety of arrangements obtains. In many cases where Canadians live close to a U.S. center, the provincial agency has arranged with the U.S. hospitals to pay directly their accounts in full, without the patient's being required to pay the account and seek reimbursement. Because of the number of Canadians wintering in Florida, such arrangements have also been made with Florida hospitals. In some cases, however, the patient is liable for the difference between the province's benefit schedule and the foreign hospital's charges. The problem involves hundreds of thousands of annual transactions but has generally been alleviated, although it is probably not one that will ever be devoid of some red tape, delays, and frustrations. The principle of portability within Canada, however, contributes greatly in melding twelve separate insurance administrations into a national program.

Public Administration

In announcing the principles on which the federal contributions would be based, Prime Minister Pearson said, "I think it will be readily agreed that a Federal contribution can properly be made available only to a plan which is publicly administered, either directly by the provincial government *or* by a provincial non-profit agency."[6] The second alternative was offered in recognition of the fact that ever since the announcement of its Statement of Principles by the Canadian Medical Association (CMA) in 1934, administration by an "independent, non-political," representative commission had been a central issue in every province when health insurance was discussed or proposed. It had also become a strongly endorsed principle of the Canadian Hospital Association (CHA). Indeed, the principle was also supported by both the Canadian Federation of Agriculture and the Canadian Labor Congress on the grounds that if the programs were administered by the Department of Health, they would be dominated by the medical profession. Accordingly, several provinces (Alberta, Manitoba, Ontario, New Brunswick, Nova Scotia, and Prince Edward Island) had adopted the commission form of administration in setting up their hospital care insurance plans. None was as independent, of course, as the special-interest groups had desired for all were responsible to the minister of health and the government, which controlled their budgets and set major policies.

When the first Medicare program was introduced in Saskatchewan in 1962, administration was assigned to a commission. Following the national Medicare Act, several provinces adopted that model: Alberta simply enlarged its Hospital Services Commission, as did Manitoba. Nova Scotia appointed another commission, as did Prince Edward Island and Newfoundland. All other provinces assigned both responsibilities to the Department of Health. In the last few years, however, a number of governments, feeling that the commissions gave too much influence on government policy to the provider interest groups, have abolished the commissions, assigning administrative responsibility to the health department and relying on advisory committees and frequent meetings with the executive committees of the respective interest groups for liaison and advice.

One of the salutary results of the nonprofit administration model is the extraordinarily low overhead administration costs—2.5 percent of total expenditures on the medical and hospital care insurance plans. We now examine methods of paying for health services, methods of financing the systems, and the health services systems that have been created.

Methods of Payment

Physicians

The vast majority of all physicians in Canada are paid by fee-for-service in accordance with official fee schedules negotiated between the provincial governments and their respective medical associations. With few exceptions the administering agencies (with strong influence from the treasury departments) simply negotiate the annual percentage increase to be added to the existing fee schedule. The allocations to general practitioners and among the various specialties is the prerogative of the medical association's tariff committee. Negotiators for the medical care plan undoubtedly have certain influence when some fee schedule items appear to be out of line.

Unfortunately for the provincial treasurer's budget projections, the total medical care expenditures invariably exceed the negotiated percentage increase because of the annual increases in the number of physicians and, frequently, in the volume of services provided by practitioners. For example, recent experience in Ontario indicates an annual increase in the number of physicians ranging from 3.0 to 4.5 percent, and an average annual increase of 2 percent in the number of services per physician.

There are exceptions to the standard practice of fee-for-service payments described above: per capita payments to health service organizations (HSOs); negotiated block payments to community health centers; isolation payments for doctors in northern communities; and in Quebec, a higher fee schedule for new graduates practicing in northern areas and a lower fee schedule for those setting up practice in urban centers.

Hospitals

At the beginning of the hospital programs, most hospitals' budgets were approved on a line-item basis, but this method induced a good deal of conflict and charges of undue bureaucratic control. Gradually, most provinces moved to what came to be called global budgets in which the plan administrators (again, with substantial treasury influence) annually announce the percentage increase in the base payment to be added to the existing budgets, giving hospital administrators more flexibility in allocating resources within their budgets. Adjustments are also made for changes in workloads (based on patient days), for changes in volume of services for life-support systems (dialysis, cancer chemotherapy, cardiac surgery, etc.), and for approved new and expanded programs. Hospitals are then paid in monthly or semimonthly installments. One result of the global budget system, now under intense scrutiny in several provinces, is that some hospitals shuffled their resources and launched new programs without approval by the Health Ministry, often duplicating programs in nearby hospitals and occasionally giving rise to deficits.

It should be noted that, in principle, the hospital plan is paying only for standard ward care for all insured patients whether in standard, semiprivate, or private wards. Accordingly, in most provinces hospitals are permitted to retain a substantial share of the revenues accruing from higher rates for superior accommodation. (If a patient must be isolated, however, he or she will be assigned to a private room without additional charge.)

In addition, to emphasize the "essential service" role of the hospitals to meet the needs of those unable to afford the charges for superior accommodation, most provinces have set limits on the proportion of beds in superior accommodation—a rule easily enforced through the Hospital Planning Division, which must approve hospitals' designs, and the substantial government provision of the capital costs. A high proportion of private and semiprivate extra charges are insured through Blue Cross, commercial insurance, and pension plans.

The method of paying hospitals in twelve or twenty-four installments eliminates an extraordinary amount of administration costs inherent in paying hospitals on a per-case basis. Although large hospitals maintain elaborate accounting systems based on "cost centers" for internal financial control, they do not have to price each item of service or prepare itemized patients' accounts. This process reduces both the hospital's internal administration costs and the overhead insurance administration costs.

Methods of Financing

The Federal Contribution

According to the Canadian constitution, the federal government cannot earmark a federal tax for health insurance because such services fall within provincial jurisdiction. Instead, the federal government must make its contributions from its general revenues. Prior to 1977, such contributions were 50 percent of the aggregate of all federally approved, provincial expenditures on the two programs. With experience, objections to this formula were raised by both parties. The provincial governments resented federal auditing to determine shareable costs and claimed that the fact of federal sharing of only two of many health programs distorted provincial priorities and decision making. For its part, the federal government was alarmed over its lack of control of its health budget (especially in the high-inflation period of the early 1970s), since it was required to match whatever expenditures provincial governments decided upon.

In 1976 the federal government offered to vacate 12.5 points of personal income tax and 1 percent of corporation income tax, creating "tax room" which the provinces could occupy. This allowance was calculated to equal one-half of the 1975–76 federal contribution to the two programs. The other half was to be a cash grant, to be escalated annually in accordance with a three-year moving average of increases in the GNP. After extended and controversial negotiations, the proposal was accepted at a federal-provincial conference on December 14, 1976, and the details were incorporated in the Federal-Provincial Fiscal Arrangements and Established Programs Financing Act, which came into force on April 1, 1977.[7]

The major effect of the act is that the federal government's contributions are no longer geared to provincial expenditures; provincial governments are therefore solely responsible for expenditures on medical and hospital care that exceed the annual percentage increase in the GNP. It also means that the federal government's contributions no longer have any steering effect on provincial governments' decision making. And the federal government got the handle on its health budget that it so strongly wanted.

Also included in the new Established Programs Financing Act was a new federal grant of twenty dollars per capita (also escalated annually in accordance with increases in the GNP) to assist provinces in providing less expensive support services including nursing home intermediate care, adult residential care services, converted mental hospitals, home care services, and ambulatory care services. By 1985–86 the Extended Health Care Grant totaled $2.87 billion.

Provincial Financing

As the provincial governments introduced their hospital insurance plans in the late 1940s and 1950s, most took advantage of the fact that the Blue Cross and Blue Shield plans and the insurance industry had "educated" residents to pay premiums for their insured health services. But British Columbia, which had introduced its hospital care insurance plan in 1949, encountered so many problems that in 1954 it abandoned the premiums system and increased its retail sales tax from 3 to 5 percent. Evidence of *bona fide* residence of one year provided entitlement to services. Quebec also rejected the premiums system, levying a payroll tax on employers and employees. Nova Scotia, like British Columbia, increased its sales tax. New Brunswick used premiums for some years and then abandoned them. Manitoba and Saskatchewan later abandoned premiums and increased their income tax levies, with Manitoba also levying an employer payroll tax on payrolls over fifty thousand dollars. Interestingly, British Columbia, which had been the first to switch to sales tax for its hospital insurance plan, reintroduced premiums for its Medicare plan. Only three provinces—Ontario, British Columbia, and Alberta—now rely on premiums, and these yield, respectively, 8, 22, and 38 percent of the costs of the three programs. (The low yield in Ontario is one of the major reasons for switching to a payroll tax in 1990.)

In 1988 the annual premium rates in the three provinces were as follows:

Province	Single	Couple	Family
British Columbia	$378	$624	$724
Alberta	$216	—	$432
Ontario	$356	—	$712

Recognizing that premiums are a regressive tax, all three provinces make provision for exemption of some groups and subsidies for others. For example, in Ontario all persons aged sixty-five and over are exempt from payment of premiums. All persons receiving social assistance (5.6 percent) are also exempt, and a further 7.5 percent receive premium subsidies. Some 11 percent pay direct, and 58 percent pay through group enrollment, many of them subsidized by employers.

Costs of the Programs

The costs of the programs are shown in table 1. In the thirteen-year period 1976–77 to 1988–89, they have increased from $8.0 billion to $25.9 billion. But what is especially remarkable is the wide variation in annual percentage

Table 1.
Federal and Provincial Expenditures on Hospital and Medical Services, 1976–77 to 1988–89

Fiscal Year	Hospital Services ($ million)	Medical Services ($ million)	Total ($ million)	Percent Increase
1976–77[a]	5,925	2,050	7,975	—
1977–78[b]	6,175	2,256	8,431	5.7
1978–79	6,733	2,551	9,285	10.1
1979–80	7,372	2,811	10,183	9.7
1980–81	8,575	3,287	11,862	16.4
1981–82	10,141	3,832	13,973	17.8
1982–83	12,052	4,440	16,492	18.0
1983–84	12,977	5,063	18,040	9.4
1984–85	13,635	5,474	19,110	5.9
1985–86	14,463	5,993	20,457	7.0
1986–87	15,734	6,725	22,459	9.7
1987–88[c]	16,816	7,402	24,219	7.8
1988–89[c]	17,991	7,957	25,948	7.1

Source: Health and Welfare Canada.
[a] Last year of 50-50 cost sharing.
[b] First year of block funding.
[c] Preliminary.

increases. An increase of 21 percent in 1975–76 had helped to trigger the federal government's income and price control program in October 1975, and the effects are clearly visible in the decline to 5.7 percent in 1977–78. With the ending of controls in 1978, the pendulum began to swing back to the earlier rates of increase, reaching 18.0 percent in 1982–83, when the rest of the economy was in recession. But the reductions in federal funding beginning in 1982 and the deficit position of many provinces ushered in a new period of restraint in 1984–85; rates of increase fell to 5.9 percent in 1984–85 and have been held to less than 10 percent since then. (A more detailed examination of program expenditures appears in chapter 10.)

Facilities and Services

As part 2 elaborates, bringing the national-provincial health insurance system into being was a long, tortuous, and massive undertaking, mobilizing resources and money on a scale seen only during World War II. Indeed, the undertaking *was* war in a sense—the funding and creation of civilian resources to fight the scourge of disease, the trauma of accidents, and the care required for inevitable death. In this section I consider the development of resources—physical and human—that enable the programs to function.

In the late 1940s and early 1950s, Canada began a vigorous campaign to renew and expand its social capital, neglected and frustrated by the depression and the war. Spurred by the federal Hospital Construction Grant under the 1948 National Health Grants Program, in the short space of five years, 1948–53, a total of 46,000 new hospital beds was added. Construction continued, so that at the end of the decade, when the national hospital insurance program became fully operational, Canada had approximately 96,000 acute-care beds and 19,000 long-term beds, or, respectively, 5.4 and 1.1 beds per 1,000 population. In the exuberant 1960s, 22,000 acute-care beds were added, reflecting an increasing population and the fact of universal hospital care insurance.

But the beginning of a new trend was evident, as 10,000 long-term beds were added. In the 1970s the trend was even more pronounced, as the number of short-term beds was reduced by 6,000, while the stock of long-term beds was increased by 20,000. By 1986 Canada had a total of 92,000 short-term beds and 63,800 long-term beds (3.6 and 2.5 per 1,000), or a total of 6.1 beds per 1,000.

Hospital utilization followed the same trend. Admission rates increased from 143.4 per 1,000 in the mid-1950s to 154.7 in 1960, a rise of only 7.9 percent. This figure is remarkably low, given that the proportion of the population insured had more than doubled. The rate rose to 165.9 per 1,000 in 1970 and then began to decline, reaching a low of 143.0 per 1,000 in 1986, just slightly under the rate of the mid-1950s. The decline in admission rates was accompanied, of course, by increases in surgical day care program visits, which reached a total of 1,166,990 in 1986.

Several factors or forces (some of them offsetting) were at work here: a gradually aging population with its concomitant needs for long-term care and the resulting increase in chronic care and nursing home beds; increasing use of outpatient and ambulatory facilities, provision of new facilities in underserviced areas, new high technology, and, not least, a widening perception that Canadians had placed too much emphasis on inpatient hospital care (in part because that service had been the first to be universally insured) and that resources should now be redeployed to preventive measures, health promotion, and noninstitutional care.

Health Services Personnel

When the Royal Commission on Health Services (RCHS) was appointed in 1961, the physician-population ratio in Canada as a whole was 1:857, ranging from a high of 1:758 in British Columbia to a low of 1:1,990 in Newfoundland. Several factors guided the commission in framing its recommendations with respect to medical personnel: the national population projections prepared by its consultants, which, based on the high birthrates and immigration of the 1950s, turned out to be grossly exaggerated (the estimate for 1986 was about 5 million too high and was due mainly to the rapid decline in the birthrate commencing in 1965—what Robert Evans has labeled "the great obstetrical contraction"); the serious disparities in medical personnel among the provinces; the higher utilization of medical services by insured persons and the fact that under universal Medicare the number of insured persons would be more than doubled; and the constant warning of medical association spokesmen that the introduction of medical care insurance, which they pejoratively referred to as socialized medicine, would lead to an exodus of doctors from the country. This prediction was reinforced during the commission's deliberations by the departure of at least 10 percent of Saskatchewan's doctors on the introduction of that province's Medicare plan in July 1962 and of another two hundred during the next eighteen months, although all had been replaced by mid-1964. Taking all these factors into account, the commission recommended that five new medical schools be created and that several existing schools be expanded.

With the financial assistance of the Health Resources Fund, introduced by the federal government in 1966 for expanding educational facilities for health sciences personnel, four new medical schools were launched and twelve others were expanded and upgraded, increasing Canada's medical-school capacity from 880 graduates in 1966 to 1,796 in 1983, an increase of more than 100 percent.

Meanwhile, however, the predictions of a mass emigration of doctors had proved wholly unfounded. From a low of 242 doctors moving abroad in 1975, the numbers increased gradually to a high of 663 in 1978 (the third year of income controls) and gradually declined to an average of 416 from 1980 to 1982. In contrast, the number of physicians immigrating reached unprecedented levels. In the five years prior to the introduction of Medicare in all provinces, the annual number of immigrant doctors averaged 470. Beginning in 1970 the numbers began to rise, reaching a maximum of 1,170 in 1973. At the request of a number of provinces, immigration regulations were changed to restrict the flow, and from 1981 to 1985 annual immigration averaged 375.

These several factors resulted in annual increases in the physician-population ratio in every province. The total number of active civilian physicians, including interns and residents, increased in the decade 1975–84 from 39,104 to 49,916, while the physician-population ratio in Canada as a whole increased from 1:585 to 1:506. The ratios ranged from 1:476 in Quebec and 1:485 in Ontario and British Columbia to lows of 1:765 in New Brunswick and 1:803 in Prince Edward Island. Nevertheless, there has been significant improvement in the less-well-served provinces, with increases over the decade in New Brunswick of 26.4 percent, 31.6 percent in Prince Edward Island, and 34.0 percent in Newfoundland. The disparities are no longer as glaring.

Although reductions have been imposed on the size of entering classes in several medical schools and in internships and residencies in a number of provinces, the ratio continues to rise. In 1988 there was one active civilian physician for every 491 Canadians.

The largest single group in the health services sector is, of course, the professional nurses, numbering in 1985 over 110,000 in full-time practice, and 84,000 part-time. Their numbers increased 38.5 percent in the period under review, which exceeded even the 32.7 percent increase in physicians. Again, as with physicians, the ratio of nurses to population varied from province to province, but the gap between the low- and high-income provinces was substantially reduced.

Perhaps no other professional group has been subject to so many changes as nurses have: the transfer in most provinces of their basic education from hospital-based schools of nursing to community colleges, assumption of responsibility for many procedures previously the domain of physicians, and greater demands for specialization in skills for intensive care, dialysis units, and other high-tech areas. One result of this upgrading of the role of nurses has been rapid expansion in baccalaureate courses in universities. In 1985, for example, there were 1,957 graduates, a 47.7 percent increase over 1975. Many nurses also completed graduate degrees in health services administration, and others completed doctoral programs for teaching and research.

A concomitant of the need for more highly specialized nurses working under unusually stressful conditions is that there is now being generated a shortage of nurses to work in intensive-care units and high-technology surgery, a problem that is partially the result of intensive recruiting of Canadian nurses by U.S. hospitals. As a result, waiting lists for such operations as open-heart surgery have lengthened, since some intensive care beds have had to be temporarily closed.

While physicians, nurses, and dentists have traditionally been the core of the health services delivery system, the explosion in medical technology and its increasingly widespread use have introduced new, specialized occupations and expanded others. Health and Welfare Canada now reports on twenty-seven different occupations in its annual *Health Manpower Inventory*. Not all these will be referred to here, but in the 1975–85 period some increases were spectacular. At the end of 1985 there were 409 audiologists (an increase of 243 percent over 1975), 4,664 dietitians (91 percent increase), 2,776 respiratory technologists (162 percent increase), 5,758 dental hygienists (267 percent increase), 19,293 laboratory technologists (24 percent increase), 10,339 radiation technologists (35 percent increase), 2,463 occupational therapists (87.7 percent increase), and 6,759 physiotherapists (54 percent increase). The list goes on, but enough has been shown to indicate the variety of health occupations and their extraordinary expansion, made possible, in the main, by publicly financed educational and health services systems.

From the foregoing it is clear that there are two major components of a health services system: (1) the organizational and financial arrangements that garner the funds and create the mechanisms to pay for services and confer entitlement to services on residents; and (2) the vast complex of facilities and personnel that provide the services. During the early 1950s there were many debates about which should come first: should hospital insurance be delayed until adequate facilities and personnel were in place? Or should trust be placed in the expectation that once effective demand had been assured through the insurance system, the necessary resources would be readily mobilized? Prime Minister St. Laurent, who was opposed to the whole idea, held firmly to the first position. But others argued that "sometimes you have to get yourself into a mess in order to get yourself out of a mess." So Canada went ahead—and there was no "mess." It was surprising that, although the proportion of insured persons had more than doubled overnight, the annual rates of increase in hospital utilization were lower after the introduction of national hospital insurance than before. Moreover, a similar scenario evolved with the introduction of Medicare, which brought such a rapid increase in medical personnel that most observers are now convinced that Canada has a surplus of physicians which will only become more serious, a subject to be examined in chapter 10.

This chapter has focused on the "inputs" to the system: the creation of the organizational and administrative infrastructure, the various ways in which financial resources are collected and disbursed, and the range of facilities and professional personnel that provide the services. What Canada does not have, however, is any accurate measure of "outcomes." We simply do not know what the impact of the expenditure of $30 billion a year has been on the health status of the population. There are some indicators, of course. Infant mortality rates have fallen from 10.4 per 1,000 in 1981 to 7.9 per 1,000 in 1985. Life expectancy has increased slightly from 69.3 years for men in 1971 to 72.9 years in 1985; and for women over the same period from 76.4 years to 79.8 years. What is not known is whether these improvements are the consequences of the health services system or simply of better nutrition, housing, and life-styles.

In 1979 Health and Welfare Canada and Statistics Canada mounted what was to have been a continuing household health survey. But in a massive budget-cutting exercise by Prime Minister Pierre Trudeau in 1979, the survey was canceled, so at present no one knows what a cost-benefit analysis would reveal.

While the experts and the provincial treasurers may be dismayed by the lack of concrete evidence of the programs' worth, that is not the case with the attitude of the general public. No other government program enjoys such overwhelming support. In the outpouring of debates and discussions on the U.S.–Canada FTA in the eight weeks preceding the election on November 21, 1988, expressions of fear of its impact on Medicare and other social programs were daily front-page news. The proponents of the agreement maintained that the fears were groundless. Since the agreement has been ratified, those who opposed it on the grounds of its threats to Canada's social programs can take only a wait-and-see attitude. Whatever the future holds, the national debate had one unanticipated and salutary outcome: whereas Canadians had tended to be complacent and take Medicare for granted, they are now acutely aware of how fortunate they are to have such programs and are united in their determination that the programs must be supported and protected.[8]

Part Two

*The Evolution
of the Canadian
Health Care System*

Chapter Three

Pre–World War II

The evolution of the Canadian system of organizing and paying for health care services has been a long, complex, and stormy struggle, often beset with extraordinary conflict and influenced greatly by the political and economic vicissitudes and crises of this turbulent twentieth century. Perhaps the most striking phenomenon in the achievement of this great humanitarian objective is that the strongest impetus to its development was war, illustrating again the paradoxical nature of humankind, so brilliantly analyzed by Carl Jung as a contradictory mix of the forces of evil and of good, of darkness and of light, of despair and of hope.

World War I contributed in two ways. First, recruiting for the armed forces revealed the abysmal state of health of young Canadian males, with rejection rates for preventable or remediable conditions in some areas ranging as high as 50 percent—alerting the nation to its lack of adequate medical care. Second, Canadians deployed overseas were introduced to the British National Health Insurance program launched by Prime Minister Lloyd George in 1912, thereby triggering, as we shall see, a spate of postwar political actions in Canada.

But World War II did more, for in the midst of that storm of violence, suffering, and death there were lightning flashes that illuminated the possibilities of recreating a society that was more humane, caring, and compassionate, one that reflected humankind's idealism, reverence for life, and desire to ameliorate the human condition. The lightning flashes were few, but they lit up the spirit of the free world with the brilliance of the northern lights as President Roosevelt declared the Four Freedoms, Churchill and

Roosevelt proclaimed the Atlantic Charter, and Sir William Beveridge in Britain and Dr. J. J. Heagerty and Dr. Leonard Marsh in Canada released their famous reports on health and social security.[1] The story of health insurance in Canada is largely about the struggle for the achievement of the ideals expressed in those documents, and it is noteworthy that such battles as did occur were primarily over means and not over goals.

The main events to be traced span a period of about one hundred years, but before beginning that contemporary survey it may be of interest to place the review in even longer historical perspective by noting that the first known medical care prepayment contract in Canada was signed over three centuries ago.

On March 3, 1655, a contract was drawn up and duly notarized before the clerk of Ville-Marie on the Island of Montreal.[2] There, Urbain Tessier dit Lavigne and sixteen others, "acting for themselves and their families and children," and Etienne Bouchard, master surgeon of Ville-Marie, came to the following agreement:

> That the said Bouchard undertakes and obligates himself to dress and
> to physic, of all sorts of illness whether natural or accidental, except for
> the plague of smallpox, leprosy, epilepsy, and lithotomy, or cutting of
> the stone, until a complete recovery, or as complete as may be possible,
> in consideration of the sum of 100 sous each year, payable by each of
> the above-mentioned persons, such payment to cover also their wives
> and children, and to treat also their children who may hereafter be
> born from the day of their birth and, in the event of the death of any
> one of the above mentioned, the said Bouchard shall nevertheless be
> paid for a full year, no matter in what season such death shall take
> place . . . and moreover, the said Bouchard shall not be entitled to can-
> cel the present agreement with respect to any persons who are suffer-
> ing from any illness unless he has first cured them or unless such can-
> cellation be with their consent.

Apparently the contract was considered mutually attractive, for one month later six other heads of families appeared before the notary to declare that they were also parties to the agreement.

A few years later, there appeared the first "in hospital" medical services contract.[3] The parties were the mother superior of the Dame Religieuses Hôpitalières and Jean Martinet de Fonblanche and Antoine Forestier, master surgeons, the latter promising and obliging themselves:

To well and truly serve the hospital of Ville-Marie, to treat, dress and physic all the sick persons who may be there and this for periods of three months each in turn and to visit such sick persons assiduously at about seven o'clock each morning and at such hours as may be necessary and this for and in consideration of the sum of 75 livres each for each year, and upon condition that the said surgeons cannot claim or seek to recover anything else whatever from the said patients. . . . And they shall furnish only their own labor and efforts, all remedies to be furnished by the hospital, and the said surgeons promise and undertake to visit the said hospital, the one in the absence of the other, when they be so required.

It will be noted that the main essentials of a modern prepayment plan appear in both contracts: comprehensive benefits with few exclusions, coverage for dependents, no coinsurance or deductibles or extra-billing, and a noncancelable contract; for the doctors, guaranteed remuneration and some of the advantages of partnership practice.

Voluntary Prepayment Plans

Despite this early experiment in prepaid health care, research to date reveals no records of other examples until late in the nineteenth century. One of the earliest "check-off" systems was introduced in 1883 in the colliery area of Cape Breton, Nova Scotia. Mining companies deducted premiums from their employees' wages, which were allocated on a capitation basis to the hospital of choice (between two local hospitals) and to doctors of choice. Similar check-off systems were later introduced among mining and lumbering communities, especially in Ontario and British Columbia, and by the railway companies across the country.[4]

The first publicly supported hospital to be built in the Northwest Territories (which became the provinces of Alberta and Saskatchewan in 1905) was the Medicine Hat General Hospital, built in 1889. As one of its sources of operating revenue, the hospital sold a "Five-Dollar Ticket" in return for a commitment "to lodge, board and give nurse and medical attendance" during a one-year period. Several hundred tickets were sold in the first year. In 1907, at the other end of the country, the Hôtel Dieu in Chatham, New Brunswick, sold three-dollar tickets to cover "medicine, medical attendance and board at any time during six months after date of this ticket."

One other form of prepayment was introduced by the burgeoning fraternal orders and benevolent societies. Many of these were offshoots of British Friendly Societies. Naylor reports, for example, that in Ontario alone there were 172,000 members of Friendly Societies.[5] They collected dues from their members and entered into contracts with physicians at rates that were deemed unfair competition by physicians in fee-for-service practice. These arrangements, known as lodge practice, became frequent targets for critical editorials in medical journals and condemnatory resolutions at annual medical association meetings.

Municipal Developments

But the thin edge of the wedge that was to lead, in very slow stages, to the national programs Canada now enjoys appeared in Saskatchewan in 1914. In that year the rural municipality of Sarnia was about to lose its only resident physician, and to induce him to stay the municipal council offered him a retainer fee of $1,500. The following year the council arranged to pay him an annual salary of $5,000 (the equivalent of $55,000 today), for which he would provide a general practitioner service including minor surgery, obstetrics, and public health services, with the right to charge discounted fees for major surgery.

In 1916 the Rural Municipality Act was amended to authorize such payments, and the "municipal doctor system" was launched. By 1930 the system had gained sufficient recognition to be studied by the U.S. Commission on the Costs of Medical Care, which analyzed its development and characteristics in a monograph written by Dr. C. Rufus Rorem.[6] In 1948, at the peak of its development, 107 municipalities, 59 villages, and 14 towns had contracts with 180 doctors.[7]

Parallel to the municipal doctor plans was the beginning of municipal hospital care plans, although on a much more limited scale. Under the various municipal acts, and true to Elizabethan poor-law tradition inherited from Great Britain by both the United States and Canada, municipalities were required to grant "aid or relief to any needy person who is a resident of the municipality." In addition to providing hospital care for indigents, a number of municipalities began paying the hospital bills of all their taxpayers (in Canada, "ratepayers," or property owners) and collecting the necessary revenues through the property tax. By 1919 ten such municipal hospital plans were in operation, although at the time there was no legislative authorization for such expenditures.[8]

But a third thrust was to provide new impetus. In both Alberta and Saskatchewan, legislative provision was made for rural municipalities, villages, and towns to combine into hospital districts to establish a special local authority for the purpose of financing the erection and maintenance of hospitals. In Saskatchewan the Union Hospital Act was passed in 1916. By 1920 there were ten such districts; by 1930 there were twenty, and at the present time over half the population is served by facilities provided by Union Hospital districts.

In 1919 legislative decisions were taken in both Alberta and Saskatchewan to enable the town of Lloydminster, which straddles the Alberta-Saskatchewan boundary, to provide funds for "the maintenance and extension of the Lloydminster Union Hospital" and "for the payment of the expenses of their respective ratepayers and residents when patients in the said hospital." It was the first provincial legislation in Canada authorizing government-operated hospital insurance. By 1945, eighty-eight rural municipalities in Saskatchewan were operating municipal hospital care plans and were to have a major impact in the development of the provincial SHSP in 1947.[9] (Union Hospital districts and Municipal Doctor plans also appeared in Manitoba and Alberta but never on the scale they did in Saskatchewan.)

Commercial Insurance

Commercial insurance also got off to an early start, at first mainly through the sickness and accident casualty companies which became organized, after World War II, in the Association of Accident and Health Underwriters. The casualty companies concentrated on selling individual policies and only later began to compete for group contracts. The life insurance companies concentrated on group policies and were organized in the Canadian Life Insurance Association (CLIA). Both types of companies issued indemnity contracts which reimbursed their beneficiaries according to predetermined fee schedules. Both imposed a deductible payment and coinsurance. In addition, in the 1950s a number of companies began to offer insurance against potentially catastrophic expenses, in contracts called major medical. These could be purchased separately or added on to basic contracts. These contracts were also characterized by a large deductible, some of which could be covered in a basic contract, and by a coinsurance payment of a percentage of the total charges above the deductible. The benefits were applicable to expenses for hospital care and medical and surgical expenses.

Provincial Beginnings

During World War I, in addition to the indigenous developments discussed above, two external streams of ideas converged on Canada, of interest mainly to leaders of the medical profession and especially to those in public health. These were the British launching of national health insurance and the brief period of interest in health insurance in the United States. Initially, leaders of the CMA cast a wary eye on the British experiment. The 1913 CMA president, Dr. H. A. McCallum, called for a membership drive to head off any parallel action in Canada. The 1914 president, Dr. A. R. Munroe, observed in his farewell address that the application of the method of insurance to medical services "is perhaps the largest problem that the younger generation of medical men will have to solve in their day and generation. It is worth every man's while studying."[10] In 1917 President A. D. Blackader urged the formation of a strong committee to study health insurance,[11] and in the fall of that year the Canadian Public Health Association mounted a special symposium on health insurance at its annual meeting in Ottawa.[12]

The other influence was the growing public interest in health insurance in the United States, spearheaded by the American Association for Labor Legislation (AALL), which had been instrumental in the adoption of workmen's compensation laws by several states and by 1913 was directing its attention to health insurance. In 1916 two state commissions reported favorably on health insurance, and another six commissions were examining the AALL proposals. Even the American Medical Association had a committee evaluating health insurance. As we shall see, these rumblings in the United States had significance for Canadian leaders.

Following the war, in 1919, two major events occurred: the first major demand for action on a provincial health insurance program, and an electoral commitment to health insurance by a national political party. The call for provincial action came in the legislature of British Columbia from a medical doctor, Major J. W. McIntosh, who had been impressed by the British National Health Insurance program while stationed in England. A member of the opposition, he introduced a resolution calling on the government to express its policy on the issue.[13] At first, the government resisted, but under pressure from a number of interest groups, including several veterans' organizations, it made the typical Canadian governmental response and announced that "before committing the province to so radical a change in her social fabric, a Commission should be set up to inquire into all details of the situation."[14]

The commission was duly appointed, held hearings throughout the province, and included among its studies reports and draft legislation from several of the American states. Its final report, outlining a proposal for a government-administered health insurance program, was submitted on March 18, 1922, but was not signed by the representative of the British Columbia College of Physicians and Surgeons. Strangely, the report did not see the light of day at all, as the government decided not to release it.[15] Only a typescript of the report, copies of the many briefs submitted, and documents from several American states occupy a file in the provincial archives.

However, in the same year (1919) that the British Columbia commission was appointed, another, more significant event transpired: the election of a new leader at a national convention of the Liberal party, William Lyon Mackenzie King. King had been appointed deputy minister of labor in 1900, a position he occupied until 1908. In 1909 he entered politics and became minister of labor in the cabinet of Sir Wilfred Laurier, only to be defeated with the rest of the government in the election of 1911 over the issue of free trade with the United States. He then became research director for the Rockefeller Foundation, establishing a solid reputation in industrial relations and becoming a lifelong friend of John D. Rockefeller. Although living in New York, he maintained his apartment in Ottawa and continued working on behalf of the Liberal party. In 1919 he published his book *Industry and Humanity*. In a chapter entitled "Principles Underlying Health," he briefly reviewed the underlying philosophy of, and the need for, such programs as workmen's compensation, unemployment insurance, sickness insurance, widows' pensions, and maternity and infants' benefits.

On August 6, 1919, the Liberal convention of 1,400 delegates convened, and King was in the midst of it, serving on the important resolutions committee. Using his many contacts with labor leaders, he persuaded the convention to adopt the following resolution as Liberal party policy: "That so far as may be practicable, having regard for Canada's financial position [two typical King phrases, indicating his cautious nature], an adequate system of insurance against unemployment, sickness, dependence in old age, and other disability, which would include old age pensions, widows' pensions, and maternity benefits, should be instituted by the Federal government in conjunction with the governments of the several provinces."[16] To top it off, Mackenzie King used material from his book in his speech to the convention, which led to his election as national leader. He would be reminded of his party's commitment to social programs, including health insurance, for years to come.

During the early 1920s the issue of health insurance in Canada, as in the United States, faded from the public agenda. But in 1929 Dr. Horace Wrinch, a member of the opposition in the British Columbia legislature, was finally successful in persuading the government to appoint yet another royal commission on health insurance.[17] This one also took three years to complete its work, and on February 13, 1932, it submitted its report.[18]

Asserting "an overwhelming desire on the part of the public for the introduction of state health insurance and maternity cash benefits, and an undeniable and acute necessity for the inauguration of such a scheme," the commission recommended that the program be compulsory for all employed persons (and their dependents) whose income was up to $2,400, with voluntary enrollment of other persons who wished to enter. Financing would be either wholly by employees or by joint employer-employee contributions. The program would provide medical and hospital benefits, a maternity benefit of thirty-five dollars, and consideration of sickness cash benefits; a central board would administer the plan.

The report was favorably appraised by the press, and hopes were high that the government would act, especially in the light of an upcoming election. The election returned a Liberal majority of thirty-six of the forty-seven seats under the leadership of Andrew Pattullo, committed to immediate action on enacting a measure of state health insurance.

Drafting of the legislation and negotiations with the British Columbia College of Physicians and Surgeons and the British Columbia Hospital Association began in 1934 and continued through 1935. Significantly, at its 1934 meeting the CMA had received a comprehensive report entitled "Medical Economics" from its Committee on Economics, which set forth nineteen principles that should obtain in any government program.[19] These were accepted by the government and the College of Physicians and Surgeons Health Insurance Committee as a basis for the program's design. More important, the secretary of the CMA's Committee on Economics, Dr. Grant Fleming of McGill University in Montreal, who had been the main draftsman of the report, was named chief negotiator for the college. Finally, in March 1935 the proposed bill was introduced in the legislature.[20] Because of its significance as the first program of its kind in Canada, and the first to result in confrontation with the medical profession, its provisions are important.

The salient features were as follows: compulsory coverage would be for all employees earning two hundred dollars a month or less (including their dependents), with voluntary coverage of all others with the same income ceiling. Benefits would include medical and hospital care and, as financial conditions permitted, drugs, diagnostic services, home nursing care, and sickness cash benefits. Contributions by employers were not to exceed 2 percent of their payroll, and those by employees were not to exceed 3 percent of income; the government would contribute on behalf of indigents at one-half the normal rate. A limit of four dollars per insured person per year was to be placed on expenditures for general practitioner services. This payment would have created a fund of a fixed amount. If physicians' total billings exceeded that amount, the payments would have had to be prorated. (In Canada this is known as the ceiling principle.)

With the introduction of the bill, it was decided that a legislative committee should hold public hearings. These were held at eighteen centers, at which 161 briefs were presented. Of these, 111 approved the proposal, 27 believed the contributions were too high, 10 stated that the time was not opportune, 9 opposed cash benefits, and 4 opposed the whole idea. Unfortunately for the government, one of these four was the College of Physicians and Surgeons. It criticized the $2,400 income ceiling as too high, noting that "it seems perfectly clear that the person earning $200 a month with or without dependants needs no assistance." It also objected to the fact that the government did not propose to underwrite the program. It also contended that cash benefits should not be included and insisted that payment should be on a fee-for-service basis at full rates. Although the college's representative, Dr. Fleming, had assisted in drafting the legislation, and the principles of the CMA had served as its structural base, the letter accompanying the brief stated that the physicians "are unanimously and unalterably opposed to the present enactment."[21]

The legislative committee held private sessions to revise the proposals, with these results: the income ceiling should be reduced to $1,800; the employee's contribution should be reduced to 2 percent of income and the employer's contribution be reduced to 1 percent; full payment should be made in respect of services to indigents; and sickness cash benefits should be postponed. Despite these proposed major changes, opposition continued to mount, the college being joined by the British Columbia Manufacturers' Association, which argued that no such program should be introduced during the depression and stressing the burden that an additional tax would have on the mining and lumber exporting industries of British Columbia. There were also indications of a split in the cabinet and of possible defections among other Liberal members.

The amended bill was reintroduced on March 3, 1936, and incorporated the recommendations of the legislative committee. In addition, the ceiling on annual expenditures for general practitioner services was increased from

$4.00 per insured person to $5.50. But the government also removed one of the main provisions of the 1935 draft: the inclusion of indigents as beneficiaries through the payment by the government of contributions on their behalf. Clearly the depressed revenue resources of the government and the vociferous opposition of the two major interest groups had forced a weakening of the proposal. But the changes in no way lessened the opposition, which in fact continued to increase, especially from the profession over the removal of indigents—mainly the vast numbers of unemployed—as beneficiaries. Ironically, it was the profession's demand that the income ceiling be reduced which deprived the program of the higher-income levies that would have contributed to the subsidy of the costs of care of the indigent.

Despite the opposition, the bill passed second reading on March 26 by a vote of 28-10. Five Liberals bolted the party, but six members of the newly launched party the Cooperative Commonwealth Federation voted with the government. The final vote on third reading on March 31 was 25-14, and on April 1, the act received royal assent.[22]

Administration of the program moved into high gear under the newly appointed Health Insurance Commission, chaired by Allon Peebles, Ph.D., who had served as a researcher for the U.S. Commission on the Costs of Medical Care. Registration of employers was completed in July, and enrollment of some 110,000 employees was begun in September. On January 8, 1937, the premier announced that the program would go into effect on March 1, with benefits to be available on March 29, 1937.[23]

Meanwhile, negotiations with the profession were deadlocked, the college announcing on February 1 that the profession, by an almost unanimous vote in a referendum, refused to work under the program. Finally, it became clear that the project was just too much. The depressed economy, the expenditures for welfare, the pressures from the manufacturers' association, the vehement opposition of the profession, combined with dissension within the Liberal party and criticism in the press, forced the premier to announce on February 9 that the program would be postponed until after an election, which he later called for June 2, 1937.

In addition to listing the local candidates, the ballots also contained the question, "Are you in favor of a comprehensive health insurance scheme progressively applied?" The Liberals were returned to power with thirty seats (a loss of four), the Conservatives, eight, and the CCF, seven. Of the total of 264,446 voters replying to the referendum question, 147,837 voted yes and 116,609 voted no, for a majority of 31,228 in favor, clearly a much narrower margin than the act's proponents had hoped. Despite the majority vote in the referendum, the Pattullo government took no further action on the legislation other than to continue appropriations for the secretary of the commission, who was still in office when I interviewed him in 1947.

So the high hopes engendered by World War I, expressed in briefs to two royal commissions, affirmed in those commissions' recommendations, and incorporated finally in legislation, had failed to achieve an operating program. But it was an experience from which many lessons had been learned, especially by a Vancouver member of Parliament, the Honorable Ian Mackenzie, who later became Canada's wartime health minister.

There was one other attempt to achieve health insurance at the provincial level, this time in Alberta. The campaign began there in 1929, the same year that the second campaign was beginning in British Columbia, and, as in that province, the initiative came from the opposition ranks. Since the government party—the UFA—had endorsed health insurance during its first successful election campaign in 1921, the debate in Alberta was less acrimonious than in British Columbia. Nevertheless, events moved just as slowly. A legislative committee studied the issue for two sessions, followed by the appointment of a commission in 1932. It submitted a final report in 1934.[24] Legislation was passed in early 1935 recommending action in two stages: (1) emphasis on municipal doctor and municipal hospital plans, and two demonstration units—one rural and one urban—to gain experience with health insurance, and (2) provincewide health insurance at a later date. With the defeat of the government in an election in August 1935 by the newly formed Social Credit party, which believed that with its "social credit dividend" such measures as health insurance would be unnecessary, no action ensued on Alberta's health insurance act of 1935.

Federal Beginnings

Although there had been sporadic discussions of health insurance by the House of Commons Committee on Industrial Relations in the late 1920s, it was not until the final days of R. B. Bennett's Conservative government (1930–35) that social insurance legislation reached the statute books. Obviously influenced by President Roosevelt's New Deal legislation, and in a last-ditch move to restore his government's falling reputation, the prime minister succeeded in getting his radical (at least for the Conservatives) employment and social insurance legislation passed in June, shortly before the election.[25] (Bennett's brother-in-law W. D. Herridge was minister in the Canadian embassy in Washington, D.C. Some wag observed that "obviously, a red Herridge had been dragged across Bennett's trail.")

The act created an administrative commission, and in addition to its responsibilities for introducing an unemployment insurance system, it was also authorized to "assemble information on medical and hospital care and sickness cash benefit programs." The commission may "submit to the Governor-in-Council [the cabinet] proposals for cooperation [with the provincial governments] by the Dominion Government in providing any of these benefits . . . for such action as the Governor-in-Council is authorized to take."

In the ensuing election, the Liberals, still under the leadership of Mackenzie King, were victorious and, winning the next four elections, were to hold office until 1957. But the social insurance legislation provoked a constitutional challenge by the Province of Ontario. In a landmark decision in 1936, the Employment and Social Insurance Act was struck down by the Supreme Court of Canada.[26]

Despite the legal decision, the financial morass and the confusion over the respective constitutional jurisdictions of the federal and provincial governments, as well as the economic and social crises to which the legislation had been addressed, remained in their stark and paralyzing reality. Faced with the twin problems of the depression and the constitutional impasse, the Liberal government decided that a major national inquiry should now be launched into the constitutional and financial foundations of the federal system. Accordingly, in 1937 the Royal Commission on Dominion-Provincial Relations was appointed. Its report, submitted in 1940, was without doubt the most extensive examination of any federal system undertaken to that time.[27]

Its most important recommendations focused on the distribution of revenue sources between the two levels of government and on the unequal capacities of the respective provinces to finance a minimum national standard of services. It will be recalled from chapter 2 that the commission also believed that while old-age security and unemployment insurance were federal responsibilities, health insurance was a provincial responsibility. The commission also rejected conditional grants-in-aid as a device for solving the provinces' financial problems.

Clearly, in the collective wisdom of the prestigious royal commission, the role of the federal government in any organized health services system was indeed to be limited. And the failure of the dominion-provincial conference, convened on January 14–15, 1941, to consider the commission's recommendations, underscored that reality.

But there was now present a new and more dramatic reality: events had overtaken the commission's analyses and prescriptions, for Canada had declared war on September 10, 1939. One of its first casualties was the minister of defense, the Honorable Ian Mackenzie, who was transferred to the more tranquil portfolio of Pensions and National Health.

The interwar years had been turbulent and included the problems of integrating veterans and defense workers into the civilian economy, the stock market crash of 1929, and ten years of depression depriving hundreds of thousands of needed medical care while doctors stacked their unpaid bills as empty legacies for their heirs. The hopes engendered by the sacrifices of World War I, including comprehensive health services inspired by the British model, had been frustrated. Now Canada was at war again. What would the future bring?

Chapter Four

Wartime Planning

Ian Mackenzie, the new minister of pensions and national health, was deeply disappointed at his demotion as minister of defense on September 19, 1939, but his ebullient spirits seemed undampened; there were other campaigns to be fought, new terrain to be occupied, greener fields to conquer. And the serendipitous happened, as he discovered that the second-ranking official in the department, Dr. J. J. Heagerty, the director of public health services, had long been a student of health insurance, thus reinforcing with solid knowledge Mackenzie's own awareness of the issues gained during his observations of the aborted attempts to introduce health insurance in his native British Columbia in the early 1930s. They were to become the ideal team so essential in the Canadian parliamentary system—the informed political leader, advised and supported by the expert public servant.

With the war a little more than three months along, on December 27, 1939, Mackenzie wrote to the prime minister urging that in the light of the burden and sacrifices to be imposed on the Canadian work force, unemployment insurance and health insurance be immediately introduced as wartime measures, arguing that "unemployment insurance will be indispensable in coping with the reestablishment problems [at the end of the war] . . . and a demand for a health insurance system is inevitable."[1]

The prime minister took the proposals to the cabinet, but that body had more pressing priorities, and the proposals were rejected, although unemployment insurance would shortly resurface. Mackenzie then acted on his own, proceeding slowly and cautiously. He first asked Dr. Heagerty to expand his studies on the design and the strategies for introducing a nationwide program. The second step was to alert the provincial governments, the professions, and consumer groups to the need for their studying the issues. The opportunity presented itself at the annual meeting on June 14, 1941, of the Dominion Council of Health, a statutory advisory body chaired by the federal deputy minister of health and composed of all the provincial deputy ministers of health and representatives of the CMA, and labor, farmers, and urban and farm women's associations. The minister suggested that the subject of health insurance be discussed with the objective of assisting the provinces in formulating comprehensive health plans. The responses were positive, with general agreement on the need for health insurance, and the representatives of the CMA indicated their willingness to grant every assistance in the formulation of a plan.[2]

Mackenzie then requested Dr. Heagerty formally to invite five health profession associations and nine consumer associations to appoint committees to advise the ministry. On February 5, 1942, the minister appointed an Interdepartmental Advisory Committee on Health Insurance, chaired by Dr. Heagerty and with representatives from the departments of finance, justice, and trade and commerce (an actuary) and from the Dominion Bureau of Statistics (now StatsCan).[3] There was thus created an internal task force which, with the assistance of the fourteen profession and consumer-group committees, would produce in less than a year the first blueprint ever drawn for a national health insurance plan for Canada.

Shortly after the appointment of the committee, there appeared a document that was to receive international acclaim and have a major impact on all Western nations—the report of Sir William Beveridge on social insurance in Britain.[4] So comprehensive was its review and so innovative and farsighted were its concepts that it not only provided a ready-made base for the committee's deliberations but also inspired it with a new sense of the importance of its work.

In addition to the Interdepartmental Committee on Health Insurance the government also appointed a Committee on Post-War Reconstruction, chaired by Dr. Cyril James, the president of McGill University. He commissioned Dr. Leonard Marsh, who, as a graduate student, had worked with Professor Beveridge, to prepare a comprehensive survey of social security for Canada. His report, submitted a year later, is a remarkable document, particularly when assessed in the light of the limited time for its preparation and the influence it, too, would have on the development of Canada's safety net programs.[5]

Meanwhile, Dr. Heagerty was directing the research and planning of his committee and meeting with his fourteen advisory committees, especially with the CMA's "Committee of Seven." Finally, in December 1942, the committee submitted to the minister the most comprehensive report on health insurance ever produced in Canada, with sections on health insurance programs in other countries, public health agencies operating in Canada, a statistical survey of the health status of Canadians, the economic status of Canadians, and estimates of the costs of a national-provincial program. It also presented two draft bills, one for Parliament and a model bill for the provinces, both incorporating most of the CMA's nineteen principles referred to in chapter 3. Most significantly, it ignored the reservations of the Royal Commission on Dominion-Provincial Relations as to the workability of conditional grants-in-aid and recommended such grants as the only feasible method of enabling all provinces to introduce the proposed programs.[6]

Almost three years to the day since he had first proposed health insurance to the prime minister, Mackenzie was armed with specific proposals, draft legislation, and supporting information. He was now ready to act.

The first weeks of January 1943 were crucial for Mackenzie's objectives. The proposal, including the draft legislation, was presented to the cabinet on January 8.[7] The cabinet made no decision but referred it to the powerful Economics Advisory Committee (which had established its reputation through its superb management of war financing), chaired by the deputy minister of finance, W. C. Clark, for a more thorough examination of its financial implications. On January 20 the cabinet received the report of the economics committee, which reflected Clark's conviction that the three social insurance programs of unemployment insurance (then in place), old-age security, and health insurance should be financed and administered in the same manner.[8] This arrangement would have required a constitutional amendment (as had been necessary to achieve a national unemployment insurance program), a stratagem already considered, and rejected, by the Heagerty Committee. The report ended with a recommendation that the bill be deferred for further study.

Mackenzie immediately responded with an angry letter to the prime minister, characterizing Clark's report as "just a stalling by a financial group of two years' work done in the Health Department." But recognizing that the views of the economics committee would likely prevail, he offered a compromise—the appointment of a special committee of the House of Commons to consider the whole question of health insurance, including the draft legislation.[9] To this the cabinet agreed.

The forty-one-member, all-party House of Commons Committee on Social Security held the first of its public hearings on March 16, 1943, with Mackenzie outlining the main features of the proposals.[10] The first offer was provision of a series of grants to enable the provinces to strengthen their depression-ravaged public health services. There were six grants: public health, tuberculosis, mental health, venereal disease, physical fitness, and professional training for physicians, nurses, and sanitary inspectors. The second proposal was for federal subsidies to provincially administered health insurance programs, which would be financed in part by a 3.0 percent income tax levy, increasing to 3.7 percent for a family of two and 4.3 percent for a family of three or more to a maximum of seventy-eight dollars per annum. The balance of costs would be shared by the federal and provincial governments on a formula to be decided later.

The draft legislation also provided for the organization of administrative health regions within each province to make certain that preventive and treatment services would be available outside the urban centers. The central administration would be under the direction of a commission representing the government, the public, and the medical profession, with a medical doctor as chairman, and the deputy minister of health (invariably also an M.D.) an ex officio member.

Then began a parade of 117 witnesses representing thirty-two organizations that would occupy the committee over the next four months. There thus occurred in Canada in 1943 public hearings that would be replicated in the U.S. Congress in 1945. But there was a major difference. It was known that consumer interest groups would strongly support—indeed demand—the legislation, but the surprise to many was the equally strong support of the CMA, the CHA, and the CLIA.

Indeed, Ian Mackenzie's strategy of involving both provider and consumer groups in the planning process had paid off handsomely. Because of the centrality of the medical profession's role in this and all future episodes, it will be worthwhile to examine the evolution of the CMA's policy.

The 1934 report of the CMA's Committee on Economics, already referred to, was a comprehensive and objective report, including a review of health insurance programs in Germany, Great Britain, France, and South Africa and of the reports of the U.S. Committee on the Costs of Medical Care. Its survey of Canadian conditions, worsened by the depression, is a clinical record of the economic malaise of the 1930s as experienced by the medical profession.

The general tenor of the committee's report was that government health insurance was necessary and, in view of the obvious interest of the public in it, probably inevitable. It was imperative, in its judgment, that the views of the profession should be heard. Accordingly, the CMA should design a plan. This would be strategically very important, for "in this as in other matters, it is the body which has prepared a concrete proposal which may expect this proposal, with modifications, to be accepted and to provide the basic plan for the final scheme." And with disarming confidence in its own objectivity and wisdom (and anticipating "Engine Charlie" Wilson of General Motors, who once said, "What is good for General Motors is good for the U.S.A."), the committee observed, "This is not a selfish motive, because what is best for the medical profession must be best for the public."

There were other homespun observations, some of which, in hindsight, one might wish had had more opportunity to prevail in the future. All but the first were reversed in later policies.

We are not making full use of the knowledge we do possess, as evidenced by the number of preventable diseases which continue to occur.

Medical services in their medical aspects should be under the control of the medical profession. The business part of any organized services will naturally be controlled by those who pay for the services.

The proposed plan supports the principle of a state insurance fund with the elimination of other insurance carriers [as in the British system].

Arguments are advanced in favor of requiring some payment by the insured for each illness to prevent abuse of the medical benefit. This is not viewed sympathetically, because the main objective is to remove any economic barrier which now keeps doctor and patient apart.

There does not seem to be any reason why a uniform system of payments should be advocated. It seems much more reasonable to allow the medical practitioners of each area to choose which system they desire to use. *There is a sum for distribution; the method used will neither decrease nor increase it, otherwise the fund would not be solvent.* (emphasis added)

But the most important contribution of the report, as has been indicated, was a series of nineteen principles to guide the development of any Canadian plan of health insurance. In summary, the major principles were that health insurance should be administered by a commission, the majority of whose members should be representatives of organized medicine; that the plan be compulsory for persons having up to a specified level of income, usually set at $2,400 annually; that all indigents, as well as dependents of insured persons, be included; that contributions to the insurance fund should be made by the insured, employers, and the government; that physicians be remunerated by the method or methods they select; that the schedule of fees be under the complete control of the organized profession in each province; that no economic barrier be imposed between patient and doctor; that the plan be periodically actuarially approved; and that a pension plan for practitioners be provided.

Despite the general approval of the principles and increasing discussion of health insurance, the executive felt that the CMA was in no position to promulgate either a policy or a plan. But in late 1942, with the imminent release of the report of the Heagerty Committee, the executive decided that an official policy must be declared. Accordingly, it took the unprecedented step of convoking a special meeting of general council, the "parliament" of the profession, on January 18–19, 1943—eight weeks before the hearings of the House of Commons committee were to begin.

There can have been no other meeting of the CMA council, before or since, so marked with idealism and harmony.[11] Each member had copies of the two draft bills and a copy of the CMA principles. Moreover, the meeting was attended by Dr. Heagerty and W. G. Gunn, the Health Department attorney, as well as by the CMA's solicitor, Arthur Fleming. The special meeting was obviously slated to grapple with details as well as with broad principles.

The president, Dr. R. I. Harris, paid tribute to Dr. Heagerty's splendid leadership. The minister of health, Ian Mackenzie, and the minister of defense, J. L. Ralston, attended the meeting briefly, and both praised the profession for its cooperation. It was an extraordinary and, as we shall see, unique example of cooperation and good feeling based on mutual trust between the profession and the government. The overwhelming impression one gains is that the elected representatives of organized medicine in Canada were fully reconciled to, if not enthusiastic about, a new system of medical care financing which, they anticipated, would have a major impact on medical practice.

So out of ten years of independent analysis and study and a year of collaboration with the Heagerty Committee, there had come agreement of organized medicine not only on the principle of health insurance but on the details of two draft bills, which incorporated in extraordinary degree the CMA principles. The wisdom of the observation in the report of the economics committee in 1934 that whoever presents the first draft generally wins the day was once again confirmed. That the health of the nation and expansion and upgrading of the medical profession were among the central objectives, there could be no doubt.

The climax of the special meeting was the unanimous endorsement of these two resolutions:

The Canadian Medical Association approves the adoption of the principle of health insurance.

The Canadian Medical Association favors a plan of health insurance which will secure the development and provision of the highest standard of health services, if such plan be fair both to the insured and to all those rendering the services.[12]

It came as no surprise then, when the CMA president and general secretary presented their brief to the House of Commons committee on March 18, that they ended their statement with this ringing note of cooperation: "The CMA desires to assure the Committee that our entire organization, stretching from sea to sea, stands ready to render any assistance in its power towards the solution of one of the country's most important problems, namely, the safeguarding of the health of our people."[13] It was Canadian organized medicine's finest hour.

The representatives of all the other interest groups were equally positive in their support of the proposed program, and many offered suggestions for improvements. One of the highlights of the hearings was the appearance of Sir William Beveridge. He lauded Dr. Marsh's report on social security and emphasized that the objective was not social insurance but, rather, social progress. And this could be achieved, he said, by attacking what he called the five "giant evils" of Want, Disease, Ignorance, Squalor, and Idleness.[14] Although in his presentation and in the question period that followed he provided few technical answers, his presence clearly inspired the committee with a vision of a brighter future and enhanced its conviction that it was engaged in one of the most important policy proposals ever to come before the Canadian Parliament.

On July 23, 1943, the committee submitted its report. It approved the general principles embodied in the draft legislation, recommended that senior officials visit the provincial governments to provide them with full information, and proposed that a conference of federal and provincial representatives should be held. It also recommended that study of the bill be continued by the House of Commons committee and by the interdepartmental committee.[15] What was unique about the whole exercise was, of course, that it was not a government bill; it was simply a proposal and not government policy. That would have to come later.

The exigencies of the war resulted in only desultory action on the health insurance proposals. The recommended visits by officials to the provinces did not take place. The House of Commons committee was reconstituted in February 1944, considered minor amendments mainly related to the financing arrangements, and heard representatives of a number of organizations. There was some dissension in the committee as opposition members criticized the fact that they were not considering a government-sponsored bill and that a conference with the provinces had not been held. However, on May 8 a conference of health ministers and their deputies, the House of Commons committee, and the Heagerty Committee was convened. All the provincial ministers approved the principle of health insurance and favored its early adoption but stressed that each province should be permitted to introduce each benefit in its own time, and should also be permitted to raise its share of the funds in any way it saw fit.[16] On July 28, 1944, the committee submitted its final report to the House of Commons, approving, with minor amendments, the two draft bills prepared by the Heagerty Committee.[17]

But as 1944 progressed, it became clear that the issue of health insurance would not be decided on its own but would become enmeshed in a whole gamut of issues—the most important being the division of tax fields between the two jurisdictions—and would have to be negotiated at a federal-provincial conference which, Mackenzie King decided, could not take place until after an election. Moreover, there was a major change in the actors. Ian Mackenzie's four-year campaign to achieve a health program for Canada had produced a conceptual design for federal-provincial cooperation, draft legislation, cost estimates, assurances of professional cooperation, provincial government support, and a much better-informed public opinion resulting from the two sessions of the House of Commons committee. But like Moses, he was not to lead the movement to the promised land. On June 13, 1944, the cabinet approved the establishment of a new Department of National Health and Welfare, to which Brooke Claxton was named minister, with Mackenzie becoming minister of the newly created Department of Veterans' Affairs.[18]

In 1945, with the end of the European war in sight and an election due, the tempo of activity in preparing for a dominion-provincial conference, which would have to be held soon after the election, was greatly accelerated. Claxton was appointed chairman of a new cabinet committee on dominion-provincial relations, and as the new minister of health he decided that the health insurance strategy must be drastically altered. The original policy would have involved substantial intervention in provincial decision making by requiring uniform legislation based on the model bill. With the inclusion of health insurance in a comprehensive package of proposals, that strategy could no longer be followed. The offer must appear more attractive and less interventionist.

The major decision was to abandon the entire concept of a model bill for the provinces and, particularly, any precondition of any specific method of provincial financing. It was decided that a full range of services would be provided by provinces in two stages. The federal share would be set at a maximum of 60 percent of the *estimated* cost of each service. Given the shaky base of costs data, it was clearly a trial-and-error method in which the federal government's errors would have become the provinces' trials.

Claxton's decision was an abandonment of a whole series of positions built up over more than four years by the Health Department. It was obviously a bitter disappointment to the CMA, for now the battle for its principles, particularly administration by independent commissions, would have to be fought on nine separate fronts. (Newfoundland would not become the tenth province until 1949.)

During the election, called for June 11, 1945, health insurance was a major issue, endorsed by all four political parties in response to public opinion. A Gallup poll taken in March 1944 reported an 80 percent affirmative response to the question, "Would you contribute to a national hospital-medical insurance plan?"

It had been obvious to the Liberal party strategists that the electorate, weary of all the wartime regulations, and particularly, Quebec voters' anger over the divisive issue of conscription, would threaten the government's majority—indeed, might defeat it. And it was close, with the Liberals winning 125 seats (a loss of 53); Conservatives, 67 (a gain of 28); CCF, 28 (a gain of 10); Social Credit, 13; others, 12. It was a slim majority, but at least the Liberals would form the government. There were two major casualties, however, with both the prime minister and his recently appointed minister of defense, General MacNaughton, losing their seats in Saskatchewan, where the CCF increased its representation from 5 to 18. (There the CCF formed the first social-democratic government in North America following the provincial election in 1944.)

The promised Dominion-Provincial Conference on Post-War Reconstruction convened on August 6, 1945—a date better known in history for the dropping of the atomic bomb on Hiroshima. There on the conference table in the magnificent setting of the House of Commons—borrowed for the occasion—fresh from the King's Printer in their green covers, neatly arranged in front of the four federal ministers and the nine provincial premiers, were copies of the dominion government's design for a new postwar world for Canada—the now-famous Green Book Proposals.

The delegates were there as the spokesmen for ten governments to consider the future of Canada, and the differences among them were as varied as the regions from which they came. There were the representatives of the central government grown both powerful and confident—some would have said arrogant—in the exercise of wartime authority, the representatives of large provinces with great resources, and the premiers of small and less wealthy provinces with the depression economy still vividly etched on their minds. They were leaders of ten political parties bearing five different labels, some fresh from new electoral mandates, some allied with the federal Liberal party, and others committed to its frustration and embarrassment. They were the main players about to enter into a new bargaining game in which the stakes were extraordinarily high: restructuring of the tax system, millions of dollars of revenues for new programs, the future balance of forces in the scale of federal-provincial relations, political party fortunes, and, not least, personal political careers—all and more hung on the outcomes.

It was a pregnant moment as Prime Minister Mackenzie King intoned his welcoming statement and sought the cooperation of the provinces in the strategies of a new war against ancient foes. "The enemies we shall have to overcome will be on our own Canadian soil. They will make their presence known in the guise of sickness, unemployment and want. It is to plan for a unified campaign in Canada against these enemies of progress and human well-being that we have come together at this time. This may well be the most important Canadian Conference since Confederation."[19]

The mood was not lost on the premiers or the 150 advisers. The dreams, hopes, and aspirations of the Canadian people were now focused on their leaders, who had the power and authority to convert those dreams into the realities of policies, agreements, legislation, and operating programs. The realities, even at their best, could never, of course, match the hopes engendered by ten years of depression and six years of war. There was a mood of rebellion against the universal risks of unemployment and sickness, disability and old age, widowhood and poverty, a pervasive dissatisfaction with precarious minimum wages, drought-stricken farms, grudgingly granted relief payments and a suspiciously administered, means-tested old age pension.

It is impossible for anyone under the age of forty today, protected as we now are with a full panoply of social insurance programs, to appreciate, or perhaps even to comprehend, the threats to individual and family independence and integrity that characterized the thirties and extended, to a declining degree, into the forties and fifties. But to millions the threats had been real and, for hundreds of thousands, had come to pass. The hopes of a nation—ambivalently balanced between the confidence born of a magnificent war effort and the fear of the return of a depression—were now centered on these key actors in the unfolding drama.

The Honorable Louis St. Laurent, minister of justice, took over as acting chairman (Mackenzie King had been called out to be told of the atomic bomb) and introduced the proposals in these words:

In familiar terms, our objectives are high and stable employment and income, and a greater sense of public responsibility for individual security and welfare. Realization of these objectives for all Canadians, as Canadians, is a cause in which we hope for national enthusiasm and unity. The Government has clear and decided views on how these objectives can be attained;

First, to facilitate private enterprise to produce and provide employment;

Second, to promote bold action by the state in those fields in which the public interest calls for public enterprise in national development;

Third, to provide, through public investment, productive employment for our human and physical resources when international and other conditions adversely affect employment;

Fourth, to provide, on the basis of small regular payments against large and uncertain individual risks, for such hazards and disabilities as unemployment, sickness, and old age.[20]

These, then, were the goals and the means, as formulated by the federal government and, it was hoped, to be accepted by the provinces. They were broad in scope and called for new thrusts and initiatives as well as federal-provincial cooperation on a scale never before envisaged.

Our concern here is with the health proposals which were presented by Health Minister Claxton in the evening of the first day. They were four in number.

1. *Planning and organization grant.* This provision was to enable each provincial government to establish a full-time planning staff to prepare for and organize health insurance benefits within the province.

2. *Health insurance.* This proposal was designed to put provincial governments in a position to develop and administer a comprehensive health insurance program worked out in stages on an agreed basis. The various benefits, their estimated per capita costs, and the proposed federal contributions are outlined in table 2.

The proposed federal contribution to the cost of each benefit was (1) a basic grant of one-fifth of the *estimated* cost of each service, and (2) one-half of the additional actual cost incurred by each provincial government for each benefit, provided that the total federal contribution did not exceed the amount stated in the table for each service. The maximum would therefore be $12.96 per person when the complete program was in operation; that is, for each benefit the federal government contribution could reach 60 percent. For the first three years the cost of each benefit would be taken to be the amounts shown in the table. These figures would be replaced after each three years by the actual average cost of providing each benefit. It was, for the federal government, a fail-safe formula, with the provincial governments being solely responsible in any three-year period for costs in excess of the estimates.

3. *Health grants*. The health grants were substantially the same as those which have been discussed.

4. *Financial assistance in the construction of hospitals*. This offer was entirely new and provided for federal loans with the interest and amortization payable out of the hospital care benefit.[21]

It had been a long and eventful day, with the prime minister's spirits being dramatically lifted as he learned of his victory in a by-election in the Glengarry constituency of Ontario. But for the provinces, the price tag would be revealed on August 7.

Prior to the war, both the federal and provincial governments had access to personal and corporate income taxes and succession duties (that is, estate taxes). But in an agreement with the provinces worked out in 1940, for the duration of the war and one added year, the federal government had "rented" these three revenue sources by paying the provincial governments per capita amounts. It now proposed to extend the system, making its offer in these terms:

1. That after the war-time agreements the provincial governments should by agreement forego the imposition of personal income taxes, corporation income taxes and succession duties, leaving the Dominion government full and exclusive access to these revenue sources.

2. As a condition of such agreement the Dominion would substantially expand its present payments to the provincial governments under an arrangement which would ensure stable revenues and provide for their growth in proportion to increases in population and per capita national production.

3. There should be an agreement under which the provincial governments would commit themselves not to withdraw before an initial trial period of, say, three years.[22]

Clearly, these and a host of other proposals were too much for the wealthier provinces (Ontario, Quebec, and British Columbia) to swallow—as attractive as the health insurance and social security proposals had been. The

Table 2.
Basis of Federal Contributions for Health Insurance
(Dollars per Capita)

Service Provided	Estimated Average Cost of Service[a]	% of Total Cost	Basic Dominion Grant	Maximum Additional Dominion Grant
First Stage				
General practitioner service	6.00	28	1.20	2.40
Hospital care	73.60	17	0.72	1.44
Visiting nursing service	0.60	3	0.12	0.24
Total first stage	10.20	48	2.04	4.08
Later Stages				
Other medical services (consultant, specialist and surgical)	3.50	16	0.70	1.40
Other nursing services (including private duty)	1.15	5	0.23	0.46
Dental care	3.60	16	0.72	1.44
Pharmaceutical (drugs, serums, and surgical appliances)	2.55	12	0.51	1.02
Laboratory services (blood tests, X rays, etc.)	0.60	3	0.12	0.24
Total all stages	21.60	100	4.32	8.64

Source: Dominion-Provincial Conference, 1945, *Proceedings*, p. 90.

[a] Estimated cost to be revised on basis of actual costs after three years.

conference and its committees dragged on their work for the next nine months, ending in failure on May 3, 1946. The price tag had been too high.[23]

But there were positive outcomes that would bear fruit in the future: the vastly expanded public awareness of the effect on the health status of Canadians of the lack of adequate medical services, the disparity among Canadian provinces and between urban and rural populations in access to medical services, a new public understanding of the device of insurance in pooling risks and resources, and new commitments by political parties and other organizations that action must be taken to remove the financial barriers to essential health services. In fact, in Saskatchewan, action had already begun.

Chapter Five

Voluntary and Commercial Insurance

As noted earlier, there were uncounted numbers of arrangements by which people "prepaid" part or all of their health care costs—mining and railway company plans, lodge practice, cooperatives, and, of course, the municipal doctor and municipal hospital plans in the prairie provinces. But there was now to be an unprecedented new thrust for health insurance as hospital associations, medical associations, and commercial insurance companies leaped into the vacuum of unfulfilled expectations following the collapse of the Dominion-Provincial Conference on Post-War Reconstruction.

The Blue Cross Movement

Some early examples of hospitals selling hospital "tickets" have already been noted. During the 1930s hospitals in several cities set up cooperative plans with two or more hospitals joining together to offer prepayment contracts. In Edmonton, four hospitals joined together; in Lethbridge, Alberta, two others; and in Kingston, Ontario, there were also two. By 1934 there were twenty-seven such plans operating in six provinces,[1] and these were to form the nuclei of the Blue Cross movement in Canada, following the rapid expansion of such plans in the United States and the formal establishment in 1937 of the Blue Cross Hospital Service Plan Commission by the American Hospital Association, of which a number of Canadians were directors. The first Blue Cross plan in Canada was launched in Manitoba on January 1, 1939, under the sponsorship of the Central Council of Social Agencies. It was followed by Ontario in 1941, Quebec in 1942, in three Maritime provinces and British Columbia in 1943, and in Alberta in 1948.

Most of the plans were sponsored by their respective hospital associations, but Manitoba and Quebec were the exceptions, with broad community representation on their boards. But the difference may not have been significant, since the sponsoring hospital associations with their broad representation of trustees could also be said to be strongly community based.

The Blue Cross plans, in contrast to commercial insurance, had pioneered the *service* contract; that is, their basic benefit was defined in terms of eligible days of care, whatever the individual hospital's basic per diem charges were. All Blue Cross plans offered two levels of contract, one providing standard ward care, and the other, semiprivate accommodation. As a control measure, dollar limits were placed on certain special services, such as radiology tests, special drugs, or maternity care. Limits were usually placed on the number of benefit days for each unrelated illness and on total days of care in any one year, although as contracts were continued, additional benefit days were accumulated, so that only in rare long-stay cases or readmission for the same diagnosis did patients find themselves uninsured for part of the hospital account.

There can be no doubt about the contribution of the hospital leaders, trustees and administrators alike, who launched the Blue Cross plans that served well both patients and hospitals. By 1953, when the public debate on national hospital insurance began to heat up, the six Blue Cross plans had enrolled over 3 million subscribers, or approximately 25 percent of Canada's population outside of British Columbia and Saskatchewan, where universal government programs were in operation.

Blue Cross had introduced two innovations. The first was the service contract, noted above. The other was standardization of the premium rates across all employee groups. This policy resulted, of course, in the subsidization of high-utilization groups by low-utilization groups, as occurs in all governmental social insurance programs. But as we shall see, the policy frequently handicapped Blue Cross in its competition with commercial insurance companies.

The Voluntary "Not-for-Profit" Medical Care Prepayment Plans

The first voluntary nonprofit medical care prepayment plan was launched in Ontario in 1937 under the leadership of Dr. J. A. Hannah, a former senior official in the Ministry of Health. With the aid of small loans from the Ontario Civil Service Association and the Ontario Medical Association (OMA), he was able to organize the Toronto-based Associated Medical Services, Inc., and offer contracts to individual subscribers covering both medical and hospital benefits. In 1945 this organization began offering contracts to groups, reaching a total enrollment of just over 100,000 by 1954.

The other undertaking, also launched in Ontario in 1937, was Windsor Medical Services, sponsored by the Windsor and Essex County Medical Society. As the pioneering physician-sponsored plan in Canada (seven of its ten directors were physicians), it was highly successful, achieving an enrollment of over 150,000 by the mid-1950s. It offered a service contract (for individuals with an income of $4,000 or less and families with an income of $6,500 or less) and an indemnity contract (i.e., permitting extra-billing by the physician) for subscribers with incomes above those limits.

In 1940 the Manitoba Medical Association (MMA) joined forces with the Blue Cross plan, enabling it also to sell medical services benefits, but the relationship was never harmonious, and in 1942 the MMA launched its own sponsored plan, Manitoba Medical Services. In Saskatchewan in 1939, the Regina Medical Society was the only other physicians' group to organize a prepayment plan before the war. Its enrollment grew very slowly.

But the most aggressive action to put the profession into the health insurance business was that of the British Columbia Medical Association (BCMA), still shaken from its bitter, though successful, battle against the British Columbia government's proposed program from 1934 to 1937. Now keenly aware of the aroused public opinion favoring health insurance, the BCMA decided to develop an organization that would sell a service contract to employee groups through their employer, who would be required to contribute a minimum of 50 percent of the premium, a stratagem with two clear advantages: a premium that would sustain higher fees, and the added incentives for unions to demand coverage in their annual contract bargaining. Moreover, in another brilliant stroke of public relations, it was the only sponsored prepayment plan not to insist on a majority of medical members on the board of directors. Incorporated under the Societies Act on April 16, 1940, the charter of British Columbia Medical Services Associated (BCMSA) called for a board of eight directors, two representing the profession, two the employers, and four the unions. The contrast with Physicians' Services Inc., a group established later and sponsored by the OMA, having two lay members on a board of seventeen, was remarkable, and this act of faith paid off in that BCMSA-profession relations were invariably more harmonious and the British Columbia fee schedule, in comparison with other provinces, among the highest. By the midforties BCMSA enrollment reached over one-quarter million subscribers.

The close collaboration of the CMA's "committee of seven" with the Heagerty Committee in 1942 and 1943 had clearly alerted CMA leaders to the possibilities inherent in the insurance model. (It is noteworthy that six of the seven members of the CMA's committee subsequently became presidents of the CMA.) And with the end of the war and the imminence of a government plan, the CMA leaders now urged all of its provincial divisions to launch profession-sponsored plans. As a result, new plans were organized in Saskatoon, Saskatchewan (1946), Ontario (1947), Alberta (1948), and Nova Scotia (1948).

But in their competition with the insurance industry, the prepayment plans suffered a very serious handicap: they could not offer a blanket contract to employers with employees in two or more provinces. The CMA leaders responded by calling a meeting of all the plans in 1947 for the purpose of creating an umbrella organization that could negotiate on behalf of several or all of the plans. The negotiations were difficult and protracted, and it was not until June 1951 that the CMA president was able to announce the formation of Trans-Canada Medical Plans (TCMP), with seven participating plans.[2] But there was still a major problem. The objective of those sponsoring TCMP was to limit its membership to plans sponsored and controlled by the respective provincial divisions of the CMA. But there was no physician-sponsored plan in Quebec, and the associations in Prince Edward Island and New Brunswick had approved the offering of indemnity medical benefits by Maritime Blue Cross–Blue Shield, which operated in those two provinces and in Nova Scotia. Finally the CMA realized it could not provide nation-wide contracts solely through plans controlled by the profession. Accordingly, in 1955 the TCMP bylaws were amended to state that "the Plan shall be sponsored, endorsed, approved or designated by a provincial medical association as a plan acceptable to its standards." Both Quebec Blue Cross–Blue Shield and Maritime Blue Cross–Blue Shield became approved members.

The growth of the medical prepayment plans was quite impressive. Between 1950 and 1961 they achieved a fourfold expansion, increasing the number of subscribers from 1.2 million to 4.8 million.

The development of the prepayment plans was important in several major respects. First, they offered a comprehensive contract; that is, unlike most commercial insurance and the profession-sponsored Blue Shield plans in the United States, they included office and home calls in their benefits package—probably attesting to the political clout of general practitioners in the provincial medical associations.

Second, they required, for the first time, an extraordinary degree of cooperation on the part of the vast majority of the profession. The associations had to negotiate a uniform, provincial fee schedule, and every participating physician was required to sign a contract agreeing to accept the plan's payment as payment in full. Only nonparticipating physicians could extra-bill, and any of their patients who were subscribers were required to submit a receipted bill to the plan in order to be reimbursed in accordance with the fee schedule.

All associations agreed that there should be a deduction of 10 percent of the fee to cover the administrative costs of the plan. The rationale for this provision was that the plan was, in effect, acting as a collection agency for the doctors, and most physicians rarely collected even as much as 90 percent (of the official fee schedule) from noninsured patients.

Finally, like the Blue Cross plans, most of the medical care plans also established a standardized provincewide premiums structure, with the same result that high-utilization groups were subsidized by low-utilization groups.

Commercial Insurance

As indicated earlier, the second major force seeking to fill the void following the failure of the 1945–46 dominion-provincial conference was the commercial insurance industry. So rapidly did it expand in the postwar period that by 1959 there were 119 companies selling health insurance benefits. They were of two types: (1) the life insurance companies, then organized in the CLIA, which concentrated on sales to groups, and (2) the casualty companies, then organized in the Association of Accident and Health Underwriters, which also sold group contracts but concentrated on sales to individuals. Both issued indemnity contracts which reimbursed their beneficiaries according to predetermined fee schedules that, while based on medical association fee schedules, typically required deductibles and copayments by patients.[3]

The commercial companies, in addition to selling contracts for hospital expense, separated medical from surgical benefits and insured each under separate contracts although, of course, both were frequently sold together. Table 3 reports the enrollment in the various types of prepayment organizations in 1952. Note that commercial medical and surgical enrollments are reported separately and undoubtedly represent some amount of duplication.

There was aggressive competition among the various companies and, of course, between the companies and the voluntary prepayment plans. Each

Table 3.
Estimated Enrollment in Voluntary Commercial Insurance and Prepayment Plans, 1950–52

Type of Insurer	Hospital Benefits			Surgical Benefits			Medical Benefits		
	1950	1951	1952	1950	1951	1952	1950	1951	1952
Insurance companies									
Group policies	1,269,000	1,635,000	1,870,000	1,242,000	1,670,000	1,926,000	526,000	800,000	1,904,000
Individual policies	642,000	706,000	833,000	316,000	348,000	420,000	130,000	143,000	169,000
Blue Cross plans	2,702,000	2,949,000	3,020,000	560,000	656,000	793,000	412,000	509,000	716,000
Medical care plans	55,000	70,000	60,000	662,000	871,000	1,084,000	661,000	871,000	1,084,000
Co-op plans	82,000	134,000	160,000	14,000	20,000	46,000	4,000	5,000	10,000
Grand totals	4,750,000	5,494,000	5,943,000	2,794,000	3,565,000	4,269,000	1,733,000	2,328,000	3,073,000
Less estimated duplication	319,000	390,000	450,000	208,000	267,000	311,000	88,000	124,000	166,000
Net totals	4,431,000	5,104,000	5,493,000	2,586,000	3,298,000	3,958,000	1,645,000	2,204,000	2,907,000
Increase during year		15.2%	7.6%		27.5%	20.0%		34.0%	31.9%
Percentage of population insured	32.0%	35.9%	37.6%	18.7%	23.2%	27.1%	11.9%	15.5%	19.9%
Adjusted population[a]	11,876,000	12,210,000	12,564,000						
Percentage of adjusted population insured	37.3%	41.8%	43.7%						

Source: Canadian Life Insurance Officers Association.

[a] "Adjusted population" equals the population of Canada less that of British Columbia and Saskatchewan, where compulsory provincial government hospital care plans exist. No deduction has been made from "adjusted population" for the estimated 770,000 covered by government plans in Alberta and Newfoundland nor from the numbers with voluntary insurance for duplication with government plans.

had one major advantage. The prepayment plans offered the advantage of the service contract, which normally paid the charges in full and required no paperwork on the part of the patient. The advantage for an insurance company was that it typically "experience-rated" its group contracts, which meant that in competing for a contract for, say, hospital insurance in a company with a high proportion of young, healthy adults, the insurance company could offer premiums considerably below those of Blue Cross.

But as successful as the voluntary plans and insurance industry had become, leaders of both groups recognized that it was a race for time if they were to prevent further expansion of government programs. By 1950 two provinces (Saskatchewan and British Columbia) had programs covering the entire population, and two others (Alberta and Newfoundland) had programs covering about half their residents. Moreover, despite imaginative efforts by Blue Cross, especially in forming groups of nonemployees, and massive sales campaigns by the insurance companies, by 1952 only 37.6 percent of the population outside Saskatchewan and British Columbia were protected against hospital costs, and less than one-fifth of the total population was protected for medical or surgical expenses. And, of course, the task of expanding enrollment became increasingly difficult as the number of viable employee groups becoming insured increased. The importance of group enrollment through employers was underscored by the 65 percent hospital insurance enrollment of the population in highly industrialized Ontario.

The dilemma for the prepayment plans and insurance leaders was acute. The more successful they were in demonstrating the advantages of insurance, the greater the public demand that it be available to all, and two provinces had demonstrated not only that a government plan was as feasible as it was desirable, but it could also achieve universal coverage with far lower overhead administrative costs. Public demand could only intensify in 1953, the year of a national election.

Chapter Six

National Hospital Care Insurance

The collapse of the Dominion-Provincial Conference on Post-War Recon-struction in May 1946 had dashed the hopes of millions of Canadians whose expectations of health insurance had been galvanized by the extraordinary publicity surrounding the public hearings of the House of Commons select committee in 1943 and 1944 and the announcement of the federal govern-ment's health insurance offer in the 1945 Green Book Proposals. Chapter 5 chronicled the major responses of the private sector to fill the gap. But there were also actions in the public sector that would be, in the end, of even greater significance, as three provincial governments picked up the torch, illustrating again the genius of federalism in that social programs are not solely dependent on initiatives by the federal government before progress can begin.

The Saskatchewan Hospital Services Plan, 1947

It will be recalled from chapter 1 that the CCF, the depression-born party, had won a spectacular victory in the Province of Saskatchewan in the election of June 15, 1944, routing the Liberal party by taking forty-seven of the fifty-two seats. The leader, Tommy Douglas, became premier, and to emphasize the priority to be given to health services, he also assumed the portfolio of minister of health.

The government began immediately to act on its health policy and other commitments and in August appointed Dr. Henry Sigerist of Johns Hopkins

University as commissioner to provide a series of explicit objectives and priorities. The commissioner reported on October 4, 1944, outlining the need for the development of health regions, provision of a number of health services, the introduction of a provincewide hospitalization program, and the creation of an HSPC.[1]

The legislature was called for a fall session, and the Health Services Act was passed in November.[2] It provided for the HSPC and, among other responsibilities, authorized the government to pay for health services for "such classes of persons as might be designated by the Lieutenant Governor in Council" (that is, the cabinet).

Three appointments were made to the planning commission, with Dr. Mindel Sheps as secretary. The HSPC began negotiations with several health professions and the Saskatchewan Hospital Association, and on January 1, 1945, all recipients of old-age pensions, mother's allowances (similar to AFDC), and blind pensions and wards of the province were entitled to prepaid medical, hospital, dental, and drug benefits.[3] The government had been in office six months, but there was now in place a program of comprehensive benefits for approximately thirty thousand people.

Planning for a provincewide hospital services system now shifted into high gear, with much of the burden falling on Dr. Sheps. The difficulties were prodigious. Saskatchewan, which borders on Montana and North Dakota, had then a one-crop economy which had markedly improved since the dustbowl days of the 1930s. Most of its population of 850,000 was spread over the vast prairie farmland and organized in eighteen-mile-square rural municipalities, dotted with villages, small towns, and four cities. But there was also a major advantage in this grass-roots local government structure for the administration of a program seeking universal enrollment in that, as has been noted, many of those municipalities had been involved over many years in managing their own municipal doctor and hospital plans. Because of the precarious economic base of such small units, that experience had led the influential Saskatchewan Association of Rural Municipalities (SARM), a group with three hundred members, to urge the provincial government to adopt a provincewide program. At its 1944 annual meeting the SARM had passed this resolution: "The municipalities should make their services available for the purpose of collecting the personal tax from their residents and should assume some measure of responsibility in this respect." Here was a ready-made premiums collection system in which the rural municipality, village, town, and city clerks could reach the entire population.

The HSPC was charting new ground; nothing on such a scale had ever before been attempted by a provincial government. Because it was the first universal hospitalization program in Canada, which would set a pattern that other provinces would emulate, it is desirable to examine briefly the decisions the government made on the major issues.

Beneficiaries

There seems never to have been any thought other than that the program should be universal, that is, compulsory. Although the CMA and the British Columbia College of Physicians and Surgeons had insisted on an upper income limit ($2,400 and $1,800, respectively) to compulsory coverage, the Saskatchewan college had opposed such restrictions. The premise on which the government operated was that all should be covered and that all who could, should pay the premiums.

Benefits

The principle underlying the decision on the range of benefits was not dissimilar to that underlying universal coverage: within reasonable limits, all essential services of the hospital should be included, those at the standard ward level and as many of the other services that, in the Blue Cross plans, were designated as extras (and billed separately)—operating room, delivery room, anesthetic services, radiology, laboratory services, drugs, and so forth. The same principle obtained on the decision on benefit days: no limit on the number of days to which an insured would be entitled, as long as they were "medically necessary." Charges could continue to be made to patients choosing superior accommodation, but the majority of beds should be standard ward.

Estimates of Costs

Although it would be possible to refine estimates later when the 1945 hospital returns were submitted in 1946, it was essential for the cabinet to receive a ballpark figure as soon as possible. There was little experience anywhere to go on. No one knew what the effect of universal coverage would be, particularly the insuring of all the aged. Blue Cross data were limited largely to the working-age population. The data on some of the better municipal hospital plans were examined, and in the absence of more reliable data, the estimates accepted by the subcommittee working on the health proposals at the dominion-provincial conference later in the year were accepted: 1,500 days per 1,000 insured. The commission applied that rate to the 850,000 residents and multiplied that by its newly calculated average per diem rate to yield a preliminary estimate of $4.4 million. As 1945 data became available in 1946, these estimates were increased.

Sources of Revenue

It was agreed that the province should contribute to the hospitalization fund an amount equal to the per diem grants it, like most all the other provinces, was currently paying to all hospitals to assist in the care of nonpaying patients. It was also agreed that the province should continue to pay into the fund the actual costs of hospital care of those persons (old-age and blind pensioners, mothers' allowance recipients, etc.) whose health services were being provided under the Health Services Act. It was also agreed that apart from these government contributions, the hospital services plan should, as far as possible, be self-supporting.

As the planning passed midsummer of 1945, it was clear that the federal Green Book Proposals introduced new emphasis on what the SARM had referred to as a personal tax. Those proposals required the provinces to provide for a "registration fee" to be paid by or on behalf of every person. A registration fee of any size was, in effect, an insurance premium, with the implication that nonpayment disqualified one from entitlement to benefits. Apparently, in expectation of action by the federal government, no other alternative was seriously considered, and the premium or personal tax (or poll tax) system was decided upon.

But a registration fee, or "hospitalization tax," as the forthcoming act was to call it, paid on behalf of every person, is a regressive tax. About 12 percent of Saskatchewan households at the time had more than four members, and these accounted for just under one-third of the population. The HSPC considered that a reasonable maximum should be set to reduce the burden on large families, and it prepared alternative premium structures to raise the estimated required revenues.

Paying the Hospitals

How to pay the hospitals equitably for services rendered to beneficiaries constituted without doubt the most complex question the HSPC faced. The simplest answer was that hospitals should be paid their costs of operation, but the chief obstacle to this proposal was the lack of a uniform accounting system among the provinces' hospitals and, indeed, in some hospitals of any intelligible accounting record. A second proposal was to classify hospitals according to size, paying them on a graduated scale (a system later adopted by Alberta). This method was rejected on the grounds that it could not be demonstrated that there existed a high correlation between size and per diem costs of operation.

But a new and unconventional method, referred to as the units-of-credit system, had been recently proposed by Dr. G. Harvey Agnew, executive director of the Canadian Hospital Council, in an article which appeared in *Canadian Hospital* (November 1943) and had been reprinted in the January 1944 issue of the U.S. journal *Hospitals*. As described by Dr. Agnew:

> In essence, the proposal is to grade hospitals according to the facilities and services provided. The *per diem* payment for each patient would be based on the number of "points" credited to each hospital and would be multiplied by the number of patient days recorded to give the total amount to be paid.
>
> Each hospital would be credited with so many points, according to the extent to which it provides operating rooms, delivery rooms, laboratory tests, X-rays, etc; and a basic number of points would be allocated for in-patient nursing care, dietary, and housekeeping services. The hospital would be paid so many mills for each unit or point credited to it. For example, one hospital might warrant 400 units and another, 500 units. If the rate be, say, 7 mills ($0.007), the first hospital would receive $2.80 per patient day and the other $3.50.

Dr. Agnew claimed a number of advantages for the system. First, all hospitals would be paid according to their ability to provide services. Then, the plan would stimulate improvement in equipment and in expert personnel. Third, size alone would not be a factor, as it would be in a system in which larger hospitals were paid a higher daily rate. Finally, by using different monetary values for the "unit of credit," varying amounts of payment adapted to varying cost situations (e.g., as indicated by the cost of living index) could be calculated. Although there were doubts and misgivings about the Agnew system, given the state of accounting among many small hospitals, the HSPC decided to recommend the system to the government. (It may be noted here that the Agnew point system was abandoned at the end of the first year, and from then on hospitals were paid on the basis of their approved budgets, a policy made possible by a new accounting system.)

On each of these major issues, planning briefs presenting alternative policies were presented to the cabinet for decision. In contrast to several of the future episodes to be examined, there was a minimum of conflict within the province and no protracted negotiations with the federal government, although it was considered essential that the plan be designed to meet anticipated federal requirements. Indeed, experts from the Department of National Health and Welfare and the Dominion Bureau of Statistics participated in the planning, to their mutual advantage, in this new learning experience.

The strategy of implementation was directed primarily to creating the administrative organization and to eliciting the cooperation of all the affected groups who must make the system work: the municipalities, the hospitals, and the medical profession. Moreover, the strategy had to be executed in such a way as to overcome the suspicions and reduce the opposition—both within the interest groups and among a segment of the public—to anything about to be "perpetrated by a socialist government."

The first approach to the hospitals had occurred early on—in the fall of 1945—when Premier Douglas was invited to give the keynote address at the hospital association's annual meeting on October 30.[4] There he had attempted to allay any fears and to direct the members' thinking about the future. His main points were (1) an assurance of the continuation of ownership of hospitals by municipalities, religious orders, and other voluntary groups; (2) a regional concept of hospital development; (3) proposals for provincial grants to assist in financing hospital construction (the first such program in Canada, and somewhat ahead of the Hill-Burton Act in the United States); (4) the need for chronic care hospitals; and (5) the desire of the government to assist in the development of a comprehensive hospitals system.

Beginning the Program

One of the most critical decisions—inherent in all major policy thrusts—was that of timing of the launching of the program in relation to the election which could be held in 1949 but which, for election strategy reasons, should be held in 1948. If the program was to be introduced before the election, it must be seen to be operating successfully not later than the spring of 1948. But time was required (1) to create the administrative organization and procedures, (2) to complete as many as possible of one thousand hospital beds approved for construction, and (3) after the introduction of the program, to correct any major defects that would inevitably appear before the voter evaluation in the election would take place.

The alternative was to postpone the introduction until after the election, which would give time for more thorough preparation in creating the administrative organization and in expanding facilities and would thus greatly reduce the risks of foul-ups. On the other hand, it had grave political disadvantages in that the government would certainly be accused of failing to fulfill its election commitment. It was decided, therefore, that the program must begin on January 1, 1947, which would require passage of the legislation during the session beginning about the first of February 1946, or several months before the outcome of the then-meeting dominion-provincial conference and the prospect of federal cost-sharing would be known. It was an extremely short critical path.

In the meantime the HSPC appointed two administrative committees whose work would be critical to the operation. The first, chaired by a member of the HSPC, C. C. Gibson, the former administrator of the Regina General Hospital, began evaluating the hospitals on the Agnew point system. The second, chaired by a chartered accountant, G. W. Myers, began the development of a uniform accounting system for the hospitals. This was a most significant project that would, after its completion in Saskatchewan, be taken over by the CHA and in collaboration with the Department of National Health and Welfare, would lead to the publication of the Canadian Hospital Accounting Manual and be adopted by all the hospitals in Canada.

In view of the population changes which had taken place since the 1941 census, it was considered essential that the entire population be preregistered. This would be done by the rural municipality secretaries and the village clerks, and in the towns and cities by the enumerators of the annual voters' lists. From these lists, the Saskatchewan Hospital Services Plan (SHSP), the name designated in the enabling act, would prepare the hospital services entitlement cards, which would then be forwarded to nearly nine hundred municipal secretaries and village, town, and city clerks for distribution to those who paid the prescribed tax.

The premiums structure was finally settled at five dollars per person, annually, with a maximum of thirty dollars for a family. The collection period was designated from September 1 to November 30, 1946, coinciding with the farmers' sale of their crops. Late payment would be penalized by a six months' waiting period, and an eligible resident who failed to pay the tax would be subject to wage garnishment or prosecution. With respect to persons receiving public assistance, the tax would be paid on their behalf by that agency of government—municipal, provincial, or federal—responsible for their medical and hospital care.

There was one major organizational decision to be made. Which agency should be responsible for administration? The most obvious was the Department of Public Health, but none of its senior personnel had experience with health insurance or, indeed, with any operation of such magnitude. Moreover, as a staff agency, the HSPC had been responsible for all the planning and the negotiations. It was therefore decided that HSPC should become both a line and a staff agency. A new division, the SHSP, would administer the hospitalization program. In addition, the Hospital Planning Division and the Medical Services Division (which administered the Social Assistance Health Services Program) would be transferred from the Department of Health to the commission, and an expanded research division would be created. Both HSPC, with the deputy minister of health an ex officio member, and the Department of Health were responsible to the minister of health.

In September there were important personnel changes. In March 1946 Dr. Cecil Sheps (husband of Dr. Mindel Sheps) had been released from the army and became acting chairman of HSPC. But on September 1 the Doctors Sheps resigned to accept fellowships for postdoctoral study in the United States. Dr. Frederick D. Mott, a senior officer in the U.S. Public Health Service, an American citizen who had graduated from McGill Medical School in Montreal and had married a Canadian, became chairman, and Dr. Leonard S. Rosenfeld, also an officer in the U.S. health service, became vice-chairman and executive director of SHSP. Both were fortunate choices, which became clear as they accelerated preparations for "the appointed day." The accounting manual was finalized; the point-system evaluation was completed; the tax collection procedures agreed upon by the rural and urban municipalities; scores of secretarial, clerical, and tabulating personnel were appointed and trained; and a massive publicity program was mounted to encourage early registration and tax payment.

It was a period of feverish activity, reminiscent of mobilization for war in 1939. The only office space available was an ancient, vacant store building; clerical desks were long rows of plywood on trestles, with clerks sitting elbow-to-elbow, processing the registration and tax-collection payments according to a system that, although using keypunch and mechanical tabulating equipment, was quite primitive. As January 1, 1947, approached, the feelings of excitement—mixed with apprehension—mounted, with hospital personnel and doctors waiting for the onslaught of increased demand, and Premier Douglas, his cabinet, and caucus hoping that the policy decision "to go it alone" would have positive rather than negative political results.

Apart from those already in the hospital on December 31, the first patients to be admitted under the program were Mrs. R. Hunt, wife of a Regina doctor, who gave birth to a baby boy fifteen minutes past midnight, Mrs. Joseph Safazakis, whose child was born at 5:45 A.M., and Mrs. Charles Reid, whose baby was born at 8:20 P.M.[5] All three children automatically became insured beneficiaries for the year 1947. A social idea had been translated into an operating reality; the first universal hospital insurance program in North America had been launched. For Saskatchewan there was no turning back.

There were important outcomes from the Saskatchewan initiative. From the political point of view, the gamble to introduce the program before the federal policy had been decided upon paid off. Although there were strains in the system, resulting from the shortage of hospital beds, and much criticism in the antigovernment press, the minor crises were weathered. By the time of the election in 1948, the plan could be said to be operating successfully. With hospital revenues assured by the SHSP, communities throughout the province began to develop new facilities, or to expand existing ones. They were assisted by provincial hospital construction grants for approved projects. With the planning and the controls introduced by the HSPC, there began to emerge a coordinated system of community, district, and regional hospitals based on the two major centers of Regina and Saskatoon, where construction of a new university hospital was begun in 1949. The ratio of hospital beds to population increased from 4.8 per 1,000 in 1946 to 6.5 per 1,000 in 1951.

The hospital utilization rate increased rapidly until it was the highest of any prepayment plan in Canada.[6] This resulted from many factors: the shortage of physicians and a consequent pattern of practice that provided few home calls; the difficulties of transportation in rural Saskatchewan; the combination of large families, low incomes, and poor housing; the failure (or impossibility, in the early stages) to introduce outpatient benefits; the almost total lack of alternative chronic care hospitals, nursing homes, or home care programs; and the fact that, unlike the voluntary plans, SHSP insured all recipients of social assistance and the aged.

The costs of the plan and, therefore, the provincial subsidy from general revenues were considerably in excess of estimates. The tax collection system, on the other hand, was successful to a degree unexpected for a regressive poll tax. (In 1972 Saskatchewan abandoned the premiums system and increased its revenues through the income tax.)

All of Canada benefited from the Saskatchewan experience. From its inception until the Quebec Hospital Plan went into effect in 1961, no provincial government failed to send its officials to Regina to learn firsthand how the program operated and what policies and procedures could be adapted to their home provinces. In the educational process through which Canadian governments learned how to administer universal hospital insurance, Saskatchewan paid most of the tuition fees.

The British Columbia Hospital Insurance Service, 1949

The decision to introduce hospital insurance in British Columbia was taken in 1947 by a badly divided Liberal-Conservative coalition cabinet. The premier, known as "Boss" Johnson, and the minister of health, George Pearson, were Liberals, but the powerful minister of finance was a Conservative. George Pearson had been a member of the cabinet during the ill-starred attempts to introduce health insurance in the 1930s, and he was determined on two things: to crown his long career in provincial politics with at least part of a health insurance program and to avoid what he considered to have been the mistakes of his predecessor.[7]

The legislation was passed in 1948, and the minister appointed a public health official, Dr. J. M. Hershey, as commissioner and Andrew Pitkethly, an official in Public Works, as executive director. Although the program was scheduled to begin on January 1, 1949, Hershey and Pitkethly did not visit Regina to study the administration of the Saskatchewan plan until July 1948. They spent one week interviewing officials and returned to Victoria with organization charts and boxes of forms. (I was research director for HSPC at the time and recall discussing my apprehensions with Chairman Mott on their departure.)

Because of the mountainous terrain of British Columbia and the concentration of the population in the three cities of Victoria (the capital), Vancouver, and New Westminster, with a large part of the rest of the population in unorganized territory serviced by provincial government agents, it was not feasible for the province to adopt the very efficient Saskatchewan municipal collection system. Moreover, although Blue Cross had been in operation since 1941, it had enrolled only 110,000 subscribers, and although its equipment and most of its staff had been taken over by the British Columbia Hospital Insurance Service (BCHIS), it was apparently impossible to expand the administrative system rapidly enough to permit payroll deduction collections of the premiums from all other employee groups. It was therefore necessary for BCHIS to create a second collection system: what was termed by the few voluntary plans that insured individuals as "pay-direct." This arrangement entailed monthly or quarterly billings, an inefficient and expensive system in comparison with Saskatchewan's annual payments. Because of the lack of foresight and appreciation on the part of the government of the magnitude of the administrative operation, the two collection systems had to be set up almost overnight.

The combination of lack of advanced planning, inadequate time for training of new staff, and two complicated collection systems created an administrative nightmare. Many were uninsured. Many who had paid their premiums did not receive their entitlement cards; some who had not paid did receive them; the change-of-address and change-of-employers procedures bogged down. As time went by, the problem of arrears of unpaid taxes snowballed. By the summer of 1952, for example, a person entering the system could owe as much as $147.50 in addition to current premiums. The resentment of delinquent taxpayers and of employers forced to act as tax collectors grew exponentially.

A proportion of the uninsured were hospitalized and unable to pay their accounts; hospitals' costs increased, as did their deficits. The public and the press responded with increased criticism. The debates in the legislature grew more acrimonious, leading to investigation by a formal Hospital Insurance Inquiry Board, resignation of the commissioner, transfer of the executive director, and, finally, resignation of the minister, ending his dream of a triumphal conclusion to his long legislative career.[8]

Under a new minister, Douglas Turnbull, who appointed a new commissioner, Lloyd Detwiller, from the Finance Department, the situation began to improve. On April 1, 1951, coinsurance payments ranging from $2.00 to $3.50 per patient-day (depending on the size of hospital) were imposed. The maximum for any one family was set at ten days' payment per year—creating yet another administrative problem. Despite the shortcomings of the premiums system, by the end of 1952, over 83 percent of hospital accounts were insured by BCHIS, and another 8 percent were the responsibility of other agencies or of legitimate self-paying patients.[9]

But the imposition of coinsurance, together with premium increases in both 1950 and 1951, merely added fuel to the flames of public reaction to high premiums in general and the arrears question in particular. Added to the opposition and newspaper charges of inefficiency in the BCHIS administration and rumors of a split in the Liberal-Conservative cabinet over the entire program, the net effect was to make hospital insurance the most emotional and controversial issue in the 1952 election campaign. The result was defeat of the government. (One might contrast the experiences in the two provinces by noting that in Saskatchewan the hospital insurance plan became popular before it became expensive, whereas in British Columbia the reverse was true.)

The new Social Credit government, under Premier W. A. C. Bennett, adopted a number of changes. The six months' prepayment and waiting period was abandoned; liability for and collection of arrears were abolished, and thus, except for those persons subject to compulsory payroll deductions, participation in the plan became, in effect, voluntary. The coinsurance payments were abolished and replaced by a one-dollar-per-day charge, without limit. Rising hospital charges, which made insurance more desirable, and the removal of the liability for tax arrears brought thirty thousand new residents into the system.

By early 1954 the system was working tolerably well. But on April 1, the beginning of the fiscal year, a new policy (on which the BCHIS commissioner had been neither consulted nor informed)[10] was announced, abolishing premiums for hospital insurance and increasing the social services retail sales tax from 3 to 5 percent. The dollar-a-day coinsurance was retained.[11]

With the changed revenue system, all the headaches, frustrations, waiting periods, payroll deductions, direct billings, uninsured hospital accounts, and three hundred BCHIS administrative and clerical positions were ended. The turmoil, bad publicity, and political repercussions of the insurance phase of BCHIS were over. Although the savings in administrative overhead were minimal (the increases in commissions to retailers for collecting the higher sales tax was not much less than the savings in administrative salaries), there was no doubt as to the greater efficiency of the new system. Proof of residence for one year was all that was required for entitlement to insured hospital benefits. (After this experience, it came as a sharp surprise when the British Columbia Social Credit government introduced its Medical Plan in 1965 that it again resorted to the premiums system, but only for the medical benefit.)

British Columbia had also paid part of the tuition costs in educating Canadian governments in the formulation of effective policies and procedures in this most complex of the social insurances. It had demonstrated the dangers in trying to import an administrative system from another jurisdiction differing in both its economic and political organization. It had alerted other provincial governments to the necessity of a much longer lead time for planning and design of the program and for creating the administrative organization and its procedures. But the popularity of the policy of universal prepayment, as distinct from its maladministration, could not be doubted. Like Regina, Victoria became a Mecca for health authorities in all other provinces in the mid-1950s as they prepared to introduce their own programs.

The Alberta Municipal Hospital Plan, 1950

With government-sponsored hospital insurance programs operating in provinces on either side, it was not surprising that Alberta decided to introduce a program on July 1, 1950—the Alberta Municipal Hospital Plan (AMHP). One element of a provincewide program was already in place. In 1944 the Alberta government had introduced a maternity hospitalization program providing standard-ward care for all resident maternity patients, paid directly from the provincial treasury. Later, full payment for all poliomyelitis cases was provided. Hospitalization benefits for recipients of social assistance were introduced on January 1, 1950.

But the new program did not replicate the bold new thrusts that characterized the Saskatchewan and British Columbia decisions to develop a centrally administered program providing universal coverage. Rather, Alberta followed the Lindblom incremental model by building on the handful of municipal hospital plans that had been developed over the years. The government decided to subsidize municipal plans that provided standard ward care, but not including the "extras" that had been part of the British Columbia and Saskatchewan benefits packages. The extras would be added at a later date.

The legislation provided that when a municipality had passed the required bylaw, all taxpayers and their dependents would be entitled to public-ward accommodation in any hospital with which the municipality had entered into a contract.[12] All nontaxpayers (i.e., tenants) could voluntarily participate in the plan by purchasing a hospital ticket at the low cost of ten dollars per year for an individual or a family.

All hospitals in the province were classified into five categories, and a uniform per diem rate was established for each category. Each patient was required to pay a coinsurance charge of one dollar per day, and the province and the municipality shared the balance. Later, when the extras were included as benefits by a municipality, the coinsurance charge was raised to two dollars per day.

Because not all municipalities established local plans, the program was estimated to cover approximately 75 percent of the population by 1953.[13] Hospitals were responsible for any deficit, which meant that municipalities owning hospitals would be responsible. Hospitals owned by religious groups or voluntary organizations were particularly vulnerable, since they had no such tax base to fall back on.

The contrast in the effectiveness of the three provincial plans in solving the twin problems of patients and hospitals is revealed in the financial data on sources of hospitals' income in 1954. In that year, hospitals in British Columbia received 73.0 percent of their revenues from the BCHIS; in Saskatchewan, SHSP payments were 85.7 percent of all income; in Alberta, however, only 38.6 percent of hospital revenues were paid by the AMHP.[14]

The Newfoundland Cottage Hospital System

When Newfoundland entered the confederation in 1949, it joined the ranks of Saskatchewan and British Columbia as a province with a hospital services plan. It was, in essence, what other Canadians would have called state medicine in that it provided services through provincially owned hospitals and physicians paid by salary, most of whom were recruited from the British Isles. The service was limited to the isolated outports of Newfoundland. Entitlement to services was conditional on payment of a modest annual premium. Approximately 47 percent of the population was insured under the program.

New Beginnings at the Federal Level

By the end of 1950, four of the ten provinces had programs that covered almost half or three-quarters or, in British Columbia and Saskatchewan, nearly all of the population. With this background, we now shift to the national scene, where the last noted event had been the collapse of the Dominion-Provincial Conference on Post-War Reconstruction in May 1946. With that failure the federal government's ambitious and idealistic plans for postwar Canada were in disarray. So, too, was the financial position of most of the provinces. In the next two years decisions were taken to go at least part of the way with respect to taxation arrangements and health services. The first decision was to negotiate taxation agreements with those provinces that wished to do so and to separate entirely the earlier interdependence between the financial arrangements and the Green Book social security and health proposals. By 1947 taxation agreements with seven provinces were in place, with the two largest provinces, Ontario and Quebec, still not on board (although they, too, would sign agreements in 1950). Those agreements provided for the transfer to the federal government of jurisdiction over personal and corporation income taxes and succession duties in return for substantial federal per capita grants to the provinces.

The second decision took a little longer. In December 1946 Prime Minister Mackenzie King made a major change in the Health and Welfare portfolio by transferring Brooke Claxton to the Ministry of Defense and promoting Paul Martin from his position as secretary of state to minister of health and welfare. The new minister had been interested in health insurance even before his parliamentary career began in 1935 and had spoken on a number of occasions in the Liberal caucus on the party's long-standing commitment to health insurance. Among those who knew the minister well, there was no doubt that he would move forward on the health proposals as rapidly as the cabinet would permit. But the failure of the 1945–46 conference had created a wave of pessimism among cabinet members, dashing any earlier confidence in the possible success of major federal initiatives in fields of provincial jurisdiction. Moreover, as the nation grappled with the immediate problems of reemployment of service personnel and defense workers, those dreams of a better postwar world envisioned in the Green Book Proposals seemed to be just that—only dreams.

Martin was determined, however, that as a new minister in the health portfolio, he must make some progress. In January 1948 he had a long discussion with Prime Minister King and endeavored to persuade him that he should not end his long parliamentary career without at least initiating the program of health insurance that he had persuaded the Liberal party to adopt as a commitment at the 1919 convention. As the conversation continued, the maximum first step on which King would agree was introduction of part of the 1945 proposals—the health grants. The proposal was taken to the cabinet by Martin, and that body agreed. On May 18, 1948, the prime minister announced in the House of Commons what came to be known as the National Health Grants Program.[15]

The format of the grants followed the 1945 offer, with two exceptions— one minor, the other major. Perhaps owing to Mackenzie King's proclivity for caution, the former planning and organization grant, which hinted of action to come, was converted into the more neutral title of "health survey grant." The other was the hospital construction grant, a matching grant that replaced the loans for hospital construction proposed in 1945. The annual grants were as follows:

General public health	$ 4,395,000
Venereal disease control	275,000
Mental health	4,000,000
Tuberculosis control	3,000,000
Cancer control (matching grant)	3,500,000
Crippled children	500,000
Professional training	500,000
Public health research	100,000[16]
Hospital construction (matching grant)	13,000,000
Health survey grant	645,000

The health survey grant was provided for three purposes: (1) to ensure the most effective use of the other grants, (2) to plan the extension of hospital accommodation, and (3) to plan for the proper organization of hospital and medical care insurance. "These grants," said Mackenzie King, "represent the first stages in the development of a comprehensive health insurance plan for all Canada."[17]

For the provincial health departments, the grants were a welcome source of new funds. Here were revenues available for long-delayed health measures, free from the annual battles with provincial finance officials who were, too frequently, still scrutinizing Health Department budget requests in terms of increments to the paltry depression and wartime appropriations. The full story of the impact of the health grants, which were phased out in the 1960s, has never been told, but it is fair to say that they did constitute, as the prime minister had described them, "the fundamental prerequisites of a nation-wide system of health insurance." One of the spin-off effects was that the meetings of provincial health officials held periodically in Ottawa to review annual expenditures and new proposals provided opportunities to compare ideas, report solutions to mutual problems, and exchange plans for new projects on a scale never before known. The grants program thus had a catalytic effect on nationwide health services planning and development, not anticipated when it was launched.[18]

Most of the provinces assigned the health survey function to committees representing the professions, the public, and the health department.[19] Since one of the intended tasks was to "plan the proper organization of hospital and medical care insurance," the committees helped to keep the issue very much in the forefront of public attention.

But there were now major changes in leadership that had the effect of postponing action at the national level for several years. Mackenzie King, prime minister over a span of twenty-eight years, decided to retire, and his choice for successor fell on Louis St. Laurent, his justice minister and member of Parliament for Quebec City. St. Laurent reluctantly agreed to stand for nomination. The Liberal convention elected him leader on the first ballot on August 7, 1948, and he became prime minister on November 15. As one journalist observed, "When a man seeks an office it isn't news, but when an office seeks a man it is."[20] St. Laurent had become leader of his country without political commitments. A former corporation lawyer, he "seemed hardly the man to lead the more impatient members of his party in what they considered was the true orientation of Canadian liberalism, a sustained campaign of progress and reform. . . . He believed in free enterprise as the most efficient means of assuring full employment . . . [and] he accepted social welfare legislation as a means for caring for the weaker members of society."[21] Government action to bring about a universal program of health insurance that would have the effect of removing the field from private enterprise would fit most uncomfortably within such philosophical parameters.

The second change of actor was the election of George Drew, then premier of Ontario and the major figure in the failure of the 1945 dominion-provincial conference, to leadership of the Conservative opposition party in Ottawa. An implacable foe of Mackenzie King, Drew's political philosophy was clearly more in harmony with that of St. Laurent, and he, too, favored a private-enterprise solution to the economic problems of health care.

The departure of Drew from Ontario led to the third change of actors when Leslie Frost, a lawyer and provincial treasurer, became premier of Ontario. His philosophy, too, accorded with that of St. Laurent, but he had a much keener sense of the obligations of the largest and richest province in the design of confederation than had Drew. He quickly moved to end the acrimonious relationships between Ottawa and Ontario that had characterized the King-Drew period. He wrote to St. Laurent to congratulate him on his election as leader. St. Laurent immediately telephoned him, and a few days later they met in Ottawa to talk, discovering that they held many views in common.

In the 1949 federal election, the new Liberal leader spoke mainly in generalities and made no firm commitment to health insurance. The Liberal party platform reaffirmed the party's commitment to social security and health insurance.[22] The Conservative platform also stated the party's commitment to health insurance in general terms but gave no indication of how or when, if elected, it would act. The CCF, as expected after the successful launching of hospital insurance by the Saskatchewan wing of the party, included a lengthy statement on health insurance, saying, in part, "The CCF believes that the Federal Government should take the leadership in, and assume the major responsibility for, the establishment of a comprehensive health service which will provide for all citizens hospital, medical, dental and optical care, irrespective of their incomes." And the Social Credit party was also committed, stating in part, "A Social Credit Government would establish a non-contributory system of national health insurance to assure all citizens of access to necessary preventive medicine, medical and hospital care, free from any bureaucratic regimentation of patients, doctors, nurses or hospital authorities."

The results for the new prime minister were overwhelming. The Liberals obtained 190 seats, the Conservatives 41 (a loss of 26), the CCF 13 (a loss of 15), and Social Credit 10 (a loss of 3).

With such minor emphasis given to health insurance by either of the major parties, the results of a Gallup poll released shortly after the election seem paradoxical if one assumes some direct relationship between strong public opinion and responses of political parties. The question was phrased, "Would you approve or disapprove of a National Health Plan whereby you would pay a flat rate each month and be assured of complete medical and hospital care by the Dominion Government?"[23] The responses, with the 1944 responses for comparison, were:

	1949	1944
Approve	80%	80%
Disapprove	13%	16%
Undecided	7%	4%

The majority of four out of five supporting the proposal duplicated that of 1944. But the majority view was obviously not reflected in the election mandate.

One other important event in 1949 had great influence on the shape of things to come—a major shift in policy by the CMA. It will be recalled that in 1943 the CMA had participated in the drafting of the Mackenzie-Heagerty proposals and had given a ringing endorsement of a government program during hearings of the House of Commons select committee. But with seven profession-sponsored plans already in place, the CMA decided to reverse that policy, favoring now the extension of the voluntary plans to cover all Canadians, with governments paying the premiums on behalf of those unable to provide for themselves.[24] That declaration was followed by similar reversals of policy by the CHA and the CLIA. They, too, now urged that the proper role of government was to pay the premiums in whole for those in receipt of social assistance and subsidize those with low incomes. These new policies would dominate the debates over the next fifteen years.

But there was one more 180-degree turn that shocked the interest groups supporting health insurance: a policy shift by the federal government itself. Although St. Laurent had been chairman of the cabinet committee that had drafted the health and social security sections of the Green Book Proposals in 1945, his philosophy of the role of government, as we have seen, was opposed to such intervention and, as prime minister, he was now in a position to have his views prevail. He gave two reasons for his position. First, he did not believe that there were enough hospital beds to meet the demand if all were insured, and as a lawyer, he felt it unethical for the government to make a commitment it could not fulfill. (This was a dubious explanation, for, with the aid of the hospital construction grant, in the period 1948–53 more than forty-six thousand beds had been added. Indeed, just before the 1953 election, the hospital construction grant was cut in half and the funds allocated to other health grants.) Second, it would be unjustifiable for the federal government to levy taxes on all citizens for the benefit of a minority living in provinces that had plans in place. Accordingly, the 1953 Liberal election platform, reflecting the prime minister's views, stated: "The Liberal party is committed to support a policy of contributory health insurance to be administered by the provinces when most of the provinces are ready to join in a nationwide scheme." That, as the pundits said, "puts the ball in the provinces' court."

What it really did, however, was put the ball in Ontario's court, for if St. Laurent insisted on a majority of the population being covered before federal funding could be justified, then either Quebec or Ontario would have to have a program in place or at least about to begin, and everyone knew that Quebec's Premier Duplessis was adamantly opposed. That meant that the one man who would make the decision was Premier Leslie Frost of Ontario, a man supremely in control of his cabinet. But Frost did not need hospital insurance as a political carrot in an election platform. He had a very comfortable majority in the legislature, and the party's prospects were bright.

The combination of all these developments had created a totally different environment from that of 1945. One person whose role both enabled and required him to be alert to such changes as they might affect government policy was George Gathercole, provincial economist for Ontario and Frost's closest official adviser. His primary concern was the fact that no one in the Ontario government was involved in any planning about health insurance. Accordingly, on April 7, 1954, I was invited to meet with Premier Frost and Gathercole. (I was then an associate professor in the Department of Political Economy in the University of Toronto.) They requested me to prepare an analysis of the situation with respect to hospitals and physicians, the methods of financing health services with emphasis on insurance, and alternative methods of extending health insurance to all residents of Ontario, together with estimates of the costs of so doing. The study was begun at the end of the academic term, and a 186-page report was submitted on August 31.[25]

The major premises on which the report was based were as follows: that all the costs of sickness and injury are borne by society in two ways, negatively through misery, disability, and premature death, and positively through the costs of preventive and treatment services; that it is in the interests of society as well as of the individual to reduce the negative costs by expanding and improving health services; that increasing costs will inevitably fall on the provincial treasury; that wise planning and leadership on the part of the government could contain the size of that burden by preventing the lopsided development of certain health services; that the introduction of universal hospital insurance would necessitate strict controls to prevent the overbuilding of facilities; that professional and hospital services flourish in an environment of freedom, including freedom from excessive bureaucratic control; that government and private activity in the field of health are neither incompatible nor mutually exclusive, since there is more to be done than both together can do; that it is easier for members of the community to pay more for health services while they are well than if only the sick pay for them; that in the words of the World Health Organization (WHO) Charter, "informed opinion and active cooperation on the part of the public are of the utmost importance in the improvement of the health of the people."

The report was distributed to all members of cabinet and to senior officials in the Departments of Health, Welfare, and Municipal Affairs. Premier Frost considered it a confidential document, and it was therefore not released to the legislature, a decision I keenly regretted.

The report analyzed the economics of hospital and medical care in Ontario, including the extent and effectiveness of voluntary and commercial insurance, current expenditures on health services, and hospital utilization of insured and noninsured residents. (The admission rate of insured residents was 40 percent higher than that of the uninsured, but the average length of stay of the uninsured was 40 percent longer.) The report examined the services desirable in a comprehensive system and presented estimates of costs of introducing them in stages. It then examined alternative methods of administration and financing. Major emphasis was placed on the desirability of providing as much medical care as possible through group practice clinics and on the dangers of introducing hospital insurance alone. I persuaded George Gathercole to visit New York's Montefiore Hospital's home care program with me, and he too became a convert under Martin Cherkasky's spell. Although we also convinced Frost of the importance of introducing a home care program simultaneously with hospital insurance, it did not happen for another twenty years.

Two special studies were undertaken in the preparation of the report. The first was conducted with the collaboration of the Ontario Hospital Association and Statistics Canada, in which a randomly selected sample of fourteen thousand hospital accounts was analyzed to ascertain the size of the account, by whom it was paid, and, if paid by an insurance agency, what proportion of the account was in fact insured. The results of the survey indicated what would be expected, that the proportion of the hospital account paid by the insuring agency varied inversely with the size of the account, with the proportion declining according to whether it was insured by Blue Cross, commercial group insurance, commercial individual insurance, or a cooperative.

What was evident was that with respect to the larger accounts, when protection was most needed, even Blue Cross began to falter, and the other types of coverage fell even further behind. In short, having two-thirds of the population insured for hospital benefits did not mean that two-thirds of the population were fully protected. It also showed that the protection fell off when it was most needed—for the long-term illness and the serious accident.

The second study centered on the question of the costs of protection, or on how much the insurance system added to the costs of health services. In simplest terms, what was the difference between the premiums that insured subscribers paid and the benefits that insuring agencies paid out? This study, conducted by a chartered accountant, was based on the annual reports of the superintendent of insurance. The analysis showed the following relationship between premiums and benefits:

Type of Insurer	Benefits as percentage of premiums	Premiums as percentage of benefits
Blue Cross	85.0	118.0
Commercial (group)	76.5	130.7
Commercial (individual)	58.2	170.8
Cooperatives	85.8	116.5

The insurance mechanism, therefore, added to the costs of hospital services 18 percent in the case of Blue Cross, 30 percent in the case of commercial group contracts, 70 percent in commercial individual contracts, and 16 percent in the case of cooperatives. (By comparison, overhead administration costs in the BCHIS were 5.7 percent and in the SHSP, 5.0 percent.) The data also confirmed the much higher costs of selling and servicing individual contracts which, as shown earlier, also provided the least degree of protection.

With the information and alternative proposals for expanding health insurance coverage for all residents of Ontario contained in the Taylor Report, Premier Frost was in a much better position to plan his future strategies. But although, as noted above, he felt no organized pressure to act on health insurance, nevertheless there were factors to be considered. The first might be called the idea of progress, an inchoate feeling abroad in the land that the 1945 agenda for a better life in Canada had not been completed, that there were next steps to be taken along the road to what Premier Frost came to describe as human betterment. It was linked to the growing public belief that health insurance worked and that the goal of universal coverage was as attainable as it was desirable.

The second factor stemmed from the first—the increasing public attention being paid to health insurance. Donald MacDonald, leader of the CCF party in Ontario, never allowed the legislature to forget the success of the SHSP, nor that a much less wealthy province had introduced its program without federal subsidy.

With the overwhelming Conservative majority, the sallies of the opposition parties might be easily disposed of, but as the year 1954 was ending, the issue had become more serious. The reason was that an election must be called in 1955. The Ontario Liberals and the CCF had both campaigned strongly for health insurance in the election of 1951. With the St. Laurent election campaign strategy in 1953 that had transferred the onus for initiative to the provinces, it could be anticipated that both parties would emphasize that the most significant provincial decision would be that of Ontario, and that, if elected, each would be committed to make the choice. From Frost's point of view the time might not be ripe for a decision, but it was time to remove the blame for delay from his government and return it to St. Laurent and the national Liberal party, which had held out the promise of health insurance since 1919.

The pressures were indeed mounting. As noted earlier, the very success of Blue Cross and commercial insurance raised demands by those unable to join in payroll groups and those unable to pay the high premiums for individual contracts that governments must act. Moreover, many newspapers, notably the high-circulation *Toronto Star*, maintained a strong editorial policy favoring government action. Finally, on March 23, 1955, during his budget address, Frost, who had retained the Treasury portfolio when he became premier, said:

> Health insurance for the people of Ontario is inevitable, but lack of as-surance of federal participation and overwhelming cost make it impos-sible at the present time. Whether the Federal government will con-tribute to such a plan is conjecture. So far, they have not undertaken to pay for any portion of the cost of hospital insurance plans operating in three other provinces, and it is unlikely they will make any contribution until health insurance is established on a national basis. However, the question is not one of whether health insurance will come—come it must and will. The only question is—when is the right time for it?[26]

But as he thought about his government's policy, knowing that he would encounter the greatest opposition to any positive action from within his own Conservative caucus and from business leaders in his party, his most con-suming passion was to put the onus for action back on the federal Liberals— where it belonged.

The opportunity came in April 1955. The taxation agreements to which all provinces had become signatories in 1950 required renegotiation every five years. That meant that there must be a federal-provincial conference in 1955 so that the enabling legislation could be passed by the eleven governments in 1956. Aware that the provinces had been most resentful of the federal government's domination of the agenda at both the 1945 and 1950 conferences, St. Laurent, although aware of the pitfalls, decided that he had no alternative but to call an agenda conference prior to the main event. Invitations were sent to the provincial premiers for a meeting beginning April 29, 1955.

In his opening statement the prime minister endeavored to limit the agenda to two items: the taxation agreements and some fine-tuning of the unemployment insurance program. It was then the turn of Premier Frost and he made it clear that there were other important subjects—six in all, including health insurance—with which the conference must deal.[27] His inclusion of health insurance was later strongly supported by Premier Douglas and Premier Bennett. But the real battle of the titans occurred at the in camera session on the second day over the issue of whether health insurance should be on the agenda at the main conference. The stronger Frost pressed, the more strongly St. Laurent resisted. Only the formal overlay of parliamentary courtesy thinly veiled the tough political battle being waged. (I attended as Frost's adviser on health insurance, and it was fascinating to watch the struggle.)

Following a strategy meeting of the federal government's delegation during the lunchtime break, St. Laurent agreed that the item should be placed on the agenda under the noncommittal term "health and welfare services." Only much later did it emerge that during the strategy meeting Health Minister Paul Martin had informed the prime minister that his opposition to the inclusion of the item was contrary to long-held Liberal policy and that if St. Laurent persisted, Martin would have to resign. Newspaper reporters were aware of the political struggle behind the closed doors and a typical headline shouted, "Provinces Win!" Frost had adroitly returned the ball to the federal court.

The federal-provincial conference reconvened in Ottawa on October 3, 1955. (Readers may be interested to note that the term "dominion" was in the process of being phased out and of being replaced by "federal" in designating the national government.) Prime Minister St. Laurent opened the conference by discussing first the federal government's position on the taxation agreements and then turned to health services, concluding by saying, "It has been suggested that the next logical step to be taken might well be the provision of radiological and laboratory services."[28] It sounded indeed like small potatoes.

Premier Frost spoke next and also, after having dealt with the taxation agreements, turned to the issue of health insurance. He reminded the conference of the length of time that health insurance had been proposed, of the 1945 federal offer, and particularly of the need for this conference to bring the subject "out into the open for joint study and action." He observed that in the absence of concerted action, the federal and provincial governments would continue to move in different directions, creating a hodgepodge that no one would be able to disentangle. "A few years more and an integrated plan will become an impossibility." He then outlined the components of a plan he would be willing to support: (1) inpatient and outpatient diagnostic services; (2) inpatient care in general, convalescent, and chronic care hospitals; (3) inpatient care in mental hospitals and tuberculosis sanatoriums; and (4) home care services. In concluding, Frost stated that Ontario was willing to come into a national plan along the lines suggested, and he recommended that a committee be set up to provide intensive studies of health insurance and report back to the conference at a later date.

The Frost statement, with its specific proposals, had an almost electrifying effect on the conference delegates. The negotiation of new and more favorable tax agreements for the provinces was still the main item on the agenda. But never before had there been such a specific proposal from the largest province. Even so, the responses were mixed. Quebec's premier, Maurice Duplessis, did not comment on the proposal. The others responded as expected: the four provinces having programs, with strong endorsement; those not, with promises or indications of cooperation if requisite finances were forthcoming (from anticipated increases in the taxation agreements).

The rest of the conference was held in camera, and at its conclusion the prime minister announced the appointment of a committee on health insurance composed of the ministers and deputy ministers of health and finance of both levels of government to make a comprehensive study. Several meetings of senior officials were held at which cost estimates were a major concern, and the final meeting of ministers, deputy ministers and other officials was held in Ottawa on January 27, 1956.[29] When the provincial delegates arrived, they were surprised to see a solid phalanx of federal ministers from many departments sitting behind the chairman, Health Minister Martin, and over dinner the delegates surmised that the conference was being held as much to educate the cabinet ministers as it was to discuss a proposal—but such is the necessity in a system of collective cabinet responsibility.

Indeed, much of the discussion focused on the experience of Saskatchewan and British Columbia, so it was a genuine learning experience for many of the delegates—and the federal ministers. But "Paul Martin's Seminar," as it came to be dubbed, could not go on forever, and on Thursday at 2:00 P.M., Martin outlined the federal offer to the delegates while, at the same time, the prime minister made the announcement in the House of Commons.[30] Its main points were as follows:

1. The federal government is willing to assist with technical support and financial assistance any provinces wishing to proceed with hospital insurance plans, as soon as a majority of provincial governments representing a majority of the Canadian people are ready to proceed.
2. Priority at this time should be given to diagnostic services and hospital care.
3. Provincial hospital plans should (1) make coverage universally available to all residents of the province; (2) include provision of specific diagnostic services to inpatients and within an agreed period of time to outpatients; (3) limit coinsurance or "deterrent charges" so as to ensure that an excessive financial burden is not placed on patients at the time of receiving service.
4. The federal contribution would be a specific portion of normal operating and maintenance costs of hospital care at the standard ward level but would not include capital costs.
5. The federal contribution would not be made in respect of care in mental hospitals or tuberculosis sanatoriums.
6. The federal contribution to each province in respect of its shareable costs would be (1) 25 percent of the average per capita costs for hospital services in Canada as a whole, plus (2) 25 percent of the average per capita costs in the province itself, multiplied by the number of insured persons in the province.
7. No contribution would be made in respect of provincial expenditures for the costs of administering a hospital insurance plan.

With the announcement of these details of the proposals, a number of delegates asked for clarification on several points, the meeting was adjourned, and the provincial ministers and their officials departed for their respective capitals to conduct the orthodontic analysis of examining this gift horse in the mouth.

There were many criticisms, all of which would be debated when the requisite legislation was introduced for debate in the House of Commons: the failure to include mental hospitals and tuberculosis sanatoriums (the federal position was that these services were, in the main, already funded by provincial governments), the failure to share administration costs, the excluding of capital costs (inclusion of depreciation on equipment was provided for), the requirement of six provinces to have plans in operation before payments to any plan would begin, and the meaning of "universally available," which most officials assumed to mean "compulsory."

The Honorable Paul Martin now had to wait for the provincial responses—decisions in which he had a major stake. He had finally persuaded his cabinet colleagues to fulfill part of the Liberal party's long-standing commitment, and they had done so, although minimally, and with very strict conditions. If health insurance was as economically desirable and as politically attractive as Martin had always insisted, then to maintain his credibility in cabinet, there should be an immediate and favorable response by the provinces.

But the required quota did not appear, and in fact, the controversy over hospital insurance seemed to expand as its prospects became more imminent. From its announcement in the first month of 1956 until the passage of the legislation sixteen months later, the hospital insurance offer never ceased to arouse emotional comment. Like a smoldering brushfire, there was always some smoke and some heat, and intermittently it flared up in brilliant flames of rhetoric, argument, charge, and countercharge. Hospital, medical, and insurance associations as well as political parties, provincial ministers, the labor unions, and every newspaper and commentator in Canada defended, praised, criticized, or denounced some or all of it. It was too much, it was too little, it was too soon, it was overdue, it drained the federal treasury, it did not offer enough to the provinces, it was the road to socialism, it was the beginning of a new day, it would not represent any additional expenditure, it would bankrupt the nation, it would jam the hospitals, it was the only way to get more hospital beds.

A review of newspaper editorial headings of the day reveals the confusion of tongues at the time: "it implies compulsion"—"it's not universal"—"ill-advised"—"the fairest remedy"—"road to chaos"—"many advantages"—"too much haste"—"do it now"—"remove the roadblock"—"supplement, don't supplant"—"year's biggest bargain"—"it won't be free"—"election bribery"—"a necessary solution"—"costs no more"—"the deceptive bargain"—"a welfare state"—"where is the end?"—"let's think this over."

Despite the opposition of the insurance industry and the chambers of commerce and the failure of the CMA to endorse the legislation, on April 10,

1957, the HIDS act was passed unanimously by the four political parties then represented in the House of Commons. The mood of the House was captured by the Toronto newspaper the *Globe and Mail*: "To tumultuous applause, the Commons tonight gave third and final reading to the proposed national hospital insurance plan. Cheers echoed through the Chamber as the House voted formally 165 to 0 for the program. Prolonged desk-thumping broke as Prime Minister St. Laurent rose to vote. More applause greeted Health Minister Paul Martin, Opposition Leader Diefenbaker, Mr. Stanley Knowles [CCF] and Mr. Hansell [Social Credit] as they voted in their turn."[31] On April 12, the bill was passed by unanimous vote in the Senate, and on May 1, the act was proclaimed the law of the land. There would still be delay—more than a year—before there was an operating national program.

The HIDS act was, indeed, a historic measure, not alone because of its own substantial history. It was the largest government undertaking since the war, and it would require federal-provincial cooperation on a scale never before known. It had been characterized by extraordinary controversy, not only on the question of whether it should happen at all, but in its timing, nature, and shape. It bore the marks of the deep conflicts within the cabinet, in which it had been conceived, and the turbulent and critical environment in which it emerged.

With the promulgation of the regulations fleshing out the act in February 1958, the degree of federal control was quite extraordinary. Every essential requirement for the operation of a program was prescribed by the federal government. The provincial government must establish a hospital planning division; it must license, inspect, and supervise hospitals and maintain adequate standards; it must approve hospitals' budgets; it must approve the purchase of equipment by hospitals; it must collect the prescribed statistics and submit the required reports; and the province must make insured services available to all residents on uniform terms and conditions. All these conditions were incorporated into an agreement which both parties must sign. Moreover, all of a province's expenditures on hospitals were subject to federal audit to ensure that they were "shareable costs." It was indeed a tough contract that provinces were required to sign, almost as if the federal government were retaliating for being pushed into a proposal it had not wanted. But a more charitable interpretation would be that it was warranted in its concern about the open-ended nature of its financing formula, in which it was required to match the aggregate total of provincial spending which, in the halcyon days of the 1960s, reached ever higher levels.

The "uniform terms and conditions" requirement effectively prevented any province from adopting the CMA-CLIA proposal of subsidizing individuals to enable them to pay premiums to the voluntary plans or commercial insurance. Any program that required means-testing of a part of the population would obviously not be available on uniform terms and conditions. In several provinces Blue Cross continued to thrive, offering insurance for semiprivate care and such other benefits as dental services.

Two features of the financing formula require further comment. The formula of 25 percent of the national per capita cost plus 25 percent of the provincial per capita cost was touted as a benefit to low-cost provinces, since it resulted in their receiving more than 50 percent of their costs, while high-cost provinces received less than 50 percent. In reality, however, it meant that high-cost (read "high-income") provinces received higher per capita payments (as much as 20 percent higher) from the federal treasury than did low-income provinces, an inequity that was not corrected until 1979. The second was in the treatment of coinsurance payments. Payments by patients were not recognized as "shareable costs," and therefore for every thousand dollars that patients paid, the province lost five hundred dollars in matching payments. Only two provinces, Alberta and British Columbia, ever imposed inpatient coinsurance fees, and these were ended, as we shall see, in 1987.

With the passage of the Hospital Insurance Act in April 1957, the Liberal government of Prime Minister St. Laurent had to face the electorate in June. Despite the positive achievement of national hospital insurance legislation, there were simply too many debits accumulated by a party that had governed continuously since 1935 and now appeared arrogant, old, and tired. The government was soundly defeated, losing sixty-five seats. The Conservatives, under the leadership of John Diefenbaker, formed a minority government that would achieve a sweeping victory in an election forced upon it in 1958. The Honorable Paul Martin was, like the former minister Ian Mackenzie, not destined to lead his movement to the promised land. The Conservatives removed the six provinces' requirement, and federal funds began flowing to five provinces on July 1, 1958. By 1961 all ten provinces and the two territories were in the system.

Contrary to most predictions, there was no grand rush to the hospitals. In fact, the annual rates of increase in days per 1,000 population declined. From 1953 to 1958, the annual rate of increase had been 2.0 percent. From 1958 to 1962 the rate was 1.7 percent, and from 1962 the rate has been 1.1 percent annually.

The decision of the federal government not to include mental hospitals in the cost-sharing program had, in the end, a salutary effect, as provinces added psychiatric wards to general hospitals where the costs were shareable.

This contributed immeasurably to bringing the treatment of mental illness into the mainstream of health care.

Although it is difficult to make judgments with respect to changes in quality over time, and perhaps impossible for the nonmedically trained, nevertheless it seems reasonable to assert that there has been a marked improvement in the quality of care arising from increased resources made available through the insurance program. Probably the most important indicator is the number of hospitals accredited by the Canadian Council on Health Facilities Accreditation. In 1954 there were 254 accredited hospitals; by 1987 there were 632 accredited hospitals with 122,567 beds, or 91.7 percent of all acute care beds in Canada.[32]

Although British Columbia had abolished premiums and begun financing its program through an increase in the retail sales tax in 1954, it seems reasonable to say that an unanticipated outcome of the national program was the extent to which the provinces abandoned the insurance or premiums system. By 1973 only one province—Ontario—continued to require the payment of premiums for hospital insurance, and these premiums, in 1988, contributed only 8 percent of the total cost. Moreover, citizens over sixty-five, recipients of public assistance, and those on low incomes have their premiums paid on their behalf by the provincial government. All other provincial hospital insurance programs are financed from general revenues collected through combinations of income and sales taxes and, of course, from the federal subsidy. In those provinces, therefore, it seems more accurate to describe them as hospital services programs rather than hospital insurance programs.

One unanticipated outcome of the national program was that with the federal contribution to Saskatchewan, relieving it of 45 percent of its expenditures on the SHSP the Saskatchewan government decided to introduce its long-promised and long-delayed medical care insurance program. The lengthy battle that characterized the introduction of a national hospital insurance program was now to be repeated over the next decade as the nation grappled with the issue of medical care insurance.

Chapter Seven

Saskatchewan Medical Care Insurance

Given the extraordinary support of the Canadian people for a national health insurance program—80 percent favored it, according to the public opinion polls—two events were crucial to its achievement by 1971: the pioneering, once again, by the CCF party of Saskatchewan, of medical services as the second stage of its health insurance program; and the phoenixlike rise from the ashes of the national Liberal party in 1963, following its overwhelming defeat at the hands of the Conservatives in the elections of 1958. This chapter will examine the Saskatchewan episode.

As we have seen, the CCF party had come to power in Saskatchewan in 1944 with a firm commitment to a broad range of health services programs. Its greatest achievement had been the launching of the SHSP, the prototype of the programs now in place in all provinces under the subsidizing umbrella of the national Hospital Insurance Act of 1957. But the Saskatchewan economy, although vastly improved, had not been able, in the assessment of the government, to underwrite the costs of a universal medical care program in the 1950s.

There had been other important advances, however. Saskatchewan was recognized as a leader in both the development of regional public health services and of its enlightened mental health programs and services. It will be recalled that it had also introduced the first comprehensive health services program for all the province's recipients of social assistance, and three other provinces had followed that lead.

And there was one other glittering, though small, experiment that had attracted a good deal of attention, especially by the CMA. The Health Services Act, 1944, had established the HSPC, which, among its other duties, was responsible for organizing twelve health regions outside the three major cities. The regions were responsible for administering a broad range of public health services (with provincial subsidies) and could, following a majority vote, introduce medical or hospital services.

The first region to be organized was Swift Current Health Region No. 1, based on the small city of Swift Current and including a population of some fifty thousand, organized in rural municipalities, villages, one town, and Swift Current, in the southwest corner of the province. With an able administrator and a highly competent board elected from municipal councils, the board immediately decided to introduce both medical and hospital benefits on July 1, 1946, even though the hospital operations would be taken over on January 1, 1947, by the SHSP.

When the program was introduced, there were nineteen general practitioners in the region, a number of them qualified in surgery, and several on salaried municipal doctor contracts. When the registrar of the College of Physicians and Surgeons, in Saskatoon, learned of the invitation of the regional board to all the doctors in the region to attend an organization meeting, he wrote to each of them, asking that they decline to attend. However, the negotiations between the board and the local medical society continued. The college council became alarmed and immediately appointed a committee of four Saskatoon and Regina specialists to meet with the premier to find out what this socialist government was up to and to press its case for administration of health services by an "independent, nonpolitical" commission on which it would be adequately represented.

Confronted by the extreme shortage of physicians in Saskatchewan and by the threat that, if the government proceeded, many would leave, Premier Douglas agreed to the formation of a commission which, he said, could wait for establishment until the outcomes were known of the Dominion-Provincial Conference on Post-War Reconstruction, still in session. (A representative commission was not appointed until 1962.) But he also agreed that the college would negotiate on behalf of the profession on such matters as "arrangements whereunder the profession will provide medical services."[1] This meant that the threat of fragmentation of the profession through negotiations of local medical societies with regional boards was ended, as was any threat to the fee-for-service method of payment.

The Swift Current program, financed from a combination of premiums and property taxes and a 10 percent subsidy from the provincial treasury, was reasonably successful. By the end of 1949, the number of doctors practicing in the program had increased to thirty-five, giving the Swift Current Region the highest doctor-population ratio in any rural area of the province.

Surprisingly, the experiment received favorable comment in the medical journals. Dr. C. P. Howden, who practiced in the region, wrote in the *Saskatchewan Medical Quarterly*, "As there is free choice of doctor and patient, and as the work is done on a fee-for-service basis, there has been almost no disruption of the present personalized system of private practice."[2] And Dr. Arthur Kelly, the then deputy secretary of the CMA, wrote a comprehensive review of the program for the *Canadian Medical Association Journal* in 1948. "An observer gathers the impression that here is a successful experiment in the large-scale provision of medical care, courageously applied, efficiently managed, and remarkably free from attempts to make the facts fit preconceived ideas, financial or otherwise."[3]

But while the Swift Current experiment was tolerated by the profession, attempts by the government to organize two additional regional medical care plans in 1955 met with defeat in two referenda, following massive publicity campaigns and lobbying by the college and the two profession-sponsored prepayment plans.

That battle had two consequences: it alerted the profession to the government's commitment to fulfill its promise to introduce medical care insurance at an early date, thereby rekindling the solidarity of the profession and strengthening its determination to use its newly acquired political clout to thwart that objective by expanding as rapidly as possible the two prepayment plans the profession controlled. Strenuous efforts were made to join the two plans, based in Saskatoon and Regina, but that goal was never accomplished.

It is now necessary to examine the unique organization of the medical profession in Saskatchewan at that time. In all other provinces, there were two organizations: the College of Physicians and Surgeons, and the provincial medical association. The colleges, established by law, have two purposes: (1) to protect the public by prescribing the qualifications of practitioners, licensing annually those so qualified and providing penalties for those who violate the standards or for those who practice medicine without being licensed; and (2) to delegate the responsibility of administering the act to those to whom it applies. By virtue of such legislation, such groups are referred to as self-governing professions, but it is clear that in exercising these functions on behalf of the public, the colleges are, in fact, quasi-governmental agencies administering functions that the government might well exercise itself.

In addition, like other such groups, the profession is organized to protect and promote its own interests, through the national CMA and its ten provincial divisions. These are the political arms of the profession.[4] But in Saskatchewan the two roles were combined, the result of a decision in 1937 concurred in by the then Liberal government that the profession could not afford to sustain two bodies. As a consequence, the council of the college, whose primary function was to exercise the governmental responsibility of protecting the public interest, was composed of precisely the same members whose duty it was to protect and enhance the interests of the profession. From the point of view of the practitioners, their annual license fees of $150 were also their membership dues in their professional association. Membership in the association was thus "universal and compulsory"—two terms that were anathema when it came to discussing health insurance. The union of these two bodies in Saskatchewan had a number of effects. Through universal membership, the association was assured of adequate revenues from the compulsory annual license fee. No physician could opt out by simply not paying his association dues. This meant that it was much more difficult to register dissent from an association policy; one could not simply "vote with one's feet" by electing not to join or continue membership. But most serious of all, it completely obscured that distinct line when the collective medical body was acting in its own interest rather than in the public interest.

However, it seems clear that it was not alone the combining of these two roles in one organization and one council that accounted for the extraordinary political power of the college. What had emerged over the years in Saskatchewan was, in essence, a unique "private government"—the College of Physicians and Surgeons. Its legal base rested on the Medical Profession Act. Its economic base lay in the profession's control of the expanding prepayment plans, for which it determined the policies respecting enrollment, benefits, methods of payment, and, to a large extent, the amount of payment. It was unique, in that unlike other private governments, membership was not voluntary. As Grant McConnell states in the chapter entitled "Private Government" in his book *Private Power and American Democracy*, "Equally important in defining a private government is the individual member's right to resign. Resignation is the individual's ultimate recourse and the element that distinguishes the private association from the public body."[5] Saskatchewan doctors did not have that option.

The Saskatchewan College of Physicians and Surgeons thus resembled the state, in which the only alternative to jurisdiction of the government is to emigrate from the territory. In fact, in July 1962 a *Montreal Star* editorial called the Saskatchewan College "a state within a state." One can push the analogy too far, but one could say that in Saskatchewan there were two governments in the field of health, a private and a public one, each with its own legislature, cabinet, bureaucracy, revenue system, territorial domain, and political ideology. Any action by one to encroach on the territory of the other was to invite certain conflict.

But in 1959 a decision must be taken. There would have to be an election in 1960, and the CCF government must refurbish its image as a party of progress. And there were now at hand those windfall revenues of almost half of the costs of the hospital insurance plan provided by the federal treasury. Here were new funds that obviously should be allocated to the health sector; now was the time to fulfill the long-delayed commitment to medical care insurance.

And so, on April 29, 1959, in a speech during a by-election campaign in the Kinistino constituency, Premier Douglas announced the government's decision "to embark upon a comprehensive medical care program that would cover all our people." He also announced the intention of appointing a representative committee which would make recommendations to the government on a program that would best suit Saskatchewan's needs.

The announcement quickly prompted a request from the registrar of the college for more information about the government's proposals,[6] to which the premier replied, indicating that as soon as its own studies had reached a point where concrete proposals could be considered, it was "the Government's intention to call in representatives of those giving the services and of the general public in order that we may have the benefit of their advice before any policy decisions are made."[7]

The government thereupon appointed an interdepartmental committee with instructions to draft terms of reference for the advisory committee and to draft a proposed bill for cabinet consideration. The minister of health was requested to appoint the advisory committee before the end of the year.

The 1959 fall convention of the College of Physicians and Surgeons provided the first opportunity for the organized profession to respond to the premier's announcement. The leaders were aware not only of the work of the interdepartmental committee but of a draft bill that had already been presented to the minister. Indeed, part of the government's continuing problem in executing both its strategy and tactics resulted from the communications system available to the college through government leaks. Within hours, sometimes minutes, of a meeting of government officials or even of cabinet, the college's strategists were informed. Occasionally, but apparently with less frequency and certainty, the government, too, received intelligence from sources inside the council. The college leaders were angry, for they interpreted the existence of draft legislation as indicating that the promise of prior consultation had not been kept. Now in conclave, the profession issued its warning by unanimously passing the following resolution:

Whereas, we the members of the College of Physicians and Surgeons of Saskatchewan know that medical care has always been readily available to the public regardless of ability to pay, and that no one has ever been denied medical attention because of his financial position, and

Whereas, recently much publicity has been given to the possibility of the introduction of a plan for a compulsory government-controlled, province-wide medical care plan, and

Whereas, we firmly believe the standards of medical services to the people will deteriorate under such a system, and

Whereas we feel that some misunderstanding of the profession's position on this matter may exist, Therefore be it resolved, that we oppose the introduction of a compulsory government-controlled, province-wide medical care plan and declare our support of, and the extension of health and sickness benefits through indemnity and service plans.[8]

The next step was the premier's. On December 16, 1959, he devoted an entire public affairs radio broadcast to the issue, stressing the need for such a program and outlining the basic principles: (1) the prepayment principle, (2) universal coverage, (3) high quality of service, (4) a government-sponsored program administered by a public body responsible to the legislature, and (5) a program that is acceptable to both those providing the service and those receiving it.[9]

With the premier's announcement confirming their worst fears, the college council issued another policy statement defining the parameters within which health insurance might be accomplished. It is a lengthy statement, but because of its importance in setting forth not only the rights and responsibilities of the profession but also those of all citizens, it contributes greatly to an understanding of the cataclysmic events that were to follow. In essence, it was a declaration on the part of the private government of the profession to the government and people of Saskatchewan that the college was prescribing unilaterally the rules of the game. The statement follows:

The College of Physicians and Surgeons of Saskatchewan believes that the preservation of the basic freedoms and democratic rights of the individual is necessary to ensure medical services satisfactory to the people of Saskatchewan.

The maintenance of health by the prevention and/or treatment of disease is the primary concern of the medical profession and of fundamental importance to all citizens of Saskatchewan.

The people of Saskatchewan as recipients of physicians' services, and the members of the medical profession as providers of physicians' services, have certain rights and responsibilities which must be respected if a satisfactory medical service is to be continued.

The people of Saskatchewan as the recipients of physicians' services have the right to determine:

1. whether or not they wish to prepay the costs of physicians' services;
2. the insuring company or agency;
3. the comprehensiveness of coverage.

The individual citizen must have the following rights and responsibilities:

1. freedom of choice of doctor;
2. freedom of choice of hospital;
3. freedom of recourse to the courts in all disputes with whatever party;
4. freedom to choose the method by which he will pay or prepay his medical care.

The medical profession acknowledges its privilege and duty to care for the health needs of the citizens of Saskatchewan regardless of race, color, creed or ability to pay. As providers of physicians' services, the medical profession must have the right and in the public interest, the responsibility to:

1. ensure that a high standard of medical care is maintained;
2. have its composite opinion considered by those responsible for legislation in the health field;
3. refuse to participate in any plan which in its opinion is not conducive to a continuing high standard of medical care;
4. evaluate the worth of its services and retain the principle of fee for service wherever and whenever possible;
5. maintain mediation committees to deal with complaints, from whatever source, be they medical, ethical or economic, and respect the recommendations made by these committees.

The individual physician must have the right to:

1. freedom of choice of location of practice;
2. freedom of choice of patient except in an emergency;
3. choose whether or not to become a participating physician in any insurance plan;
4. determine his method of remuneration;

5. treat his patients in and out of hospital within the limits of his competence as judged by his confreres without interference by laymen.[10]

When the statement is examined in detail, there are few points with which many would quarrel, and many that both citizen and patient would support. Citizens might object that they are not simply "recipients," a term redolent with paternalism. They might also object that, in this category of recipient, their choice of methods of payment is restricted; they are not permitted to choose, as one of their democratic rights, to make their payments through their elected government; they can choose only a "company" or an "agency."

The original version of this statement had been prepared by the executive of the OMA earlier in 1959, but because of the imminent publication of a new policy statement by the CMA, it was decided that the OMA statement should not be released.[11] The Saskatchewan version of the statement differed substantially from that of the OMA, which gave the people of Ontario more options by declaring that they had the right to determine (1) whether or not they wish to prepay the costs of medical services, (2) whether payment will be made on a voluntary or a mandatory basis, (3) the degree of participation by the government in any plan of prepayment, and (4) the comprehensiveness of any plan.

The Saskatchewan college declaration, in contrast, denied these rights to citizens and was intended, thereby, greatly to restrict the potential role of government. Its issuance at this critical stage not only revealed the wide gap between the college and the government but served notice of further conflict to come.

Now, as the government began the process of setting up the advisory committee, time was of the essence. The minister therefore informed the associations which he invited to nominate members that he wanted a report by December 31, 1960. For the profession, faced with the government's policy declaration, delay was one of its important strategies. Since the college had to assume that a public committee on which it would have only three of ten members might well endorse the government's proposal, it recognized that it might be trapped in a series of recommendations to which it was fundamentally opposed. Accordingly, its first response was to refuse to participate, but as a result of behind-the-scenes conversations with the editor of the *Regina Leader-Post*, the college was persuaded that from a public relations point of view, that position had become untenable.

Finally, on January 18, 1960, the college informed the minister that it was prepared to name its representatives—but only on the condition that the terms of reference be expanded and two more members be added to the committee, representing the Saskatchewan Chamber of Commerce and the Saskatchewan Federation of Labor.[12]

The expansion of the committee was readily agreed to, but negotiations over expanded terms of reference were difficult. The college presented a long list, extending the field of investigation far beyond the issue of medical services to include, among others, the public need of health care, the scope of benefits essential to providing such care, the means by which existing services would be integrated into any new plan, methods of remuneration, relationships between the profession and the administrative commission, and several others of lesser import. The college was thus insisting that the public inquiry be addressed to its order of priorities rather than to those of the government. It was also providing the agenda for a two- or three-year project.

Delaying tactics continued but finally on April 25—several months behind schedule—the committee and its membership were announced. The chairman was Dr. Walter Thompson, former president of the University of Saskatchewan. Three doctors represented the College of Physicians and Surgeons, one doctor from the University of Saskatchewan College of Medicine, one representative from the Chamber of Commerce, one from the Federation of Labor, four representing the government, and two representing the public.[13]

But even as the college was reluctantly acquiescing in the appointment of its representatives, it was preparing for what it considered to be the political battle of its life—the June 1960 provincial election. The college council assessed its members one hundred dollars to wage its campaign against the CCF and its promised medical care program. About six hundred of the province's nine hundred doctors paid the fee, and later the CMA contributed thirty-five thousand dollars. The College position was supported by the Liberal party, the dental and pharmaceutical associations, and the Chambers of Commerce.

In a four-party contest, it was probably inevitable that any party, whether winning a majority or a plurality of seats, would do so on the basis of a minority vote. Although increasing its number of seats to thirty-eight of the fifty-four in the legislature, the government received only 40 percent of the votes. The Liberals won 33 percent, the Conservatives 14 percent, and Social Credit 12 percent. Neither of the latter two elected any members.

What was to be read into the results? The college contended that the election, which had been virtually converted into a referendum on medical care insurance, had indicated majority opposition to the government's policy. But called by a reporter at his home in Toronto in the early hours of June 9, Dr. A. D. Kelly, the CMA general secretary, stated as his personal opinion,

"This is a democracy. . . . Our efforts will now be bent on avoiding defects we see in government plans elsewhere."[14]

But the Saskatchewan college did not interpret the election in this light and began to place more emphasis on its strategy of delay. Obviously, this tactic could now be used more legitimately, since the government had bowed to the college's demands that the terms of reference of the Advisory Planning Committee on Medical Care (note the specificity of the title which the government had insisted on retaining) be broadened to include the entire spectrum of health services. As the committee's deliberations dragged on into the fourteenth month, six months beyond the original schedule and with no end in sight, the government decided that it could brook no further delay.

There were two internal reasons for this. The first was the government's own credibility; it had been reelected with a commitment to medical care insurance, which must be fulfilled. The second was that within three years there would be another election, and the program would have to be introduced, debugged, and seen to be operating successfully before that date. In the meantime, however, a third and external reason had been introduced. That was the formation of the NDP, resulting from a new liaison between the CCF and the Canadian Labor Congress, and the possibility of Premier Tommy Douglas becoming its leader.

There were two major effects of the formation of the new party and Douglas's acceptance of the leadership candidacy. The first was to speed up the process to introduce what was now becoming known as Medicare.

The second was that there was now a third extraprovincial force interested in the outcome of the Medicare issue in Saskatchewan, the NDP, which would obviously benefit from its success. The other two external forces were the CMA and the insurance industry, both committed to its defeat. It is interesting to speculate that if there had been no external allies on either side, the resolution of the conflict might have been more amicably achieved; but such was not to be.

On June 21, 1961, a few days after his decision to stand for leadership of the NDP, the premier directed the minister of health, Walter Erb, to write to Dr. Thompson, asking for an interim report from the advisory committee so that the government could introduce "enabling legislation couched in general terms" at the fall session of the legislature. The college knew, of course, of the draft bill prepared months earlier. It was also fully aware of the desire of the founders of the new party to have a successfully operating medical care program in Saskatchewan to help launch the NDP—and Tommy Douglas— on their way. Despite the opposition of the representatives of the college and the Chamber of Commerce, the Thompson Committee responded with an interim report on September 25, 1961.[15] It included recommendations of the majority for a program providing universal coverage and a comprehensive range of medical services benefits, financed by premiums subsidized from general revenues and administered by a public commission, responsible to the government through the minister of health.

The three college representatives, supported by the Chamber of Commerce member, submitted a memorandum of dissent, arguing for the CMA policy of subsidizing low-income individuals and families to obtain coverage through existing voluntary agencies. The representative of the Federation of Labor, Walter Smishek (who, some years later, would become the minister of health), submitted a thirteen-page dissent, recommending payment of physicians by salary, financing by increases in the income tax, and opposing administration by a commission.

Despite the opposition of the profession, which was supported by the Liberal opposition party, the Medical Care Insurance Act was introduced in the legislature on October 13, 1961, and passed one month later.[16] The administration was placed in a Medical Care Insurance Commission (MCIC) of not fewer than six or more than eight members, including the deputy minister of health, and at least two of whom, not including the chairman, were to be physicians. The MCIC was authorized "to establish and administer a medical care insurance plan for the residents of Saskatchewan and the improvement of the quality of the insured services provided under such a plan." In addition, there was to be an advisory council representative of professional and other interested organizations, with powers to be consulted by the minister or the commission and to propose improvements, extensions, restrictions, or modifications of the plan on its own initiative. There was also to be a medical advisory committee composed of physicians approved by the college.

The program was to be universal and compulsory; that is, all residents were required to register themselves and any dependents. A resident became entitled to insured services by paying, or having paid on his or her behalf, the required premiums. Insured services were defined as services by physicians or surgeons in the office, home, or hospital. The patient was guaranteed freedom of choice in the selection of a physician, and the physician had the right to free acceptance or rejection of a patient. Also included were clauses providing for confidentiality with respect to reports, for the establishment of an appeals procedure, and authorization for the government to enter into any forthcoming agreement with the government of Canada.

With the introduction of the Medicare legislation, Tommy Douglas had crossed off the last item on his unfinished agenda for Saskatchewan. He had now to take up his new duties in Ottawa as leader there of the NDP. He was succeeded by the Honorable Woodrow Lloyd, who had served as minister of education and provincial treasurer. The political styles of the two leaders were strikingly different, but there is no impression of any difference in their dedication to the medical care objective.

Lloyd was sworn in as premier on November 7, and with his new mandate, his first major decision was to make an important change in the cabinet by transferring W. G. Davies to the Health Ministry and Erb to Davies's previous post as minister of public works. It was clearly a demotion for Erb which was to have serious consequences, but it was a decision that Douglas had been avoiding for some time.[17] Davies had been the executive director of the Saskatchewan Federation of Labor and a member of the Health Survey Committee in 1949–51. He was therefore not unfamiliar with the major issues or the influential personnel.

Aware that the ten months' delay in the report of the Thompson Committee had already forced the government to postpone the "appointed day" to April 1, 1962, the most urgent task for the minister was the appointment of the commission. But the college refused to cooperate or to name nominees. Accordingly, when the MCIC membership was announced on January 5, the chairman was Donald Tansley, a senior finance official. The deputy minister of health, Dr. F. B. Roth, served ex officio. A professor of public health, Dr. Samuel Wolfe (later appointed to Columbia University), and a practicing physician in Prince Albert, Dr. O. K. Hjertas, who had once served as secretary to the HSPC, were the only medical doctors who would accept appointment.[18] The commission was immediately attacked by Dr. Dalgleish, president of the college, and by spokesmen for the Liberal party.

Although creation of the administrative organization had been underway for several months, it was not until February 8, 1962, that, in the delicate matter of attempted negotiations, chairman Tansley picked up where the minister had left off, by requesting an early meeting with the college council.[19] Two weeks later, Dr. Dalgleish replied to the minister, citing another bill of particulars in which the government had acted unilaterally, ending with the passage of the Medicare Act as a form of "civil conscription," a term coined by the Supreme Court of Australia.[20] (Since the commission was the bastard progeny of an illegitimate act, the college refused to recognize it—a not unknown strategy in relations between hostile governments!)

On March 2 the minister tried again, informing Dr. Dalgleish that since the legislature was now in session, the government was willing to make changes in the act to meet the profession's objections but not repeal it.[21] Dalgleish replied, again citing a list of grievances and asking whether expected changes in the act would permit implementation of the doctors' proposals.[22] On March 22, Davies wrote again, restating the government's position that the Medical Care Insurance Act was now law and that the latest date for changes in the act was March 28, and inviting the representatives of the college council to meet on that date.[23]

In the meantime, however, the cabinet had been forced to take a decision that was to have consequences that were great, complex, and immeasurable. In its monthlong review of its administrative responsibilities and its degree of readiness, the commission had come to the conclusion that "the sheer administrative task" of setting up the program could not be accomplished by April. The minister had been informed and, after anguished discussion, the cabinet had acquiesced. (Interestingly, a similar request for postponement of the launching of the Hospital Services Plan in December 1946 had come from the top officials, but Premier Douglas had rejected the request outright and ordered the SHSP to begin on time.) The postponement until July 1, as will be seen later, was to create extraordinary problems for the government by giving opposition forces three additional months in which to mobilize.

By now, however, the college's strategy of refusing to negotiate had to undergo serious reappraisal; there was a limit to the public's understanding of the doctors' refusal even to talk, despite the apparent degree of success of the college in stalling operations and contributing to a general public impression of a faltering of purpose in the government through its postponement a second time of the plan's inaugural date. Moreover, the March 22 invitation had promised an "open agenda." A meeting would provide another forum in which to urge the college's priorities and the subsidization of membership in voluntary plans. The attendant publicity would also likely be helpful; it was decided to accept the invitation.

The meeting took place, as planned, on March 28, continued on April 1 and, briefly, on April 11. The government's proposed concessions included removal of concern "if such there is," about possible interference with professional standards and professional independence; provision for new mechanisms for arriving at fair and equitable remuneration; provision for appeal procedures; the appointment of more doctors to the MCIC; and for the first time, a major concession *to consider changes whereby the physician need not accept payment directly from the commission.*[24]

It is difficult to overemphasize—from the government's point of view—the magnitude of this concession. When fee-for-service is the method of payment in a prepayment plan, the system preferred by the insured and the insuring agency—and indeed, as surveys had shown, by a majority of physicians—is that the doctor bills the agency according to an official fee schedule, is paid directly by the agency, and accepts that payment as payment in full. The obligation is met by one transaction, and of course the administrative costs are much lower. This method—the service contract—had been adopted, as noted in chapter 5, by all the profession-sponsored prepayment plans. But as also noted, there were in each province nonparticipating doctors who were at liberty to set their own fees, and thus extra-bill.

Obviously, the government wanted the service contract, but aware of the strong opposition of the profession generally and of a hard core of Liberal stalwarts within the profession who wanted "no truck nor trade" with a commission appointed by a socialist government, it was offering a way out: doctors could bill their patients, who would be reimbursed according to the negotiated fee schedule by MCIC. The government was deeply concerned not only with the greater inconvenience for patients and the higher costs of administering an indemnity system but even more by the total medical costs a reimbursement system might entail as a result of widespread extra-billing. Nevertheless, it appeared to be a price that would have to be paid for a principle about to be abandoned. (Incidentally, it was a system that the Saskatchewan College of Physicians and Surgeons had explained to the then-sitting federal RCHS, earlier in the year, that it might be forced to adopt as a fallback position if the government persisted in its policy.)

One week later, the college presented its response. It rejected outright the government's concessions, saying, "The minor amendments do not fundamentally change the legislation. . . . This Act is completely unacceptable to the profession." As an alternative, the college offered as "the final concession we can make" a proposal that insurance be universally available through existing or new prepayment plans, that a registration board would function through the provincial auditor as an approval body, that government would pay the premiums for indigents, that all other insured persons would be subsidized by the government, that in addition each approved agency would determine and charge the premiums it required, that patients would pay their accounts directly to their doctors and would receive a refund of a major (but unspecified) portion of the expense incurred, but that no additional charges would be made to indigents.[25]

The gulf between the two positions had greatly widened, for while the government's proposals now incorporated even more fully the CMA principles, the plan proposed by the college was more complex and unattractive than anything previously proposed; in fact it was a highly retrograde step from the prepayment plans currently operating. And so the meeting adjourned, without resolution.

When the council returned to meet with the government on April 11, having spent the weekend reworking its proposal, it was evident that the government had made up its mind that further discussions on nonnegotiable issues would be fruitless. Press releases had been prepared, and the meeting with the council was peremptorily ended after the premier had read his prepared statement.

The council members were angry over their treatment, particularly the refusal even to discuss the results of the weekend's work, and over the arbitrary way in which the meeting had been terminated. It was the low point of trust in the government and the high point of frustration and anger to that date.

The government had rejected the alternative proposal, as stated in the press release, for seven reasons: (1) it required the repudiation of the commission; (2) the government would have no part in determining the total amount the people would pay; (3) it would leave to the private agencies the full right to set premiums, coinsurance charges, or extra-billing; (4) no government operating agency would be permitted; (5) there was no indication whether the Swift Current plan would continue; (6) indigents would be identified and dealt with in a separate way; (7) permitting a large number of private plans strikes at the root of the insurance principle based on substantially the whole population. The statement concluded, "It is the intention of the Government to proceed to introduce a medical care insurance plan designed to meet the needs of the people."[26]

For the government, it was the point of no return. Either it capitulated, or it put on a bold front, prepared for the launching, and hoped for the best. It chose the second course. High as the political costs might be, they appeared less than the costs of capitulating. The latter was to admit that in a contest between a public and a private government, the public government could lose. With its convictions that it had a mandate as a duly elected majority government and that it was acting in accordance with the rules of democratic, responsible government, for the government to countenance defeat was to think of the unthinkable.

But at the same time, even to contemplate that the profession might withdraw services—that they might strike—that, too, was to think of the unthinkable, and so the government did not think about it. As the premier said in the legislature on April 11, "It is the Government's belief that doctors will carry on treating their patients and accepting remuneration on the same basis as they have been doing for years in Government-sponsored plans such as treatment for cancer. This, we believe, will give the plan an opportunity to prove that it will not affect professional freedom nor lower the standards of their service. On the contrary, we believe it will give doctors an opportunity of a type they have never had to beneficially influence the practice of medicine in Saskatchewan."[27]

The recalcitrance of the college continued, with the registrar not deigning to reply to a letter from the chairman of MCIC requesting lists of general practitioners and specialists, to whom the different fee schedules would apply. The chairman replied, informing him of his legal duty to provide such lists.

Meanwhile, as the MCIC geared itself for the July 1 launching, the scene shifted once again to the political level. One week after its short meeting with the cabinet on April 11, the college announced that a two-day meeting of all doctors would be held in Regina on May 3–4. The premier requested, and was granted, an opportunity to address the meeting, attended by two-thirds of Saskatchewan's doctors.

The mood of the meeting was almost unanimously defiant, and the self-confidence of the profession was greatly reinforced by a critically significant event, the defection from the government and the CCF party of the former minister of health, Walter Erb, still smarting from his demotion to Public Works. The announcement came after a stirring and passionate address by the vice-president of the college, Dr. E. W. Barootes, and immediately before the address of the premier. Its effect was electrifying; the citadel was beginning to crumble.[28]

Few spokesmen since Mark Anthony have ever faced a more unreceptive audience as this former school superintendent, now government leader, addressed the profession. His speech was a low-key review of events to that date, an elaboration of the program, and a firm declaration by the government to administer the plan in such a way as not to interfere with the doctors' professional freedom. He ended with an appeal to their rational judgment, hoping that a calm, unemotional assessment would conclude that the program, as proposed, would meet the objectives of both the profession and the public. "My appeal has been to what has been termed 'the ancient wisdom of your profession.' We seek not to change the ends of medicine. We do seek to find ways and means to adapt the financing of medicare to twentieth century society and the legitimate expectations of that society. In this, the 'ancient mission' need not be lost. Its achievement can be advanced. I invite you to join in a bold attempt to consolidate past gains and to move towards new horizons in the field of medical care."[29]

But rational goals, eloquently and courageously expressed, could neither legitimize the government's actions in the doctors' minds nor abate in any way the rising confidence of the profession that in solidarity it would triumph. A near-unanimous standing vote was the response to the president's question as to who would oppose the medicare plan and refuse to act under it.[30] (A half dozen did not stand and were later ostracized.)

In an article in the *American Journal of Public Health* (May 1963), the assistant secretary of the CMA, Dr. A. F. W. Peart, outlined the options open to the Saskatchewan doctors as follows:

1. To accept the Act and practise medicine as the Commission dictated, which would gradually erode away the freedom of practice and would ultimately result in low-quality care.
2. To test the legislation in the courts, but legal advisers had already said there was little chance of success.
3. To leave the province for more favorable areas where one could practise with freedom and peace of mind, but many doctors were reluctant to do this as they were well established in practice and had their families to consider.
4. To protest to the Government by withdrawing normal medical services. This seemed to be the only road left open if the doctors were not to succumb to the Act.

The fourth was decided to be the only tenable course, and the meeting passed resolutions instructing the council to make plans for the establishment of emergency services in selected hospitals on July 1, when all doctors' offices would be closed. The two parties were now on a collision course.

It was now time for the government to think realistically about the heretofore unthinkable—a doctors' strike. The MCIC, however, had already begun preparations, making plans to recruit doctors from other countries. On May 4, the second day of the doctors' mass meeting, advertisements appeared in British newspapers, and Dr. Sam Wolfe, member of the commission, flew to London to begin interviewing candidates for vacant rural practices and to ascertain the possibilities of temporary recruitment in the event of a withdrawal of services.[31]

Meanwhile a newly organized grass-roots pressure group was generating enormous volumes of publicity—the Keep Our Doctors Committees (KODCs). These committees had been started when four women in Regina had been warned by their obstetricians that they would not be treated after July 1 if they were members of the government's plan. They therefore decided to act. The movement spread to other centers and quickly recruited opposition politicians, druggists, dentists, businessmen, doctors, and everyone with a grievance against the government. On May 30 a cavalcade of nine hundred people in four hundred automobiles converged on Regina to meet the premier with petitions containing forty-six thousand names.[32]

The most significant effect of the KODCs was that they provided a means by which Liberal, Conservative, and Social Credit party members could coalesce on a single issue as they could not normally do. Their press releases were constant sources of news and were given generous space in the mainly antigovernment newspapers in the province.

As the government examined its resources, it was clear that recruiting of physicians from outside the province on a temporary basis would be, if successful, the most effective means of alleviating the emergency situation. Indeed, with the actual and announced departures of doctors, the publicity given to the offers of sale of large medical clinics in both Regina and Saskatoon, and the advertisements of doctors' homes for sale, the recruiters would also have to seek candidates for permanent positions.

But as the preparations to manage the crisis continued, the government was dealt another serious blow by what became, in effect, an externally imposed referendum—the federal election on June 18, 1962. As Pat Dwyer wrote in the *Ottawa Journal*, "Saskatchewan voters, aroused to a frenzy due to fear of losing their doctors, will use the federal election as a virtual referendum in the provincial medicare crisis."[33]

For Woodrow Lloyd and his CCF government, the timing of the federal election could not have been more damaging. These were Prime Minister Diefenbaker's days in the West. In 1958 the Conservatives had won forty-seven of forty-eight seats in the three prairie provinces; in 1962 they retained forty-two of them while losing eighty-two seats nationwide. It might therefore be argued that the Diefenbaker sweep in Saskatchewan would have occurred in any event, owing largely to Agriculture Minister Hamilton's wheat sales to China and Russia, and that Medicare was irrelevant. But that was not the interpretation in the press. It was not Diefenbaker's victory; it was Medicare's defeat. And what made it so crystal clear was that Tommy Douglas, the new leader of the NDP and father of Medicare, was defeated in Regina, where he had so long governed as premier. A *Toronto Star* editorial, entitled "A Blow against Medical Plan," accepted that "Douglas had been beaten by mothers . . . fearful of a denial of medical attention to their children."[34] Premier Lloyd did his best to deflect the damage. "As far as the Medicare plan goes," he commented, "the results of a federal election can in no way be significant."[35]

The jubilation of the CMA, with its leaders assembled in Winnipeg at their annual meeting, was matched only by that of the publishers and editors of the Saskatchewan press. In his presidential address on June 17, Dr. Gerald Halpenny stated that in the medical impasse in Saskatchewan, "patients, the doctor, and the profession would all suffer. I can only hope that the unscrupulous politicians will also suffer very severely for their reckless gambling with the welfare of the citizens whom they claim to represent." The legislation, he said, made the commission "the sole provider of medical services. Our colleagues in Saskatchewan have received the unanimous support of every provincial Division across Canada . . . and we are ready to come to their aid if assistance should prove necessary."[36]

While this impassioned call to arms was delivered for the dual purpose of influencing public opinion and reinforcing professional solidarity, the behind-the-scenes discussions of the profession's position were far more calm and deliberate. Dr. Dalgleish presented a comprehensive and politically sensitive assessment of the situation to the CMA executive.

> This government . . . is so dedicated and firmly committed to the rigid course they have adopted that they would probably be willing to sacrifice the future of their own political party, the reputation of the medical profession, and the quality of future medical care in Saskatchewan. . . . It is inevitable that some of the forces in this dispute will have to give way in the very near future, and it is not likely that either faction will achieve a clean-cut victory.
>
> As yet, however, there has been no indication that the Saskatchewan government is willing to consider any significant, acceptable changes in their existing legislation, to which they appear to be more firmly committed. *Over the past two and a half years, the public in that province seems to have accepted and approved of the fact that they will be provided with some form of plan for comprehensive, all-inclusive medical care insurance.* None of the groups that have advocated delay, mediation and discussion of the disputed features of the Saskatchewan Medical Care Insurance Act have given any indication that this legislation should be completely withdrawn. (emphasis added)[37]

Despite this sobering review, or perhaps because of it, it was not surprising that the Saskatchewan division had the support of the CMA. The Saskatchewan members were now the shock troops fighting the battle for the entire profession. As the *Toronto Globe and Mail* observed, "The battle being waged is merely the opening round in a war over government medical insurance which may spread to the entire continent."[38] Elsewhere there appeared little opposition to, and in some provinces even strong indications of support for, the CMA subsidization policy. Only in Saskatchewan was there actual legislation that would wind up the operations of the profession-sponsored prepayment plans. The Saskatchewan government was being confronted not only by the Saskatchewan doctors but by a profession united nationwide. To the new uncertainties about the actual extent of the government's wavering support, there was added the certainty of the profession's determination and of its apparently growing strength.

With burgeoning confidence stimulated by the reinforcing effects of a large conclave in Winnipeg and the exhilarating results of the federal election, the profession took the offensive. Dr. Halpenny sent a telegram calling for immediate discussions between the Saskatchewan profession and the government, a meeting that the government had been seeking for a month and that already was being arranged through the good offices of the Saskatchewan Hospital Association. It was finally agreed that the council and the cabinet would meet on June 22.[39]

With the hopes and fears of so many riding on the outcomes, the meeting began in an atmosphere sated with tension.[40] Both parties were aware of the high stakes and the potentially tragic consequences of their decisions. Despite the mutual distrust, the discussion was frank, serious, and polite. There was clear recognition that time was running out, that the image of a profession and the credibility of a government, as well as the kind, and the availability, of a program of health services, hung in the balance.

The government remained firm in its conviction that, with its major concession permitting doctors to practice outside the act on a reimbursement basis, it had effectively drawn the teeth from the charge that the act imposed "civil conscription." It was equally convinced that the college's multicarrier proposal precluded any possibility of achieving the advantages of a universal program providing a genuine health services system. Convinced of the rightness of its policy and its legitimacy as the representative government of the people, it was nonetheless fully aware of the adamant stand of nearly the total profession, the mounting opposition engendered by the KODCs and the hostile press, and the damage to its apparent strength by the federal election. On the other hand, major organizations representing labor, farmers, teachers, and churches, together with letters numbering in the thousands, provided moral and political support just when it was most needed. Although the government was obviously beleaguered, its objectives were clear; although its strategy perhaps lacked balance and its past tactics were not always productive, its continuing support, though less vocal at least when weighed against the stridency of the voices of those opposed, sharpened its resolve to see the commitment through. It was now or never!

The college council, for its part, was highly confident. The KODCs had generated public support far in excess of expectations, and the routing of every CCF-NDP candidate in the federal election only a week before—including T. C. Douglas, the instigator of Medicare—all on top of the defection of the former minister of health, had provided ample evidence that many people were changing their minds, that the government was indeed on the ropes, and that a united profession having two major weapons at hand— the exodus threat, and a withdrawal of services—could achieve the accommodation it sought. The primary objective was to preserve the prepayment plans intact; some degree of government intervention might be tolerated as a short-run sacrifice, but with the demise of an already tottering government, the plans could then be unshackled and assume again their proper role in the more congenial environment of a friendly government. They must be preserved, no matter what the cost.

The meeting, therefore, was a confrontation of two groups of men, each convinced of the legitimacy of its role, the rightness of its goals, and of its power to achieve them. The premier emphasized the concessions the government had made, especially the right of any physician to practice outside the act. The college insisted on its multicarrier solution. The meeting concluded at 10:35 P.M. at an impasse, and both groups prepared their press releases.[41] Despite frantic efforts by leaders of the Saskatchewan Hospital Association and of the rural and urban municipalities associations to induce the parties to continue negotiations, their positions remained fixed. At 12:01 A.M., July 1, 1962, the withdrawal of services began.[42]

The news editor of CFQC-TV, William Cameron, described the tension in Saskatchewan in late June.

The plains of Saskatchewan bring forth men and women who learn early what it is to know struggle and discomfort. By her very nature Saskatchewan must produce a combative people. Controversy is as natural to them as their fierce love of the forbidding wilderness they have tamed. But never before has there been a greater controversy than this. All over Saskatchewan, her sons are taking sides as never before. And, like the cloud of an oncoming Saskatchewan dust storm, with equal power to strike fear into Saskatchewan hearts, there looms ever larger the date that all Saskatchewan dreads—July 1.[43]

The final stages of the government's strategy had been characterized by extraordinary attempts to dissuade the profession from withdrawing services. It had made a major concession that compromised seriously its service-plan ideal. It had publicly committed itself to make legislative changes that would enable any doctor to practice outside the act. But these concessions had not been enough, for while doctors could practice as privately as they had done before any system of prepayment (but now with assurance of payment of all accounts), the coming into force of the act would mean the abandonment of the profession-sponsored prepayment plans. It meant the relinquishing of a major part of the territorial domain of the college's private government. If the plans were completely dismantled, there would be no hope of revival under a new Liberal government. This was a prospect not to be accepted, and so the ultimate weapons—the permanent exodus of some physicians and the withdrawal of services of most of the rest—were brought into action.

The government's strategies to implement its program had failed. The issue was now, as Premier Lloyd had said, "whether Saskatchewan will be governed by a democratically elected legislature, or by a small, highly organized group."[44]

The question of whether the defeat was permanent or temporary now clearly hung in the balance, the outcome dependent on which side emerged the stronger in what most observers saw as a contest of wills. Both parties recognized the critical and determining role of public opinion and expanded their publicity campaigns to generate support. Both held daily press conferences for a corps of newspaper, radio, and television reporters that each day increased as more outside correspondents arrived on the scene.

The Canadian press divided along three lines: those who criticized the government, those critical of the profession, and those who pronounced a plague on both houses. The foreign press, however, was most critical of the profession. On July 6 the *London Observer* stated, "The medical situation in Saskatchewan is more than a doctors' strike, it is a mutiny." The *London Daily Mail* editorialized on July 4, "When doctors strike and neglect patients the voice of humanity protests. That this could happen in Britain is so inconceivable that we regard Saskatchewan with astonishment and sadness."

In the United States, the issue was more relevant for the U.S. Senate was in the process of debating and ultimately defeating President Kennedy's Medicare program for the aged. The *Washington Post* was the most critical of the profession. "Whatever the merits of Saskatchewan's new medical care Act, the strike staged by doctors throughout the province is indefensible . . . a strike by doctors is a betrayal of their profession. It reduces medicine to the level of a business. Worse, it desecrates the Hippocratic Oath which consecrates doctors to use their art for the benefit of the sick. . . . In every sense of the word this is bad medicine" (July 19).

Dr. James Howard Means of Harvard Medical School wrote a much-publicized letter to Premier Lloyd in which he stated, "I think the behaviour of the striking doctors is reprehensible." Dr. Richard Long, professor of legal medicine at Harvard, long known as an opponent of socialized medicine, also stated, "It is my opinion that no doctor has the right to strike in the present crisis in Saskatchewan."[45] And Dr. Albert Sabin categorized the strike as "contrary to everything the practice of medicine stands for."[46]

But these were the views of the international press, and however much encouragement the government was inclined to take from them, the paramount point was that, in the main, these did not reach Saskatchewan voters. At home, where press opinion would have its major impact on the government's supporters and detractors, the reaction was universally critical. Indeed, the Saskatchewan press became more defensive. An editorial in the *Weyburn Review* was typical. "Perhaps the medicare legislation looks less ferocious to people who are not ruled by a government dedicated to the destruction of our economic system. Some of the comments from afar, however, display a remarkable ignorance of what is happening in Saskatchewan" (July 12).

How to manage a doctors' strike situation? No other provincial government had ever faced such a crisis; fear was almost universal, and the lives of some citizens were obviously in jeopardy. The highest objective was to get back to the negotiating table, but the immediate task was to ensure that no citizen suffered unduly. This meant more active recruiting for the emergency—a hard decision, invoking as it would, all the emotional overtones of strikebreaking—anathema to a government now associated with the labor movement in Canada. But this was no ordinary strike against the public interest; human lives were at stake, and every means must be taken to protect them.

The commission was relieved to find, however, that outside Saskatchewan, the "strikebreaker" fear was, for the most part, irrelevant, as editorials and, as we have seen, some medical spokesmen condemned the act of disobedience of the law. By June 24 the recruiting drive in England had reached the point of signing contracts with physicians and arranging their airlift to Saskatchewan.

At the beginning of the strike, 240 doctors staffed the emergency services in thirty-four hospitals, about 35 others were estimated to be cooperating with the plan, while others continued to practice for ethical reasons. An estimated 250 went, as usual, on holidays. It was this group that posed the never-to-be-answered question: If the plan had gone into effect on April 1, how many of these might have continued in practice as a matter of conscience rather than on July 1 going as usual on vacation? That number could never be known, but whatever it was, it was one of the high costs of that postponement decision.

The second task was to renew the enthusiasm of supporters and respond positively to the increasingly vociferous and demanding outcries of the KODCs. Their success or failure in mobilizing opposition could well determine the outcome.

The KODCs held rallies at various points in the province and planned as their climactic event a mammoth rally in Regina on July 11. The premier spoke out on July 9, counseling against mass meetings "that cannot contribute a solution to the problem." But the plans went forward with advertisements in the press and with cooperation by dentists, pharmacists, and merchants whose places of business were closed so that employees, clients, and customers could attend.

On July 11 the automobiles began to pour in. The leaders carried a petition that had appeared the day before in full-page newspaper advertisements, declaring that "no rulers in a free society may coerce a minority of citizens . . . nor discriminate against them in their profession. . . . The Government alone is responsible. . . . We protest the dictatorial provisions of the Act . . . and paid mercenaries from abroad."

But the protest proved to be anticlimactic. Instead of the 40,000 to 50,000 forecast by the KODC leaders, only about 4,500 appeared. The tide of prodoctor opinion had begun to ebb. It was, clearly, the "beginning of the end."[47]

The recruiting of doctors from Britain, other provinces of Canada, and the United States accelerated, reaching a total of 110. The number of hospitals providing emergency services increased by twenty-five, and some doctors, mainly in rural areas, were returning. The 240 physicians providing emergency services in the original thirty-four hospitals—and who were charging no fees—were gradually becoming exhausted, and on July 20 college spokesmen revealed that their numbers had shrunk to 190.[48]

The stalemate was complete, but in the first week of the vacation season, communications began that were to provide the key to the unlocking of the impasse. Don McPherson, an influential Regina lawyer, now felt that it was time for some behind-the-scenes negotiations.[49] He called the Honorable Mr. Blakeney, the provincial treasurer (who later became premier), and outlined his proposal to contact a key member of the college council. If he returned with proposals, could he reach the minister by phone, and would these then be transmitted immediately to the cabinet? Positive assurances were given. He then invited Dr. J. F. C. Anderson, member of council and former president of the CMA, to his summer cottage, and there over several days he reviewed in the light of his own legal experience the provisions of the act and the new proposals of the government.

During their discussions, telephone calls (from a telephone a mile away) were made by McPherson to Blakeney, and from Anderson to the college. The fundamental issue was, from the college's point of view, the retaining of the prepayment plans (Medical Services Incorporated, Saskatoon, and Group Medical Services, Regina), and finally there emerged as a possible compromise solution the proposal that insured persons might be entitled to assign their "payment rights" to a designated prepayment plan of their choice; that is, the commission would transmit its payments to designated prepayment plans which would pay the doctors. It would be a major concession by the college, for it would mean that with respect to medical services, the plans would no longer have the right to raise revenue through premiums, and obviously a "private government" without "fiscal authority and autonomy" (the CMA's term) would be as devoid of power as a political government without authority to levy taxes. On the other hand, it would be a major gain for those doctors unalterably opposed to having any contact with the government or its commission. On the part of the government the cost was equally great, for by perpetuating a fragmented payment system, it precluded the development of a unified and integrated health services delivery system, including the further development of the regional concept. At the same time, it could go a long way in achieving the benefits of the service-type contract if, as part of the negotiations, it were agreed that those who chose to become members of the prepayment plans were not extra-billed—as current members were not.

Other strategies were discussed by the two men, of course, but the most significant effect of McPherson's intervention was that a possible compromise proposal was now being discussed at the highest levels. The cabinet strategy committee weighed the alternatives and concluded that an "informal negotiator" should be selected to discuss the issues with McPherson and Robertson, the college's solicitor, but who would not be authorized to speak for the government. If these informal negotiations resulted in a plan that was mutually agreeable, a mediator could be chosen who "miraculously" would come up with a proposal that was mutually acceptable. The seemingly complex process called for a miracle worker. Fortunately, he would come on stage in about another week.

On July 4 Premier Lloyd left on a secret mission to Toronto, Ottawa, and Montreal to discuss strategy with national NDP leaders and constitutional experts. He was also in touch with Lord Stephen Taylor, a London medical doctor who had assisted in the launching of the British National Health Service in 1948 and been awarded a lifetime peerage by a grateful Labour government. He had visited Saskatchewan in 1946 during the planning stages of the Hospital Services Plan and was therefore knowledgeable about the province and of the CCF government's health policies.[50]

He had been contacted in early June by an old friend, Graham Spry, then Saskatchewan's trade commissioner in London, who brought with him to the House of Lords Dr. Sam Wolfe, then on his recruiting mission in England, who briefed Taylor thoroughly on the Saskatchewan crisis.

On July 4 Lord Taylor received a letter from Premier Lloyd, inviting him to come to Regina to help. He agreed, on condition that the government pay his expenses, pay him no fee, but provide a week's fishing at the conclusion of his visit.

It was not for twelve days, however, that he arrived in Regina. In the meantime, he touched several bases: first a press conference for Canadian reporters in London, during which he endeavored "to build up a picture of myself which would prove acceptable to the doctors of Saskatchewan . . . that although I was being invited by the Government, my interest was in fair play all around." Next, there were conversations with the editor of the British medical journal *Lancet* and with the secretary of the British Medical Association, which led to the necessary endorsements, and finally, a cablegram to Dr. Arthur Kelly, general secretary of the CMA, which elicited the reply that he hoped to see Taylor in Saskatoon. So far, so good.

Arriving in Regina, he spent Monday evening July 16 and Tuesday morning with government leaders and the afternoon with the doctors manning the emergency services at the Regina General Hospital. Of them, he later wrote:

As I had expected, they differed in no respect from other good doctors anywhere else in the English-speaking world. They were obviously fine men but they were puzzled about what had hit them. They knew little of politics [obviously inaccurate] and had no love of politicians [obviously true]. They knew that professional freedom was essential, if they were to do their work properly. They believed it was in danger, but they could not say precisely where the danger lay.

The American Medical Association was at this time hysterically opposed to Medicare; and it endeavored, not without some success, to communicate its hysteria to the doctors and the public in Saskatchewan. . . . I think it would be fair to say that, despite its good will, the Government was quite ignorant of the pattern of thought of the ordinary medical practitioner. Its members could not conceive of people who did not believe in collective action, who were resolutely opposed to public control, and who believed that even the most benign of civil services could turn into a dangerous tyranny.

Having talked with both sides in the controversy in Regina, on Tuesday evening he traveled to Saskatoon.

There were several other important developments on that Tuesday. One was the opening of hearings on an application for an injunction against the MCIC, launched by the vice-president of the KODCs and Dr. L. M. Brand of Saskatoon. A second was the announcement that Dr. J. F. C. Anderson was flying to England to make an appeal on behalf of Saskatchewan doctors at the annual meeting of the British Medical Association. The third was the announcement of the appointment of a judicial inquiry into allegations of discrimination in the granting of hospital privileges to newly arriving physicians.[51] There were other arrivals. "The Sub-Committee on Saskatchewan" of the CMA had met on the weekend in Ottawa, and both the president, Dr. William Wigle, and the general secretary, Dr. Arthur Kelly, arrived in Saskatoon with senior officers to assist their confreres.[52]

That same evening, two other groups were meeting to grapple with aspects of the issue. The first was composed of delegates from a number of the mushrooming community health clinics—with four established and estimates of between thirty and forty in the process of organizing—meeting in Saskatoon to form the Saskatchewan Council for Community Health Services. The second group, however, was even more important—the delegates to the annual CCF party convention, who were even then debating resolutions supporting the Medicare plan and recommending the curtailment of the licensing powers of the College of Physicians and Surgeons.[53]

The coincidence that the CCF annual convention was scheduled for the third week of July was a fortunate stroke of fate, for it meant that the cabinet would be in the same city as the council of the college. Both groups had been in almost continuous session since the first of the month, but now they were only three blocks apart. If there were to be communications at all—and there had to be—the opportunities were obviously greatly enhanced. But the coincidence provided even more: an opportunity for the CCF-NDP to act as host to a spokesman for the college—a kind of reciprocal hospitality, as it were, for Premier Lloyd's address to the doctors' meeting in Regina. The initiative had come from the college by telegram and had been agreed to. Dr. Dalgleish had been chosen as spokesman. The main points of his address had already been passed to the government in a letter of July 14 which suggested a slight easing from the July 1 position. Both Premier Lloyd and Dr. Dalgleish addressed the convention on Wednesday.

Premier Lloyd's speech dealt solely with the medical care issue. As a new party leader he had been engrossed in a political battle more serious than that ever faced by a provincial premier. He was now reporting on his stewardship to the party supporters, aware from the numerous resolutions submitted that there were many who were critical of the concessions already made.

He rejected suspension of the act or the calling of an election, raised the question of the use of its power by the college, and emphasized that the issue was not the Medical Care Act alone but the "democratic process." He ventured that "there are those who are concerned not that the medical care insurance plan will not work but that it will work too well. . . . They realize that satisfaction is contagious, that Canadian public opinion is on the move in this direction and areas beyond are watching carefully the Saskatchewan scene." He reasserted, as expected, the right of doctors to practice outside the act and stated that a return to normal practice could be accompanied by a special session of the legislature.[54]

His address set the background for the speech by Dr. Dalgleish in the afternoon session. He emphasized that "it is still the College's belief that the best way to achieve a solution . . . is to suspend the Act and have doctors resume normal practice . . . but the College has decided to shift its stand in an attempt to settle the issue." In elaborating, he stressed that amendments would have to include the following: (1) a doctor who chooses may practice outside the act without any of the provisions of the act applying to him or her; (2) medical services provided outside the act could not be insured services under the act; (3) a beneficiary would be allowed to assign to any agency his or her right to payment from MCIC; (4) the commission would not differentiate between services for which a refund was requested and services for which direct payment was made to the doctor; and (5) private agencies would be recognized as collectors of the premiums levied by the commission.[55] At the conclusion of his address, which was politely, if not enthusiastically, received, Dr. Dalgleish returned to the Medical Arts Building, where he and the other members of council received their distinguished guest, Lord Taylor.

Dr. Kelly's description, written almost immediately after the event, of how Lord Taylor ingratiated himself is instructive not only on the attainment of agreement in this case but for all would-be mediators. "The consensus of professional opinion was cool if not adverse to this relatively unknown government adviser and it must be admitted at this time and in the climate of Saskatchewan any friend of government would be suspect."[56] After some other remarks, Kelly continued:

Although the guest could not be classified as a mediator, he immediately began to act as one. He told the council what he had learned in his brief stay, and very skillfully dissected the essentials of Dr. Dalgleish's speech [which he had just heard]. He said that as a doctor he was in favor of the new proposals which established the useful function of the prepayment plans and that he would endeavor to convince the Cabinet of their merits. As a politician he doubted that the Government would agree to the plans acting as tax collectors and advised the council not to press the point. By sheer force of an attractive and aggressive personality he rapidly reached the stage where council was agreeing to his transmission of the doctors' case to Government and after two hours he left to do just that. The following day he reported back that after a good deal of argument he had persuaded the Cabinet to accept the concept that the profession-sponsored prepayment plans could continue to function under the Medical Care Insurance Act.

"This," says Dr. Kelly, "I regard as a triumph of diplomacy because I was not optimistic that the Government would concede anything in this area."[57] This, of course, was part of the solution proposed earlier by McPherson, but in his memorandum on the episode Lord Taylor makes no reference to those earlier discussions.

Lord Taylor, not having been appointed a mediator, with two strikes against him (he was a socialist politician and had come at the invitation of the government) and only one positive credential (he was a practicing physician), began gradually to be trusted by the majority of council. He thus assumed the role of an intermediary, striding back and forth along the three short blocks between the two hostile forces, the one bivouacked in the Bessborough Hotel, and the other encamped in the Medical Arts Building, the latter still up for sale.

Recognizing that the doctors "were ready at the drop of a hat to put the worst possible interpretation on anything which the Government might say, I quickly decided that since the doctors and the Government were, in effect, speaking different languages, it was vital for them not to meet. If they did, there were bound to be misunderstandings and, at once, the fighting would start all over again. So I had to keep them apart at all costs, until final agreement had been reached." And this he did, laboring indefatigably for five days, interpreting, reporting, explaining, persuading, cajoling, even threatening to leave, and weaving through all of it large measures of wit, humor, and histrionics.

By Friday, with the assistance of several senior government officials, he had prepared a draft of an agreement which was approved by the cabinet. He then took it to the college council, where line by line it was discussed, debated, and changes proposed, with the college solicitor, Mr. Robertson, having similar difficulties in getting explicit instructions. As Taylor makes clear, it was slow going.

By Saturday night, it appeared hopeless, and Taylor prepared to depart but was persuaded by Dr. Dalgleish to continue a little longer. By Sunday night he felt they were ready to sign but advised them to sleep on it. Early Monday morning, he was advised that they were ready, and the agreement was formally signed. Taylor tried to obtain more drama for the event by having a public ceremony, but the doctors "had the feeling that they were making concessions in signing the document at all, and some of them retained considerable doubts in their minds. To sign the document in public was more than they could stomach."

And so, on July 23, after twenty-three days of a withdrawal of all but emergency services, the Saskatoon Agreement was signed, and the Saskatchewan Medical Care Insurance program—in greatly modified form—was achieved.[58] As befitting an agreement concluded between two hostile governments, both Lord Taylor in his reminiscent article and Dr. Kelly in his refer to the agreement as a treaty. But as is well known, a more accurate term would have been "cease-fire."

There was one major concession on each side that enabled the rest to follow. The council accepted the idea that the Medicare plan must be universal and compulsory and that the government would be the sole collector of revenues and disburser of payments. The government accepted the college's position that the voluntary plans be retained as billing and payment conduits (some referred to them as post offices) for those doctors who did not wish to deal with the commission. As Taylor says, they were to act as barriers between the government and the individual doctor, ensuring that he did not have a single paymaster with overtones of becoming a civil servant. These arrangements thus provided four ways or combinations of ways in which a doctor could choose to practice.

1. The doctor may choose direct payments from the Commission which he accepts as payment in full. These payments may be fee-for-service, salary, or a combination of the two. (Mode 1)
2. The doctor may practise partly or entirely in association with one or more of the voluntary agencies. For such of his patients who are enrolled with such agencies, he will submit bills at the agreed upon rate. The agency will transmit the account to the MCIC which will pay the agency which, in turn, will pay the doctor, who will accept the payment as payment in full. (Mode 2)
3. The doctor may practise partly, largely, or entirely outside any voluntary agency and not be enrolled for direct payment by the MCIC. He will bill patients solely at his own discretion. He is required to submit an itemized bill to the patient containing the information normally given to a voluntary agency. In this case the patient must claim reimbursement from the MCIC and pay any difference between the doctor's fee and the minimum fee schedule. (Mode 3)

4. The doctor may choose to practise entirely for private fees, provided that his patients also agree not to seek reimbursement. The patient must agree in advance and no itemized statement is required. (Mode 4)[59]

The existence and possible further development of community health services associations was accepted. It was recognized that there might be places where few or no doctors were enrolled for direct payments by the MCIC. The remedy lay in the hands of citizens themselves, with advice, if desired, from MCIC, but the citizens' role must be limited to that of landlord. The Medical Care Commission was expanded by adding three medical members, a general practitioner, a specialist, and a faculty member from the College of Medicine.

With the signing of the agreement, the withdrawal of services officially ended. Doctors manning the emergency services returned to their respective practices. Many others returned from their normal July vacations and others did not return at all. Hospitals reestablished normal operations, and the government began preparations for a one-day session of the legislature to incorporate the terms of the agreement in the Medical Care Insurance Act.

But the peaceful convalescence that Lord Taylor had also prescribed was too much to expect, for the trauma had been too serious, the emotional wounds too deep, the dislocations too severe, the compromises too galling, and the loss of trust too great for any speedy reconciliation or recovery to occur. Continuing, deep-seated suspicion clouded every action or statement by either party.

A total of sixty-eight doctors had left the province, some of them highly qualified specialists. Many of the British doctors on temporary contracts remained. A growing threat to the profession was the developing community clinic movement. By the end of July it was reported that clinics had been established in five centers, final arrangements were being made in ten more, and fifteen other associations were being organized, almost all to be staffed by recently recruited British doctors. Their development ensured a continuation of bitter division within the ranks of physicians and among citizens and neighbors in the communities involved, as well as a firm conviction in the college that they were government inspired.

The entire battle had been a tragic episode, polarizing the society in a manner never before experienced by any Canadian province. As an editorial in the *Canadian Medical Association Journal* stated on July 28, 1962: "Those who are unfamiliar with the details of events surrounding the encounters between the Saskatchewan doctors and their government can have no adequate understanding of the deep and powerful undercurrents of distrust and suspicion that bear on all relations between these two opposing forces."

Although the agreement had been signed, with major concessions on both sides, it was manifest that the college had not really accepted the drastically modified medicare act and that the government was unhappy with the structure resulting from the compromises it had made. On the day following the agreement, the *Toronto Telegram*, which had consistently supported the college editorially, reported in an article headed "MDs Won't Drop Guard" that "the CMA made it plain it is not giving up its fight against socialized medicare . . . and served notice that the profession hopes for the defeat of the CCF-NDP government."

The *Edmonton Journal*, also critical of the government, reported the same day under the headline "Doctors Claim Medical Pact Retreat Only": "The battle may be over but the war is still on. Although it is difficult to assess just who won the medical care dispute, one thing is certain; Saskatchewan doctors have not dropped their opposition to the government-sponsored plan. The doctors say they have made a strategic retreat. They are going to continue fighting Premier Woodrow Lloyd's medical care plan. They may even wreck it."

In March 1963 a statement of policy was issued in the *Saskatchewan Medical Quarterly*, saying in part: "We must be cognizant, of course, of the fact that we must live with the Medical Care Insurance Act for the time being." Clearly, the hope was that with the decline in fortunes of the NDP, a new Liberal government would be formed which would restore the prepayment plans to their rightful place and enable them to insure the entire population through government subsidies of those with low incomes.

What were the outcomes of the fulfillment of the eighteen-year commitment to medical care insurance? The first, obviously, was the establishment of the first universal, tax-supported medical care insurance plan in North America, administered by public authority. For the people of Saskatchewan the economic barrier to medical care and the fear of large medical bills had been banished. Also eliminated were the commercial insurance concepts of deductibles, coinsurance, noninsurable conditions, limitations with respect to age, employment, or membership in groups, and experience-rating—all the devices that protect insurance funds but frequently at the cost of individual hardship.

The new program retained, as one option, the physician-controlled plans as agencies for the transmitting of doctors' accounts and payments and granted them authority to act as insuring agencies for supplementary benefits. By accepting this role for the prepayment plans, the government had relinquished any possibility of developing a regionalized system of health services, as had been envisioned since 1945. Thus, although the profession had lost its near-monopoly control of the medical care prepayment system, the agreement had frozen the status quo in the profession-preferred mold. The CCF-NDP party of Saskatchewan had achieved one of the major objectives to which it had been committed since its inception. But it did so at the cost of polarizing Saskatchewan society to a greater extent than did any of its other social policies.

The Saskatchewan decision moved the subject of health insurance forward on the political agenda of the federal government and the provinces. Three provinces—British Columbia, Alberta, and Ontario—almost immediately introduced Medicare plans that conformed to the proposals of the CMA and the insurance industry.

For the first time in Canada there had been an organized withdrawal of services (most observers called it simply a strike) of the most essential group in society—and that for a political rather than an economic objective. As a host of observers asked, What did this mean for the democratic process? If the most prestigious, elite group in society could flout the law with impunity, what did the law mean? And how many other groups providing essential services would be encouraged to follow suit?

The private government of the profession had lost its revenue system. From now on, fee levels would have to be negotiated with the government rather than with the profession's own prepayment plans. Nor could such issues as coinsurance be unilaterally determined, as they had been, by the profession. On the other hand, the introduction of Medicare resulted in spectacular rises in physicians' incomes—an increase of 35 percent in 1963 over 1960, bringing Saskatchewan doctors to first place among all the provinces and $3,400 above the Canadian average.

One unexpected by-product of the withdrawal of services was the community clinic movement. It gained substantial support in a number of communities, was moderately successful in a few, caused major dissension in most of these, and, over time, began to wane. By 1974 only two clinics, cast in the original mold, continued to function successfully.

The immediate effect on medical personnel was very serious: a net loss of 68 doctors was reported in the first seven months of 1962. By the end of 1963, a total of 260 physicians who had been in practice in 1961 were no longer in Saskatchewan. On the other hand, by June 1964, as a result of new registrants, the physician-population ratio was at its highest level ever.

The preference of the physicians not to deal with the commission directly and the reluctance of potential patients to run the risk of being extra-billed through the reimbursement method (Mode 3) led to an extraordinary increase in enrollment in the prepayment plans—from 290,000 in June 1962 to over 530,000 by the end of 1963. These "subscribers" thus were assured of the benefits of the service-type contract and of additional benefits for which they paid a supplementary premium. In 1963 the proportion of physicians billing the commission directly was minimal, amounting to only 21.5 percent. By 1970 this proportion had increased to 51.5 percent, with the proportion billed through the prepayment plans declining from 68.0 percent to 40.5. With the proportion continuing to decline, in 1988 all physicians' claims were sent directly to the commission. The prepayment plans continue to sell other benefits, including out-of-country coverage, but they no longer serve as administrative intermediaries, a role that had made possible a compromise settlement of the 1962 strike.

To the strategists of the Liberal, Conservative, and Social Credit parties, it was evident that the CCF administration had run its course. After nearly two decades in office, with only one change in leadership and only minor changes in cabinet membership, it was obvious that even without the turmoil of Medicare, the accumulation of political debits now exceeded credits. As the three parties planned their strategies and deployed their resources for the 1964 election, informal agreements were made not to run candidates in every constituency in order to consolidate the opposition votes. Although the NDP retained the same percentage of votes it had received in 1960, the Liberals under the leadership of Ross Thatcher won a majority of seats on election day, April 22, 1964, and a new government took over the reins of office. But to the surprise of many of the public and the dismay of the profession, the Liberal government did not change the format of the program, and the profession-controlled plans were never returned to their prior status.

Six weeks after the election, the federal RCHS (of which more later), appointed by a Conservative government at the behest of the CMA, issued volume 1 of its report. The commission rejected outright the subsidy method so strongly pursued by the profession and the insurance industry and unanimously endorsed a program fundamentally the same as the original Saskatchewan government proposals.

For the Canadian organized profession as a whole, the Saskatchewan episode had created a serious breach in its TCMP structure. One province was now gone, but that could be considered a fluke of history, since it was the only province to have a socialist government. But it *had* happened, and there were lessons to be learned. One of those who gave the matter serious consideration was Dr. William Wigle, CMA president. In an article in the *CMA Journal*, he wrote:

The medical profession must be impressed with the fact that a large segment of the population want to prepay their medical care completely. It is also obvious that many people would have no objection to the funds being raised by taxation.

We in the profession must face these issues and act in accordance with our beliefs. . . . The prepayment of medical care in all its phases—the collection of funds, administration and payment for the services—must be diligently studied and controlled by the profession or it will be done by someone else.

The details of how these ends may be achieved must be the immediate responsibility of the profession in Canada, and the programs must be developed, debated and adopted with determination and unity, within the next few months.[60]

It was a ringing call to the profession to reinforce the private governmental structure it had created to prevent any further breach in the system. And it made very clear its fear of, and determination to exclude, any other influence in the arrangements the profession controlled.

Chapter Eight

National Medical Care Insurance

The defeat of the St. Laurent Liberal government in the elections of June 1957 initiated the most turbulent period in Canadian politics in a generation. The Conservatives under John Diefenbaker of Prince Albert, Saskatchewan (the first Western Canadian to become prime minister since Conservative R. B. Bennett, of Calgary, Alberta, in 1930), assumed power as a minority government.

The former secretary of state for external affairs, Nobel Peace Prize winner Lester B. Pearson, was elected Liberal party leader at a convention held in Ottawa in January 1958, only to lead the party to a humiliating defeat in the election of March 31, 1958, when the Conservatives won the largest majority ever achieved in Canadian parliamentary history—208 seats to the Liberals' 49 and CCF's 8. The task of rebuilding the party under Pearson fell mainly to four men: Walter Gordon, a Toronto business leader; Keith Davey, a partner in the same management consulting firm; Tom Kent, editor of the *Winnipeg Free Press*, who later became Pearson's assistant; and Maurice Lamontagne, an economist at the University of Ottawa.

The first step in revitalizing the party was to hold a "think tank" conference at Queen's University in September 1960.[1] There, two hundred participants discussed and debated a wide range of issues, and especially documents on social security measures prepared by Kent and Lamontagne. This conference contributed to the formulation of new policies for the second stage, a National Liberal Rally held in Ottawa in January 1961. Under Walter Gordon, chairman of the policy committee, resolutions were passed, creating a new platform that was more nationalist and progressive, and with a strong commitment to health insurance: "A Liberal government will establish, in cooperation with the provinces, a medical care plan for all Canadians."

But events were moving on another front—the direct result of the reelection of the CCF government in Saskatchewan in 1960 and its commitment to Medicare. Although the CMA had reaffirmed its subsidization policy in major public statements in 1955 and 1960, the CCF victory seemed to demand that the CMA take some further action to forestall the possibility of Medicare again becoming, in its term, a political football in any other province or at the federal level. There must be some way of inserting into the decision-making process a larger element of calm, deliberate, and rational judgment, safe from the intervention of politics. Accordingly, at the 1960 meeting of the CMA, the council, "taking account of the fact that all major Federal political parties are interested in medical services insurance on a tax-supported basis," resolved: "That the CMA Executive approach the Federal Government to ask them to establish a committee to study the existing and projected health needs and health resources of Canada; and to study methods of ensuring the highest standards of health care for all citizens of Canada, *bearing in mind the CMA statement on Medical Services Insurance*" (emphasis added).[2]

The letter conveying the request was forwarded to the prime minister on December 12, 1960, and on December 21, Diefenbaker responded by announcing that a royal commission would be appointed.[3] By his decision, the prime minister may well have assumed that he had removed the issue of health insurance from his active agenda for the next three years. In any event, he had enhanced the confidence of the CMA that, unlike the situation in Saskatchewan, any future decisions on health insurance would be made rationally, based on the recommendations of an independent commission, and not distorted by the pulling and hauling of politics. Moreover, during the years that the commission would gather evidence and proceed in its deliberations, TCMP would pursue the goal of expanding enrollments.

Nor would TCMP be alone. On the initiative of the insurance industry's new lobby, the Canadian Health Insurance Association (CHIA), TCMP was persuaded to join forces in a new body, the Canadian Conference on Health Care, in 1960. The rationale for this union of forces was explained as follows by Howard Shillington, the former executive director of TCMP, in his book *The Road to Medicare*.

It was suggested that the members of the Conference had a common purpose to make adequate health care available to all Canadians. A strong plea was made that government insurance was imminent, that it represented a giant monolith, and that doctors would be prisoners of such bureaucratic operation which would, thereafter, completely control the purse strings and dictate the terms of service. Related to this whole approach was the theme that the doctors' only protection lay in the retention of multiple insurance organizations in the health field and for this reason, every support should be given to the insurance companies who were fighting the profession's battle as much as were the sponsored plans.[4]

The profession thus was ideologically and politically joined with the insurance industry in its opposition to a government program, while at the same time its sponsored prepayment plans were locked in keen competition with those same companies.

Critical events were also moving along a third front, as three other provinces began introducing programs based on the profession-preferred model. On March 11, 1963, a bill was introduced by the Social Credit government in the Alberta legislature authorizing the government to pay individual subsidies to assist low-income earners to obtain voluntary coverage through either Medical Services Inc. or a consortium established by the insurance companies. The policy was a clear victory for the Canadian Conference on Health Care, with whom the details had been worked out. It was expected that between 250,000 and 300,000 would apply. The subsidy would vary from one third of the premium (for those with taxable incomes up to five hundred dollars) to one-half the premium (for those with no taxable income), and this plan would entail government expenditures estimated to be $4–6 million. Following an election, on June 16 the details were announced at a press conference, at which the plan was lauded by representatives of the CMA and the CHIA and by the premier, who said that it would give Canadians a program they could set alongside "the socialistic type of program" in Saskatchewan.

But despite the subsidies, by March 1964, when the minister of health reported to the legislature, over 200,000 out of a total population of 1.3 million were uninsured. There was also growing criticism that the income-tax exemption threshold (the base line for determining the amount of subsidy) was unfair in that by depreciation and tax allowances, wealthy farmers making heavy purchases of machinery could qualify for subsidy, while a worker with dependents, earning as little as $3,500 a year, could not.

The second major breakthrough for the CMA-CHIA policy occurred in Ontario. Late in April 1963 the minister of health introduced the government's Medicare bill, providing for a plan to assist low-income earners to subscribe to one of the prepayment plans or to become insured by an insurance company. Enrollment would be voluntary, maximum premiums would be established, benefits would be prescribed, and contracts would be "guaranteed renewable." Two standard contracts would be offered, the second at lower premiums and requiring deductibles and coinsurance. The proposal was vehemently attacked by the Liberals and the NDP as "leaning over backward to be of assistance to the insurance companies" and "a 100 percent capitulation to the insurance companies and the medical profession." The bill was not passed at that session, and during the summer, public hearings were held by an independent commission chaired by the president of the University of Waterloo. The majority endorsed the proposal and added suggestions for covering the indigent and medically indigent. The Labor representative, as expected, filed a minority report calling for a Saskatchewan-type system and stating "that the interests of the insurance industry should not be of greater concern than the well-being of the people."[5]

As a result of criticism in the legislature and in the media, the bill was amended in January 1966 in such a way as to eliminate the proposed participation of the voluntary plans and insurance companies in the task of insuring recipients of social assistance and low-income earners. Instead, the government established the Ontario Medical Services Insurance Plan (OMSIP) to insure with subsidies these categories, as well as all other self-paying individuals and families wishing to join. The cost to the government in 1967–68 for full payment of premiums on behalf of recipients of social assistance and subsidies to others amounted to approximately $55 million.

In British Columbia, which had little commercial health insurance, although the government at first leaned toward the Alberta model of subsidizing enrollment in voluntary plans, the pattern finally adopted followed that of Ontario with the creation of the British Columbia Medical Plan (BCMP). The income-tax exemption threshold was used in determining eligibility of low-income earners for subsidy. Three of Canada's most powerful provinces had now acted in such a way as to leave the majority of the population who could afford voluntary insurance to the private sector, while governments paid part or all of the costs for the "poor risks."

During these developments, all the issues became focused in the Report of the Royal Commission on Health Services released in June 1964. As noted earlier, the composition of the commission had been announced by Prime Minister Diefenbaker in June 1961. Its chairman was the Honorable Emmett Hall, chief justice of Saskatchewan. (During the course of the commission's work, he would be appointed an associate justice of the Supreme Court of Canada.)

The other members were two doctors, a dentist, a nurse, an industrialist, and an economist. I served as research consultant. In August 1962 the industrialist Senator Wallace McCutcheon was appointed to the cabinet and resigned from the RCHS.

Following three months of public hearings, the study of myriad reports, the commissioning of a score of research studies, on-site studies in other countries, and lengthy deliberations, the RCHS released its report on June 19, 1964, three years after its appointment and three days before the annual meeting of the CMA.[6] Its recommendations can best be understood in terms of the stated objective.

As we examined the hundreds of briefs with their thousands of recommendations we were impressed with the fact that the field of health services illustrates, perhaps better than any other, the paradox of our age, which is, of course, the enormous gap between our scientific knowledge and skills on the one hand, and our organizational and financial arrangements to apply them to the needs of man, on the other.

What the Commission recommends is that in Canada this gap be closed, that as a nation we now take the necessary legislative, organizational, and financial decisions to make all the fruits of the health sciences available to all our residents without hindrance of any kind. All our recommendations are directed to this objective.

The RCHS then went on to state that "this goal should be incorporated in a declaration of purpose" and recommended that a "Health Charter" it had drafted "be accepted as an objective of national policy for Canada." The essence of the Health Charter was the following:

The achievement of the highest possible health standards for all our people must become a primary objective of national policy and a cohesive factor contributing to national unity, involving individual and community responsibilities and actions. The objective can best be achieved through a comprehensive, universal Health Services Program for the Canadian people,

IMPLEMENTED in accordance with Canada's evolving constitutional arrangements;

BASED upon freedom of choice, and upon free and self-governing professions;

FINANCED through prepayment arrangements;

ACCOMPLISHED through the full cooperation of the general public, the health professions, voluntary agencies, all political parties and governments, federal, provincial, and municipal;

DIRECTED towards the most effective use of the nation's health resources to attain the highest possible levels of physical and mental well-being.

There then followed eight subsections defining and expanding upon the terms used in the main statement. For example, "full cooperation" was said to mean:

a. the responsibility of the individual to observe good health practices and to use available health services prudently;
b. the responsibility of the individual to allocate a reasonable share of his income [by way of taxes or premiums or both] for health purposes;
c. the methods of remuneration of health personnel—fee-for-service, salary or other arrangements—and the rates thereof should be as agreed upon by the professional associations and the administrative agencies and not by arbitrary decision, with an appeal procedure in the event of inability to agree;
d. the maintenance of the close relationship between those who provide and those who receive health services, maintaining the confidential nature of that relationship;
e. the provision of educational facilities of the highest standards and the removal of the financial barriers to education and training to enable all those capable and desirous of so doing to pursue health services careers;
f. the adequate support of health research and its application;
g. the necessity of retaining and developing further the indispensable work of voluntary agencies in the health care field;
h. the efforts to improve the quality and availability of health services must be accompanied by a wide range of other measures concerned with such matters as housing, nutrition, cigarette smoking, water and air pollution, motor vehicle and other accidents, alcoholism, and drug addiction;
i. the development of representative health planning agencies at all levels of government, federal, provincial, regional, and municipal, and integration of health planning.

And, lest this prescription should sound utopian, the RCHS then said, "This is what Canada and the provinces working together should do. It is not an idealist's dream but a practical program within Canada's ability, financially and practically, as subsequent chapters will show. It is what Canadians ought to strive for and expect through their governments. They should not be content with less."

It was an extraordinary call for action, coming as it did from a prestigious royal commission. Nor did the RCHS stop there. It stressed that "all these matters [on which it had made recommendations] will require careful planning and the fullest cooperation at all levels of government and with the health professions. It follows that the advisory and planning councils we recommend in Chapter 2 should be agreed upon and chosen following a Federal-Provincial Health Conference *which we urge should be called within six months* by the Federal Government."

It then defined the flexible system it had in mind. "We do not suggest that the various provincial programs be required to conform to any rigid pattern, but to qualify for federal support they need to provide, in whatever manner may be chosen, universal coverage in the province regardless of age or condition, or ability to pay, upon uniform terms and conditions, and to adhere to the basic inclusive features of each of the programs recommended."

This statement of objectives was reinforced by the first of two hundred recommendations:

1. That the Federal Government enter into agreements with the provinces to provide grants on a fiscal need formula to assist the provinces to introduce and operate comprehensive, universal, provincial programs of personal health services. The programs should consist of the following services, with the provinces exercising the right to determine the order of priority of each service and the timing of its introduction:

   Medical Services
   Dental services for children, expectant mothers, and public assistance recipients
   Prescription Drug Services
   Optical Services, for children and public assistance recipients
   Prosthetic Services
   Home Care Services

By its insistence on "uniform terms and conditions," a phrase borrowed from the federal Hospital Insurance Act, the RCHS had rejected the subsidization policy of the CMA-CHIA (and of the government of Alberta), for if millions of Canadians were subjected to a means test while the rest were not, obviously the terms and conditions would not be uniform. Calculations by the

RCHS indicated that if the maximum personal contribution were set at 5 percent of income, individuals and family heads representing 14 million people would need to be subsidized; if set at 6 percent, 12 million; and if set at 7 percent, 10 million. It should be noted that consumer surveys at the time indicated an average allocation of personal income to personal health services of 4 percent. An allocation of 5 percent would have represented a 25 percent increase.

Giving full weight to both the philosophical arguments and the practical administrative requirements, the RCHS recommended a federal subsidy of provincially administered programs. Its reasoning was stated as follows:

1. That the method of subsidy should be one that subsidizes the provincial insurance funds rather than one that subsidizes individuals.
2. That reliance on the method of voluntary insurance would be unnecessarily slow and inevitably incomplete. [It might also have added, "and much more expensive."]
3. That the number of individuals who would require subsidy to meet total health services is so large that no government could impose the means test procedure on so many citizens, or would be justified in establishing a system requiring so much unnecessary administration. The health services will make enough demands on our resources. We must not waste them.
4. That, so far as the issue of compulsion is concerned, we believe that as long as decisions of this kind are made by democratically elected legislatures, so long as they provide only the basic essentials [for example, standard-ward hospital care] and assure citizens of free choice of physician and hospital and free choice of additional items against which they may insure through private arrangements, then we have confidence that our democratic ideals will not only be protected, but, in fact, more fully realized. It is of great significance for a democratic society that the Hospital Insurance Act was passed by an unanimous vote of the House of Commons representing all political parties.
5. That the health insurance fund in each province should be administered by one agency in order to achieve full integration in effective planning of *all* health services, and thus to obtain the most efficient administration of all sectors of the proposed health services program. We have recommended that the existing hospital insurance program be administered by the same agency in each province as

administers all health services. This necessarily means rejection of any proposal that the one phase of health services, namely, payment of physicians' services, be administered by a separate agency.

The rejection of the CMA's subsidization policy was bitter medicine for the profession. Released just three days before the annual meeting of the CMA in Vancouver, the report totally dominated all nonscientific discussion at the conference. It was almost impossible to believe that the RCHS, which had been appointed at the CMA's request, would not have almost automatically perceived the superior wisdom of the CMA approach. The CMA had seen an independent inquiry as the means of removing "consideration of health and health insurance from the hectic arena of political controversy" on the grounds that "a heated and emotionally charged election campaign in which contesting parties are faced with the urge to outdo each other in the attractiveness of their projected programs, scarcely provides the ideal atmosphere for dispassionate and objective consideration of the future pattern of health care in this country."[7]

The RCHS had given such "dispassionate and objective consideration" and had reached the same conclusion that the profession had feared would emerge. Moreover, during the years of the commission's deliberations, the health insurance issue had not subsided in the political arena; indeed, the issue was being more widely and heatedly debated than ever before. The report could only add fuel to the fire and strengthen the Liberal government's commitment to health insurance on which it had been elected.

The report of the RCHS was a major challenge to the profession's policy of maintaining control of the distribution system of medical services. The commission's questioning of the underlying principle of means-testing those who could not afford the premiums of the voluntary plans as being inherently undemocratic and administratively inefficient was an attack on what had become an article of faith for the profession within the doctrines of individual freedom and the free enterprise system. In addition to pragmatic arguments, the commission had clearly used a stigma to beat a dogma. The perdurability of the profession's "private governments" (TCMP was now a federated system) clearly depended on the outcome of what was shaping up as an ideological war.

The profession's leaders surveyed the terrain and began to replan their strategy. Despite the psychological and political blows delivered by the RCHS, it was, after all, simply an advisory body, albeit one on which the CMA had pinned such high hopes; the Liberal government, despite its electoral commitment, might not accept all of the advice. Moreover, as noted above, there were extremely encouraging signs among a number of provincial governments, where jurisdiction on health matters lay. Alberta had taken the lead, adopting wholeheartedly both the profession's philosophy and its sponsored prepayment plan as one of the carriers. Now British Columbia and Ontario were joining the ranks of the converted. With three of the four most powerful provincial governments adopting the CMA-CHIA policy, the odds in favor of the market-economy approach and against the political-economy philosophy endorsed by the Commission were shifting most favorably. A massive effort must now be made to ensure that nothing interfered with this progress in provincial governments' decisions to implement the CMA-CHIA policy.

It had been impossible at the Vancouver meeting of the CMA to deal adequately with so voluminous a document and so momentous an issue. But time was running out, as the Liberal party's 1962 and 1963 election commitments attested. For the second time in its history, the CMA decided to convoke a special meeting of council to deal with the issue of health insurance. It scheduled the meeting for January 1965—twenty-two years after the 1943 special meeting—its purpose to reverse irrevocably that regrettable decision taken amid the emotional overtones of war when, in Macaulay's famous words in *Lays of Ancient Rome*, "none were for the party and all were for the state."

The executive committee had prepared a synthesis of the reports of its Committee on Economics and its Committee on Prepaid Plans, and excerpts from this document highlight the debate on the main ideological themes and provide deeper insight into the profession's thinking.[8]

Volume I of the Report of the Royal Commission presents us with proposals in the field of health insurance which differ radically from our preferred approach. . . . The Report presents a case for the transfer of expenditures for all health services from the private to the public sector of the economy and in so doing it has undertaken to demolish many of our arguments on medical services insurance which the profession advanced during the public hearings.

We have stated our belief that a tax-supported, compulsory program of medical services insurance is neither necessary nor desirable. . . .
We feel that a single source of funds with compulsory control could restrict progress in medical services.
We are confronted with a clash of ideologies and it is our view that it surely represents exaggeration to magnify the difficulties to the degree

that a compulsory, tax-supported system is presented as a preferable alternative, principally on grounds of administrative simplicity. The mainstay of the profession's proposal for the extension of medical and health services under voluntary auspices is that the costs for the self-supporting should remain in the private sector of the economy and that public funds should be employed to subsidize the indigent completely and the marginal income classes to the extent of their need. We believe this concept to be valid, acceptable to Canadians generally and consonant with what we regard as the true responsibility of government in this field.

As realists we should be aware of the attractiveness of the philosophical concept that people should be financed by governments to the best of medical care in unlimited amount. This concept is eloquently expressed in the Report of the Royal Commission and it may prove to be beguiling to our fellow citizens and to the governments which represent them. We have a duty to proclaim what we believe to be a superior system, not in our own interest, but for the continued progress of medicine and for the ultimate benefit of our patients.

The Royal Commission has presented us with an exhaustive and most valuable appraisal of Canada's health needs and resources. The fact that we cannot agree with the Commission's recommendations on the best method of insuring personal health services does not detract from our admiration and support of other features of the Commission's work.

With its policy clarified and its resolve strengthened by the provincial developments and the consensus achieved at the special meeting, the executive stepped up its publicity campaign and arranged for a meeting with the minister of health and the prime minister in Ottawa on June 9, 1965.

It was against this background of political instability, intense political party rivalry, royal commission findings and recommendations, continuing expansion of the prepayment plans, the decisions of Alberta, Ontario, and British Columbia to establish subsidized programs, and the increasing aggressiveness of the CMA and the CHIA in pursuit of their subsidization policy that the Pearson government made its decision. It is now desirable to review the factors that were instrumental in the final choice.

The major factor was the Liberal party's long-term commitment to health insurance, which had been first undertaken in the election platform of 1919. (As some wag has observed, "An election platform is like a railway station platform: it helps you get on the train but you don't take it with you.") That commitment had resulted in the 1945 Green Book Proposals, which identified health insurance not only with the party but, for the first time, with a Liberal government. Although Prime Minister St. Laurent had declared in 1955 that the 1945 offer was no longer valid, there was clearly in the minds of Canadians who thought about it at all—and members of Parliament thought about it a good deal—the sense that the commitment must some day be redeemed. This feeling had been strengthened of course by the introduction of national hospital insurance. That event created, in a sense, the "other shoe" syndrome. Hospital Insurance had been highly successful; when would its twin—Medicare—be adopted? Somehow, it had become a natural, normal expectation that awaited only the time when a unique concatenation of political forces, public attitudes, and determined leadership would reach the necessary critical mass and the dreams of 1945 would be realized. Those elements were present, as never before, in 1965.

With the return of the Liberal government to office in 1963, Prime Minister Pearson appointed Judy LaMarsh to the portfolio of minister of health and welfare, informing her that she would "be responsible for the Pension and Medicare programs and would have to fight the Minister of Finance, Walter Gordon, for money for them." But as she later observed in her book *A Bird in a Gilded Cage*, "Considering the extent of Walter Gordon's commitment to these programs as election campaign chief, *that* fight wouldn't be too hard."[9] Indeed, it was not; Walter Gordon was the only federal finance minister in the fifty-year history of health insurance in Canada to support the proposal strongly.

For those within the cabinet and caucus committed to health insurance, the report of the royal commission came not only as a surprise but as a rallying cry of support for the commitment already made. Not only did it highlight the unmet needs and document and assess the resources, but through its dramatic proclamation of the Health Charter for Canadians, it had focused new light on the goals to be achieved.

For a modern industrialized nation, the unmet needs were prodigious: still high infant mortality, high incidence of illness, inadequate supply of trained personnel, general lack of insurance and inadequacy of much of it, inequitable distribution of expenditures on health services among the provinces, and disparate financial capacities of the provinces to act. The report documented them all.

Moreover, there was now that expanding threat on the Left from the NDP, with its showpiece, the Saskatchewan Medicare plan, demonstrating that Medicare was as feasible and effective as it was desirable. True, the birthpangs of Saskatchewan Medicare had been horrendous; the government that had introduced the program had been toppled, but it was obvious that the new government would not dream of dismantling it. By 1965 the Saskatchewan example was, like Banquo's ghost, a constant specter at every Liberal cabinet meeting when Medicare was discussed. The CCF contingent in Parliament, led by Tommy Douglas, never let the government forget it. Although the Diefenbaker government had introduced no legislation while in office, its leaders could at least claim paternity of the royal commission that had helped to move public opinion forward, and they could, and some of them did, chide the government for its failure to respond.

In addition to party promises, however, and all the rational reasons adduced by the royal commission for government action, the main thrust came from the handful of new progressive leaders in the cabinet: Judy LaMarsh, Walter Gordon, Alan McEachen, Maurice Lamontagne, and, after the election of 1965, Jean Marchand. In addition, with extraordinary influence, there was the prime minister's assistant, Tom Kent, whose speech to the Kingston Conference entitled "Towards a Philosophy of Social Security" contained many of the more progressive ideas that became the Liberal government's policies. And then there was the Right Honorable Lester Pearson, whose basic humanitarian philosophy embraced Medicare and ensured his support, but who, as in so many other controversial issues, found it difficult to maintain a consistent thrust toward an agreed-upon goal.

The leadership was now present; the needs, as documented by the royal commission, were great; the goals were defined; and a road map was at hand. It was time to act.

But there were constraints. Government policy-making is never simple, but in a federal state on an issue in any way involving the constituent provinces, it takes on additional complexity, particularly when the policy area falls within the jurisdiction of the provinces, as health insurance has been assumed to do.

Even when the constitutional question has been legally settled—in this case, through the right of the federal government to proceed under its blanket power to spend—to all the normal problems created by the conflicting demands and pressures of interest groups, there are added the political realities of the differing policy positions of the ten provincial governments. Their positions are equally complex, for their views represent not only the distillations of the pressures of their respective dominant interest groups, their program priorities, and differing financial resources but as well the survival needs and expansionist desires of their respective bureaucracies.

Moreover, as has been noted, the provinces had become more powerful. Coinciding with the emergence of the new autonomy-seeking Quebec under

Premier Jean Lesage, the Liberal government in Ottawa found itself also confronting other provincial governments with strong, determined leaders backed by solid majorities. With the provinces no longer content to accept Ottawa's largesse if it meant accepting Ottawa's dictates, clearly the central-ization-decentralization pendulum that had reached its apogee during the war was commencing its backswing to the provinces, and despite the frequent references to the advancement of "cooperative federalism," the competitive and sometimes hostile nature of the relationship in the sixties was yearly being reinforced.[10] An electoral commitment to a national constituency and the corresponding expectations of the national electorate for federal action in a field of provincial jurisdiction posed a dilemma that had been resolved before, but the omens for its resolution now were increasingly dark.

The senior echelons of the Department of National Health and Welfare were, it appears, as surprised by the range, vigor, and direction of the RCHS recommendations as the medical profession itself (and, one may assume, far more delighted). But unlike a royal commission which publishes its report, folds its tents, and silently steals away, a government department has a continuing responsibility for every proposal that is translated into policy; the response is therefore less bold and infinitely more concerned with out-comes—whether predictable or fortuitous.

The Health Department established a number of committees to examine the various sections of the report, evaluate them, and comment on the feasibility of the proposals and their relationships to ongoing programs of the department and its long-range planning. The RCHS had found little criti-cism of the hospital insurance program and obviously assumed that Medi-care, if implemented, would be designed along the same lines and enjoy the same acceptance. The Health Department's committee on Medicare, too, feeling comfortable with the familiar, envisaged a federal Medicare structure closely paralleling the hospital insurance model. And these proposals were fully supported by the minister.[11] When they reached the prime minister, he immediately appointed a committee representing Health, Finance, and the prime minister's office, the latter adding new perspectives to the discussions.

With his extraordinary diplomatic skills, the prime minister was probably more alert to the changing nature of federal-provincial relations than anyone else in Canada. It was clear that if all Canadians were to be insured, federal leadership was essential. In the past, national standards had been established by the federal government's use of the conditional grant-in-aid. Both the RCHS and the Health Department had recommended that model. The prime minister, however, was aware that there was now no possibility that such a circumscribing model would be accepted by the provinces. There began, therefore, an intensive examination of shared-cost program designs that would comport with the rising objections of provincial governments to federally imposed conditions.

Clearly, the requirements of the Hospital Insurance Act of a formal agreement and provision for detailed federal auditing of provincial accounts were no longer tolerable. The proposal would have to be based on a general understanding of what a Medicare program was, an agreement only on general principles on which a provincial program could be erected.[12]

Accordingly, in the interdepartmental committee, "principles" or "criteria" were examined, rejected, refined, and reduced to the absolute minimum, until four remained: comprehensiveness, universality, public administration, and portable benefits. Gone would be the need for signed agreements and for federal audit, that irritant and symbol of provincial subordination. It was simplicity itself. Not a federal program but ten provincial programs that together with federal sharing would aggregate to a national program of uniform minimum standards for all Canadians.

There was one more fundamental issue to be resolved: the design of a cost-sharing formula that would also accord with the new realities. A fixed per capita amount, similar to the proposals of 1945, would be preferable from the federal point of view but totally unacceptable to the provinces. A second possibility was the formula of the hospital insurance program. But if the new federal stance obviated the possibility of individual agreements and federal audits, then, to be consistent, the federal government must be equally oblivious to individual provincial program costs. In short, the hospital insurance formula was unacceptable precisely because one-half of the federal contribution was geared to each province's per capita costs. The only alternative seemed to be a single national figure, applied equally to all provinces. That, of course, was the national per capita cost. If the federal government paid one-half that amount on behalf of every insured person, calculations indicated that the figure would contribute less than half the cost in the wealthier provinces and up to 80 percent in low-income provinces. It would be a serendipitous outcome that almost all would applaud.

By the end of 1964, the minority government of Lester Pearson was a beleaguered force. Rocked by scandals, almost paranoid from the incessant leaks of cabinet discussions and reports of dissension among ministers, demoralized by the puerile feud between the leader of the opposition and the prime minister, and fatigued by the long, drawn-out negotiations with Quebec over the pension plan and the protracted debate in Parliament over a new Canadian flag, the cabinet appeared to lurch from crisis to crisis.

The Christmas recess had brought a welcome respite, and the prime minister directed his attention to preparation of the Speech from the Throne, the ritual address read by the governor-general at the opening of Parliament, signaling the government's agenda for the ensuing session. He wrote to members of the cabinet seeking their advice. He reminded them that two of the three social measures promised by the party had been implemented: extended family allowances and the pension plan. The third was Medicare. Of that he said, "I do not think that we can plan to take that on, at least in any comprehensive way, in 1965. But we do need to make some plans for dealing with the greatest needs in this area."[13] Finance Minister Walter Gordon replied, stating that he agreed that Medicare could not be enacted in 1965 but that the speech should contain "some reference to Medicare to remind the public of the Government's commitment."[14]

And so, on April 5, 1965, the Speech from the Throne contained a commitment to call a conference of the provinces (as had been recommended by the RCHS) to discuss health services for all Canadians.[15] The first step in the strategy of implementation had now been decided. The proposal would be offered in the first instance in the most general terms, to avoid the possibility that immediate waves of opposition to specific details would capsize the proposal before a firm launching could be made.

On June 9, as scheduled, the prime minister, the finance minister, and the health minister met with the CMA's Advisory Committee to the federal government. The committee restated its opposition to a compulsory plan with a single source of funds. It stressed that physicians should have the right to opt out of any plan, the patient also having the right to opt out without loss of benefits. It also reaffirmed its endorsement of the programs developed in Alberta and in the process of introduction in British Columbia and Ontario, and offered to discuss similar proposals with the prime minister and his colleagues at any time.

The committee reported back to the council that it had received a sympathetic hearing and had conveyed to the prime minister views which it felt would be considered at the federal-provincial conference.[16] It did not, however, receive any indication of imminent action by the federal government.

And now, on July 19, 1965, the First Ministers' Conference opened, with the prime minister giving the opening speech. He was at his diplomatic best. The federal government would not impose its views on the provinces; rather, "it is now the responsibility of the federal government to cooperate with the provinces in making Medicare financially possible for all Canadians. The Government now accepts that responsibility."[17]

To disabuse the provinces of any idea of federal domination, the prime minister said, "I am not proposing another shared-cost program. . . . In the case of Medicare I believe it is appropriate and possible to proceed by another route. The Federal Government, subject of course to Parliamentary approval, will support provincial Medicare plans by means of a fiscal contribution of predetermined size."[18]

Of course, the federal government did have conditions, but they must not be presented as such. The prime minister therefore said, "This proposal does not require detailed agreements governing the Medicare plan. It calls only for a general Federal-Provincial *understanding* as to the nature of the health programs which will make the Federal government believe that there are four criteria on which such an understanding should be based." The four criteria or principles, as they were called, were as follows:

First, the scope of benefits should be all the services provided by general practitioners and specialists.

Second, the plan should be universal; that is to say, it should cover all residents of a province on uniform terms and conditions.

Third, I think it will readily be agreed that a Federal contribution can properly be made available only to a plan which is publicly administered, either directly by the provincial government or by a provincial non-profit agency.

Fourth, each provincial plan should provide full transferability of benefits when people are absent from the province or when they move to another province.[19]

Then, taking cognizance of the RCHS recommendations that there be increased expenditures on facilities and health professions' training, the Prime Minister announced a proposal for a Health Resources Fund which would be concentrated on medical schools and teaching hospitals.[20]

In view of the conflicts that were to come, the responses of the provinces were extraordinarily low key. Premier John Robarts of Ontario did not respond to the Medicare proposals at all but commented on the need for developments in mental health, reorganization of the health grants, and increases in hospital construction grants.

Premier Lesage of Quebec, however, simply reinforced his now-familiar independent stance. "When our plan is introduced, it will be operated outside any joint Federal-Provincial program in line with our general policy of opting out of all areas within our competence. . . . The Federal Government can make it easier for provinces to exercise their constitutional powers, for example, by rectifying the present system of sharing revenue sources in Canada."

New Brunswick fully endorsed the proposal but emphasized that "our ability, and the ability of several other provinces is limited, not by desire or intelligence, but by dollars and cents." Manitoba indicated that it was considering adopting the Alberta system of subsidizing those on low incomes. And Saskatchewan, of course, with its program already in place, welcomed the prospect of federal funds but did warn "that the extension of health services should be undertaken only when positive steps are taken by all governments, the medical profession, hospital boards, and the public to control the level of hospital and medical costs." Saskatchewan was speaking from experience and the words were to echo down the years.[21]

And so, with minimum debate, and no outright opposition, the conference adjourned. But the seeming harmony of the 1965 conference was deceptive as the opposition forces mounted. In September 1965 the BCMP became operational, insuring individuals and families, whether requiring subsidy or not, and leaving groups to the prepayment plans. In January 1966 the Ontario plan (OMSIP) was introduced, providing subsidies to those with taxable incomes below $1,000 and offering coverage to all other individuals and families not in payroll groups.

Worse, from the point of view of the federal government, were the results of a September public opinion poll on whether a compulsory plan was preferred to the voluntary approach, revealing that 52 percent preferred the voluntary approach to 41 percent who preferred a compulsory plan, with 7 percent undecided.[22]

Equally shattering were the results of the November 1965 election, which Pearson had called in the hope of achieving a majority government. The Liberals gained only two seats, still remaining a minority.[23] Walter Gordon, who had recommended the election, resigned as finance minister, and was succeeded by Mitchell Sharp, a known opponent of Medicare. In addition, Judy LaMarsh was succeeded as health minister by Alan McEachen, who, on the other hand, was a strong advocate for the program.[24]

There were thus five major factors in the decision-making process: (1) the continuing minority position of the government, (2) the increasing opposition from the insurance industry and the medical profession, (3) the increasing resistance among several of the provinces to the principles underlying the federal plan, (4) the increasing seriousness of the state of the economy in the face of rising inflation and the rising federal budget deficit, and (5) the increasing vocal support of the Liberal party for the proposal, constantly reinforced by the NDP.

But time was running out, for it was the hope of the government to have the program introduced on the symbolic date of July 1, 1967, Canada's centennial anniversary. As the legislation cleared cabinet before introduction in the House of Commons, the only opposition to be raised even by Sharp was whether the timing was right, in view of the inflation threats. The decision was to proceed.[25]

The Medical Care Insurance Bill was introduced in July, and the details followed the principles announced earlier. There was one change, an enlargement of the definition of "publicly administered." Insurance companies could serve as carriers, provided that no profits accrued to the company, their books were open to the public, and their administration was responsible to the provincial government. This was an obvious shift in strategy to placate Alberta and Ontario and to enable British Columbia, with a half dozen voluntary plans, to qualify.

In view of the strength of the opposing forces and the minority position of the government, the proposed legislation was extraordinarily bold. There was an obvious and justified assumption that support would be forthcoming from the NDP, whatever the position of the other opposition parties.

The parliamentary debates and the accompanying media coverage of the details of the proposal resulted in a reinforcing or snowballing effect, as the opponents took advantage of the summer recess of Parliament that permitted a last-ditch offensive. A focal point for the opposition was the regularly scheduled Provincial Premiers' Conference, held in Toronto on August 1–2. So strident were the tones, so angry the voices, and so vehement the opposition that one journalist summed up, "The federal government's proposed legislation lies torn, tattered, and politically rejected." And another said, "But in the end, the provinces did gang up on Ottawa so surely and thoroughly the whole future of Medicare is now in the balance."[26]

These rumbles of opposition of course were reflected in the cabinet, as the press reported a widening split. Sharp and Winters, with reputedly a majority following, were marshaling their forces in opposition to McEachen and LaMarsh in the cabinet and Walter Gordon in the caucus to change the launching date from July 1, 1967, to July 1, 1968—and they succeeded in doing so.[27]

After eight days of acrimonious debate, the bill was given second reading on October 25 with only ten Conservatives and eleven others opposed. On December 8, 1966, the bill was given third reading and was passed by a vote of 177 to 2, almost reaching the unanimous vote that had endorsed the Hospital Insurance Act in 1957.[28]

Unlike the case of hospital insurance, there was no minimum requirement of a majority of the provinces agreeing to the program before federal contributions would be made. Accordingly, on the inaugural date of July 1, 1968, only two provinces, Saskatchewan and British Columbia, qualified. Three more, Newfoundland, Nova Scotia, and Manitoba, commenced their programs at the beginning of the fiscal year, April 1, 1969. The other followed in this order: Alberta, July 1, 1969; Ontario, October 1, 1969; Quebec, October 1, 1970; Prince Edward Island, December 1, 1970; New Brunswick, January

1, 1971. The Northwest Territories' plan began on April 1, 1971, and the Yukon program on April 1, 1972.

The Liberal party's promise of 1919, formalized in the federal government's commitment at the 1965 federal-provincial conference "to cooperate with the provinces in making Medicare financially possible for all Canadians," had been redeemed. This was the federal view and was probably so construed by Saskatchewan and British Columbia. It could scarcely have been so interpreted by Ontario and Alberta, for the political costs of their cooperation were large, and they and some others considered the arrangement less cooperation than coercive political blackmail. But whatever the political and economic costs that would impinge on other provincial priorities, ten provincial programs with portable benefits came into being, and the national plan was born.

Three provinces fought hard battles to obtain concessions even after the act was passed. Alberta, opposed to compulsion, was forced to abandon its contracts with the profession-sponsored plan, MSI (which folded), and the insurance company consortium.

In Ontario, consideration was given to the future role of Physicians Services Inc. Finally concluding that there was no real contribution to be made in serving simply as a post office, PSI ceased its operations on October 1, 1969, when the Ontario plan, OHIP, began.

But the insurance-industry operations in Ontario Medicare were another matter. Given the basic philosophy of OMSIP, it was not to be expected that the insurance companies would be dropped from their place in the administration. They were, of course, reduced to serving as post offices and deprived of their profits from Medicare contracts. Their inclusion in the administration caused an enormous amount of duplication and an unnecessary additional administration cost. They were phased out in 1972.

Quebec endeavored to stay out of the program, but of course that failed. When its legislation provided for a single fee schedule for both general practitioners and specialists and prohibited extra-billing, the specialists went on strike, only to be legislated back to work on October 16, 1970.[29]

The transition in British Columbia was fairly easy to make, since the insurance industry had had a relatively insignificant part in insuring medical benefits in that province and the nonprofit prepayment plans could, with minor changes, be readily designated as publicly administered. It was necessary only to have personnel responsible to BCMP assess all medical accounts and audit financial statements.

The Atlantic provinces confronted similar, complex problems of creating new administrative agencies, dealing with the existing prepayment plans, and finding new sources of revenue. Their difficulties were only partly ameliorated by the favorable terms of the financing formula.

It had been a long political battle extending over almost half of a century since Mackenzie King had persuaded the Liberal party convention in 1919 to commit the party to health insurance. But the programs described in part 1 were now an integral part of the social, political, and economic fabric of Canada.

Chapter Nine

Changes in the System

As in all large-scale joint undertakings by the two orders of government, it was inevitable that, despite the general satisfaction with and the strong public support for the two programs, experience would dictate that changes be made. There have been two major modifications to the programs, both initiated by the federal government, the first altering the financial arrangements with the provinces, and the second affecting doctors' billings and hospital user fees. Changing the financing formula also triggered three important public inquiries.

As inflation forces and increasing utilization of health services pushed annual cost increases in the two programs over the 20 percent mark in the early 1970s, the pressures on and concerns of health and finance officials mounted exponentially. The provinces objected to the inflexible administrative details of the agreements they had been required to sign in accordance with the Hospital Insurance Act; they also resented the federal audit to determine shareable costs; and low-income provinces objected to the hospital insurance financing formula that resulted in higher per capita payments from the federal treasury to high-cost than to low-cost provinces. Moreover, the provinces claimed that the sharing of costs of only two programs effectively distorted provincial priorities and decision making.

For its part, the federal Finance Department was concerned that it had no control over its rapidly rising, open-ended health budget, since the legislation required it to match all medical and hospital care expenditures determined by provincial governments. There was also an uneasy feeling among federal officials that provincial governments were not as prudent in their decisions on 50-50 cost-shared expenditures as they were in other programs to which they must allocate 100-cent dollars. The belief that provinces were spending 50-cent dollars was widely held, but Lee Soderstrom, a health economist at McGill University, has shown that Ontario, whose expenditures had the largest impact on national per capita averages, received only eighteen cents for each additional dollar of expenditure on Medicare and only thirty-four cents for each additional dollar spent on hospital services. All other provinces received less.[1] But the myth prevailed.

There was also a growing feeling at both levels that, as a result of introducing hospital insurance first, Canada had overbuilt its hospital system, and a number of provinces began to reduce their hospital bed–population ratios, usually at great political risk. To enhance uncertainty about how high the open-ended health budget might go, a flood of health care and economics journals, as well as press reports, constantly informed Canadians of rising health expenditures in the United States, as well as of President Carter's thwarted efforts to control them. A sense of a "health costs spiral" permeated the whole system, not least the upper echelons of the Finance Department. With the growing conviction that the federal government must gain control of its health expenditures, it was clear that the stage was being set for a fundamental restructuring of the financial underpinnings of the Canadian medical and hospital care system.

It is necessary to digress briefly to take account of a secondary major financial agreement in 1972 that paralleled, but was unrelated to, the regular five-year Tax Agreements. In that year, the federal government introduced income-tax reforms that reduced the federal income "basic tax" on which all provinces except Quebec base their provincial income tax levies, expressed as a percentage of the federal basic tax, which are then added on and collected by the Department of National Revenue on behalf of, but at no cost to, the provincial governments. (Quebec is thus the only province in which income-tax payers are required to submit two returns.) With the reduction in the basic tax, provincial governments would either have to accept reduced revenues or have to bear the onus for raising their effective percentage rates.

Recognizing the provincial treasurers' Hobson's choice, the federal government agreed, for a period of three years (during which the provincial governments could gradually legislate politically painful tax increases) to ensure that the provinces would receive no less than they would have if the reforms had not been introduced.[2] This Revenue Guarantee, which became entangled, as we shall see, with health insurance financing, bedeviled federal-provincial relations for the next ten years. With the 1972 Tax Agreements and the income tax reforms out of the way, the Finance Department turned its attention to the cost-sharing formula, finally offering a proposal that would tie its contribution to increases in the GNP rather than to increased provincial expenditures. As expected, the provinces rejected the proposal. The federal government then tightened the screws. It announced that its annual contributions to Medicare (but not to hospital services) would be limited to increases of 13.0 percent in 1976–77, 10.5 percent in 1977–78, and 8.5 percent in 1978–79. It also gave the required five-year advance notice to terminate the Hospital Insurance Agreements in 1980.[3] And on Thanksgiving Day in October 1975, the prime minister announced a nationwide program of income and price controls.[4]

Negotiations of the Tax Agreements for the 1977–82 period began at a federal-provincial conference in June 1976, and there Prime Minister Trudeau proposed termination of the 50-50 cost-sharing arrangements for the two health programs and for postsecondary education. In their place he offered to vacate 12.5 percentage points of personal income tax and 1 percent of corporation income tax, thus providing "tax room" which the provincial governments could occupy. This was calculated to approximate one-half of the federal contribution under the existing cost-sharing formula. In addition, the federal government would contribute a cash grant equal to the other half of its 1975–76 payments for the three programs, escalated annually in accordance with a three-year moving average of increases in per capita GNP. Since a tax point yields less revenue in low-income than in high-income provinces, the tax points would be equalized to the national average. Moreover, in the event that revenue from the transferred tax points fell below the amount payable in the escalated cash grant, a transitional payment equal to the difference would be made.[5]

The negotiations were lengthy, often bitter, and always complex. The provincial finance ministers and their officials held an unprecedented number of joint meetings. The low-income provinces wanted the 50-50 cost-sharing formula to remain. The high-income provinces wanted the total federal contribution in tax transfers, with no federal cash payments. The federal government, of course, wanted the 50 percent cash payment in order to retain some control over the shape of the programs. Finally, the four Atlantic provinces and Saskatchewan were persuaded to abandon their position of retaining the 50-50 cost-sharing formula, enabling the provincial finance ministers to present a unanimous proposal in early December that included a demand for transfer of an additional four tax points as a continuation of the 1972 Revenue Guarantee, due to expire on March 31, 1977. (It had been extended from the original three years to five.) The demand was rejected by the federal finance minister, and the issues were left for the scheduled First Ministers' Conference, December 13–14, 1976.

While the fundamental change from cost sharing to block funding was accepted, the provinces were adamant that the Revenue Guarantee be continued. Finally, to achieve agreement on the entire package, the federal government compromised, offering an additional transfer of one tax point and its equivalent in cash, also to be escalated in accordance with increases in the GNP, or, in total, one-half the added amount the provinces had demanded.

The essentials of the agreement were incorporated in the Federal-Provincial Fiscal Arrangements and Established Programs Financing Act and became operational for the period April 1, 1977, to March 31, 1982.[6] Although the origins of the Revenue Guarantee were based in the 1972 income-tax reforms and had absolutely nothing to do with established programs financing (EPF), the Revenue Guarantee amounts (the equivalent of two tax points) were included in the EPF legislation and in all published data as part of the federal "contribution." Although this move had the short-term effect of magnifying the federal contribution, it was a political decision that would come to embarrass the government.

In addition to the provisions already outlined, the federal government introduced a new grant of twenty dollars per capita, also to be escalated annually in accordance with increases in the GNP, to assist provinces in providing less expensive support services, including nursing home intermediate care, adult residential care, converted mental hospitals, home care services, and ambulatory health services. No conditions other than information reporting were attached to this grant. However, some of this new revenue for the provinces was offset by removing nursing homes and adult residential care from the 50-50 cost-sharing provisions under the CAP. By 1987–88, the Extended Health Care Grant totaled $1.273 billion. For the effect of the shift to block funding on the respective financial contributions to the health programs by the two orders of government, reference should be made to table 4.

With the introduction of the EPF arrangements, the major objectives of the federal and provincial governments were met. The federal government obtained greater predictability and stability over its health expenditures; the provincial governments achieved greater flexibility in determining their health services program priorities. The new block grant also provided greater equity in that by the third year the per capita payments to provinces were equal, whereas under the Hospital Insurance Act formula, they had not been. However, this newfound autonomy and equity were not achieved without cost. The provinces are now solely responsible for program cost increases that exceed annual increases in the GNP; but since provincial expenditures on all health services are now 100-cent dollars, federal contributions no

Table 4.

Government Expenditures for Hospital and Medical Insurance Programs, Selected Fiscal Years, 1976–77 to 1988–89

Province	1976–77[a]	1977–78[b]	1979–80	1981–82	1983–84	1985–86	1987–88	1988–89[c]
	Provincial expenditures ($ millions)							
Newfoundland	156.0	173.1	225.7	303.2	377.8	406.2	471.0	499.6
Prince Edward Island	32.5	35.2	44.1	58.5	76.5	84.4	95.9	101.6
Nova Scotia	257.3	273.9	335.5	473.9	598.0	706.6	797.2	842.8
New Brunswick	190.7	207.8	243.8	351.5	447.5	507.5	563.8	618.0
Quebec	2,291.7	2,383.9	3,079.2	3,971.5	4,973.0	5,398.5	6,292.4	6,621.5
Ontario	2,882.2	3,036.0	3,500.0	4,729.2	6,229.4	7,471.3	9,290.3	10,045.8
Manitoba	338.9	365.4	418.2	591.0	729.8	834.7	968.2	1,038.9
Saskatchewan	292.2	320.9	370.0	487.0	626.9	697.8	772.7	808.8
Alberta	636.5	657.2	806.3	1,252.5	1,820.2	2,055.0	2,266.8	2,440.1
British Columbia	878.8	953.9	1,130.1	1,718.4	2,104.7	2,226.2	2,608.3	2,833.1
Yukon	7.0	7.5	9.2	11.0	16.2	17.1	20.4	22.2
Northwest Territories	11.7	16.9	20.9	26.2	41.0	52.4	72.2	76.3
Canada	7,975.0	8,431.7	10,183.0	13,973.9	18,041.0	20,457.7	24,219.2	25,948.8
	Federal contributions ($ millions)							
Newfoundland	90.3	95.5	129.9	161.2	200.8	229.4	252.8	263.9
Prince Edward Island	16.6	19.5	28.1	34.8	43.3	50.6	56.6	59.8
Nova Scotia	130.6	147.2	194.4	240.7	300.3	349.7	391.6	410.6
New Brunswick	106.6	116.9	159.9	197.8	246.7	281.7	316.9	331.9
Quebec	1,062.2	1,180.7	1,465.0	1,828.7	2,268.9	2,608.9	2,933.2	3,084.2
Ontario	1,341.9	1,512.0	1,962.9	2,449.7	3,075.8	3,562.2	4,124.7	4,381.1
Manitoba	171.1	186.4	237.6	291.5	365.3	427.9	480.1	503.9

Saskatchewan	148.8	163.3	219.8	275.0	346.3	406.3	451.2	469.8
Alberta	302.0	347.8	501.1	712.5	817.8	930.9	1,059.1	1,115.4
British Columbia	390.4	426.4	597.7	782.1	983.1	1,121.6	1,301.7	1,386.2
Yukon	3.2	4.1	5.6	7.2	7.8	9.4	10.9	11.8
Northwest Territories	6.7	7.9	10.4	13.0	16.9	20.8	23.0	24.1
Canada	3,770.4	4,207.7	5,512.4	6,994.1	8,672.9	9,999.5	11,401.8	12,042.6

Federal contributions as percentage of provincial expenditures

Newfoundland	57.9	55.2	57.6	53.2	53.1	56.5	53.7	52.8
Prince Edward Island	50.9	55.4	63.8	59.5	56.6	60.0	59.0	58.8
Nova Scotia	50.7	53.8	57.9	50.8	50.2	49.5	49.1	48.7
New Brunswick	55.9	56.2	65.6	56.3	55.1	55.5	56.2	53.7
Quebec	46.4	49.5	47.6	46.0	45.6	48.3	46.6	46.6
Ontario	46.6	49.8	56.1	51.8	49.4	47.7	44.4	43.6
Manitoba	50.5	51.0	56.8	49.3	50.1	51.3	49.6	48.5
Saskatchewan	50.9	50.9	59.4	56.5	55.2	58.2	58.4	58.1
Alberta	47.4	52.9	62.2	56.9	44.9	45.3	46.7	45.7
British Columbia	44.4	44.7	52.9	45.5	46.7	50.4	49.9	48.9
Yukon	46.4	54.3	60.4	64.7	48.2	55.0	53.2	52.9
Northwest Territories	57.2	46.7	49.5	49.5	41.3	39.7	31.9	31.6
Canada	47.3	49.9	54.1	50.1	48.1	48.9	47.1	46.4

Source: Health and Welfare Canada.

[a] Last year of 50–50 cost-sharing.
[b] First year of block funding.
[c] Provisional.

longer have any steering effect on provincial decision making. And the overall effect appears to have strengthened the resolve of provincial governments to greater efforts at cost containment.

With the lifting of income and price controls on July 1, 1978, the anticipated happened: the name of the game was catch-up. The latter half of that year and 1979 saw large increases in the numbers of doctors extra-billing, more militancy among nursing and other unionized hospital employees, and the beginning of charges that, as a result of the new flexibility provided to the provinces in their allocation of funds under EPF, provincial governments were diverting federal health contributions to nonhealth purposes.

Following the election of a minority Conservative government in 1979, under the leadership of Joe Clark, the new health minister, David Crombie, became the focal point of charges that the federal government was not fulfilling its responsibilities to ensure that "national standards" be maintained and that the principles of Medicare not be eroded by the spreading practice of extra-billing. (In Quebec extra-billing had been banned from the beginning.) As an indication of public interest in the threat to access to Medicare, a number of provincial health coalitions, spearheaded by the labor unions and including associations of teachers, nurses, consumers, and senior citizens, as well as church associations and others, held conferences in 1979, culminating in a National Health Coalition "SOS Medicare Conference" in Ottawa in early November. Over 250 delegates representing organizations with a combined membership of over 2 million attended. The media had been focusing on the issue, of course, since mid-1978. So heated became the issue that three public inquiries were launched, the first in 1979.

The Health Services Review, 1979–80

In the meantime, Health Minister Crombie had already begun to take action. He had three major concerns.[7] Since both hospital insurance and Medicare had been introduced by Liberal governments, he wanted to identify the Conservatives positively with the popular health care programs. He also needed answers to two questions. Were the provinces, as charged during the election by his predecessor, the Honorable Monique Begin, diverting federal funds to nonhealth purposes? And were extra-billing by doctors and hospital user fees violating the principle of reasonable access and thus eroding Medicare? A commission of inquiry could examine the issues and, if it were to be headed by the Honorable Emmett Hall, chairman of the RCHS in the early 1960s and a lifelong Conservative, that would clearly identify the new government with a pro-Medicare policy. (A commission would also give the new minister several months in which to get a better handle on his department.) Crombie then convened a meeting in July with provincial health ministers and made his proposal for a special commission with Hall as chairman. The provincial ministers, although leery about another federal inquiry into their jurisdiction, agreed—with the exception of Quebec, which, in the event, cooperated fully. The terms of reference were broad, but it turned out to be a Herculean task for which Lilliputian resources were made available.

Although the government was almost solely concerned with the two questions posed above, the public viewed the appointment of a commission on a much broader scale. After eleven years of operation of Medicare, a comprehensive in-depth examination of the system was considered imperative. Both provider and consumer groups responded with an overwhelming total of 450 briefs that, in the main, lauded the system, observed its shortcomings, complained of underfunding, criticized (and defended) extra-billing, and pointed to new directions.

I took leave from York University to become research consultant to the commissioner, responsible primarily for ascertaining whether provinces were indeed diverting federal health funds, for analyzing briefs in preparation for questioning of witnesses in the public hearings, and for preparing drafts of other sections of the report.

Without independent research staff, we relied on senior research staff at Health and Welfare Canada to analyze pre-EPF and post-EPF federal and provincial health expenditures. That group completed the monumental task of examining provincial public accounts, and all its data were submitted to provincial health and treasury officials for verification. The task was complicated by the fact that health services expenditures are made by several departments, including Social Welfare, Corrections, and others. This was followed up by my personal interviews with federal and provincial health and finance officials. The results were indisputable; provinces were *not* diverting federal health contributions to nonhealth purposes. The whole misunderstanding (some would say, fiasco) had occurred because the federal government had included the Revenue Guarantee funds as a contribution under EPF. The proportion of aggregate provincial budgets allocated to health services, before and after EPF, was identical. Revenue Guarantee funds had been spent, quite rightly, on other programs. That answered federal question number one.

On question two, whether extra-billing and user charges were endangering the principle of reasonable access, Commissioner Hall was adamant. He said:

Canadians understand the full meaning of the Hospital Insurance and Medical Care Insurance Acts. They said, through these two Acts, that we, as a society, are aware that the pain of illness, the trauma of surgery, the decline to death, are burdens enough for the human being to bear without the added burden of medical and hospital bills penalizing the patient at the moment of vulnerability. The Canadian people determined that they should band together to pay their medical and hospital bills when they were well and income earning. Health services were no longer to be items to be bought off the shelf and paid for at the checkout stand. Nor was their price to be bargained for at the time they were sought. They were a fundamental need, like education, which Canadians could meet collectively and pay for through taxes.[8]

After examining further evidence, he concluded, "If extra-billing is permitted as a right and practised by physicians in their sole discretion, it will, over the years, destroy the program, creating in that downward path a two-tier system incompatible with the societal level which Canadians have attained."[9]

But what if extra-billing were denied? What if government-profession negotiations over the fee schedule broke down? The remedy, said the former Supreme Court justice, was binding arbitration, a solution, he knew from his questioning in the public hearings, that almost every witness speaking to the issue had rejected. His views on extra-billing were a noble restatement of a fundamental principle of the Canadian health system and reflect credit on the ideals and sense of equity of a distinguished jurist. But the total report did not do justice to the terms of reference, the expectations of the public, or the fundamental need to reexamine the roles of the overextended sickness treatment system and of health-promoting alternatives.

The House of Commons Task Force

The defeat of the short-lived Joe Clark Conservative government in 1980 had brought the Liberals back to power, with the Honorable Monique Begin reinstated as minister of health. One effect of the Clark Conservatives' period in office and their return to opposition was that they now insisted on a greater role for Parliament in the upcoming negotiations for the 1982 Tax Agreements. Previous negotiations had taken place solely between federal and provincial finance ministers and their officials, with their agreements rubber-stamped by Parliament and provincial legislatures. Professor Donald

Smiley had described the process as "executive federalism," and there now appeared a determination among opposition members and Liberal back-benchers alike to reassert their roles in the parliamentary system.[10]

The Conservative opposition demanded and finally obtained agreement by the government to the appointment of an ad hoc investigative committee—an all-party House of Commons task force—to examine the entire field of federal-provincial fiscal relations, including the impact of EPF.

The committee held public hearings in Ottawa and all the provincial capitals and received briefs from a host of interest groups concerned, in the main, with financing postsecondary education and the health care system, both of which, many claimed, were underfunded. The CMA and several of its divisions cited evidence of the underfinancing of the system and urged that spending be immediately increased to at least 8.2 percent of GNP from the 7 percent characteristic of the 1970s. (In fact, Canadian spending on health services reached 8.4 percent in 1982, due more to the recession and consequent decline in the rate of growth of the GNP than to an increase in the rate of growth of health spending.) Total health spending increased 16.7 percent in 1980, 17.3 percent in 1981, and 17.1 percent in 1982, and it declined to an increase of 11.1 percent in 1983, when health expenditures reached 8.7 percent of the GNP. Public spending in Canada constitutes about 75 percent of all health spending.

Acknowledging that it was, in part, recrossing terrain already traversed by commissioner Hall's Health Services Review, the task force nevertheless conducted an intensive analysis of the relevant briefs and statistical and financial data available to it. It grappled with the issue of the role of the federal government in an area of provincial jurisdiction and finally con-cluded: "There is an overriding national interest in the operation of health insurance plans and in the effectiveness of health care delivery. The question that follows is what actions the federal government may take to serve the national interest without itself becoming directly involved in health care delivery." It concluded that "the proper role for the federal government is the formulation, monitoring and enforcement of conditions on its financial sup-port of provincial programs." To this end, it urged that the Hospital Insur-ance and Medical Care Acts be consolidated in order to establish clear program conditions supported by explicit criteria against which satisfaction of those conditions could be monitored and some withholding of federal finan-cial support to provincial plans that did not fully meet those conditions. The minister of health should report annually to Parliament the results of the monitoring and any withholding actions taken, for reference to a parliamentary committee.[11] (Their position was a quantum leap from Prime Minister Pearson's statement in 1965 that Medicare was not to be a *conditional* shared-cost program "like the others.")

The task force then examined the extent to which user fees and extra-billing violated the principle of reasonable access and concluded that, with respect to user fees, given the exemptions provided by the provinces that imposed them, it had no evidence that they constituted a barrier to accessibility to hospitals. Nevertheless, it endorsed the view of the Health Services Review that the "user pay" concept is contrary to the spirit of the National Health Program.

With respect to extra-billing, it agreed with the conclusions of the Health Service Review that if extra-billing were allowed to continue, it would over the years destroy the system. The majority recommended that "doctors not be allowed to charge fees in excess of those permitted under the plan's approved fee schedule." It then endorsed commissioner Hall's proposal that if agreement on a fee schedule was not reached, recourse should be made to binding arbitration. Finally, the majority said, "Following federal-provincial negotiations, any plan that does not meet fully all the accessibility criteria be ineligible for full financial support under Established Programs Financing." The Conservative members of the committee were not prepared to go that far (although they would in 1984, when it came time to vote on the Canada Health Bill), recommending only that if doctors wished to extra-bill any patients, they must opt out of the plan and bill all their patients directly, as already required in Ontario and Manitoba.

The final major issue was whether Canadians were committing a sufficient proportion of national resources to meet their essential health care needs. The committee carefully analyzed the claim, most forcefully argued by the CMA, that the health system was underfunded. In 1979 Canada spent 7.22 percent of its GNP on health care; of eight Western nations, only the United Kingdom and New Zealand spent less. The counterarguments submitted by the committee were as follows:

International comparisons of the percentage of GNP allocated to health services are misleading; they dwell on expenditures and say nothing about the mix of services or results. In the United States over-head insurance administration costs are four times higher than in Canada; hospital administration overhead [because of billing for each service] is much higher; there is far greater duplication of facilities and high technology.

The switch to block funding from cost-sharing had injected a major infusion of new funds into the system. In 1978–79 provinces received between 1.5 and 1.8 billion dollars more than they would have under the old formula. The federal share of *all* provincial spending on health and post-secondary education increased from 42 percent in 1976–77 to 47 percent in 1979–80. In constant dollars *per capita* spending on health increased by almost one-fifth in the decade of the seventies.[12]

In essence, the report concluded that comparisons of the percent of the GNP spent by Canada and the United States were irrelevant. "The difference is in our philosophy; Canadians are endeavouring to develop a health care system directed to health needs—not a competitive system to serve an illness market."

Noting that added spending in the acute care system yields only marginal improvements in health status, and endorsing provinces' decisions to expand their preventive, health promotion, and support programs, the committee concluded that "in aggregate, and in present circumstances, federal funding for health care services in Canada appears to be generally adequate (although) there may remain specific areas—for example, preventive care—that require expansion."[13] The task force's recommendations thus reinforced those of the Health Services Review and, indeed, by going further in the recommendations for financial penalties, paved the way for the Canada Health Act.

But the saga of EPF was not over. In the negotiations for renewal of the Taxation Agreements for the 1982–87 period, the federal government held firm to its decision (on which it had compromised in 1977) to end the Revenue Guarantee. That represented an aggregate loss to the provinces of just under $5 billion over the 1982–87 period, and although, as has been stressed, the Revenue Guarantee funds were wholly unrelated to EPF, any decline in overall provincial revenues cannot fail to affect many programs. But there was more bad news to come: EPF was to be directly attacked.

Confronted on its accession to office in September 1984 with the magnitude of the impending deficit and the ever-increasing national debt, the Conservative government through its new finance minister, Michael Wilson, announced a number of deficit-cutting measures in his budgets of May 1985 and February 1986. Acknowledging that the deficit was not being reduced at the projected rate, in May 1986 the minister announced a reduction of 2 percent in the growth rate of the EPF transfer payments, commencing April 1, 1986. The decreases in annual payments to the provinces were projected to rise from $318 million in 1986–87 to just over $2 billion in 1991–92.

Citing this reduction as but part of a comprehensive attack on the deficit problem, the minister emphasized that federal statutory spending (such as FA or CPP, but excluding EPF) would be restricted to an annual growth rate of 3.8 percent, and nonstatutory spending to an annual rate of only 2.7 percent, while EPF spending, despite the reductions, would increase annually at a rate of about 5 percent. "Federal transfer payments to provinces could not be insulated from the over-all effort because they constitute about 20 percent of federal budgetary expenditures."[14] The loss of a projected total of $5.689 billion by the provinces over the five-year period cannot fail to constrain medical fee negotiations and hospital budget-setting.

The CMA Task Force on the Allocation of Health Resources

In the meantime, there had been one other nationwide inquiry into the Canadian health care system, this one sponsored and financed by the CMA. Frustrated and perhaps even alarmed that its massive lobbying and publicity efforts and those of its provincial divisions claiming that the real problem in the system was not extra-billing but, rather, inadequate financing had won no support from either the Health Services Review or the parliamentary task force, in early 1983 the CMA budgeted approximately $500,000 to finance the Task Force on the Allocation of Health Resources. It selected a blue-ribbon committee of distinguished citizens including two doctors, former Saskatchewan attorney general Roy Romanow, former lieutenant governor of Ontario, Pauline McGibbon, with Joan Watson, former star of the Canadian Broadcasting Corporation's program "Marketplace," as chairperson.

The task force held hearings across Canada and received numerous submissions. In its report,[15] the committee concentrated on the effects on the health care system of the aging of the population, of medical technology, and of the issue of funding. The CMA and the ten provincial associations consistently stressed the serious underfunding of the system and the need to augment government spending by a greater infusion of private funds through such devices as user fees and extra-billing.

On the funding issue, the report summarized the arguments of the CMA that underfunding represented a real threat to Medicare and those of others, including Health and Welfare Canada, that funding was adequate and that what was needed was significant restructuring and reorganization of health care priorities and delivery systems. But the task force came down on the side of those declaring that it cannot be said that there is, or is not, underfunding.

The debate surrounding the issue of adequate funding levels has degenerated to the point where little is being contributed to an amicable resolution of the outstanding differences . . . what is needed is cooling the rhetoric. . . . To answer this point [of underfunding] we must again return to the proposition that spending more money on health care must be shown to provide a commensurate improvement in health, and this improvement must be shown to be greater than that which could be achieved by spending the money in some other way. The Task Force could find no evidence to clearly substantiate either of these views. We cannot assess the extent of existing inefficiencies, and because there is no guarantee that putting more money into the system is necessarily the best way of improving health, the Task Force cannot make a clear-cut recommendation.[16]

The sections of the report on the elderly and on medical technology were major contributions to public discourse on those issues, and that on funding should have lowered the temperature of the debate on that issue. But in view of the raison d'être of the task force, there must have been second thoughts on the part of the CMA about the return on its investment in a third public inquiry.

The Canada Health Act, 1984

From the introduction of the two programs, the major concerns for the provincial health ministries were related to making the systems work: deciding on the optimum allocation of resources to acute and chronic care hospitals, nursing homes, and home care programs; negotiating fee schedules with medical associations and annual budgets for hospitals; getting thousands of checks out on time to doctors, other health professionals, and hospitals; expanding preventive services and health promotion; managing the continuing financial commitments to a rapidly growing inventory of physicians and perceived oversupply of acute hospital beds; making rational decisions about the efficacy of and the need for an ever-expanding armamentarium of high technology; managing relationships with increasingly militant hospital workers' unions and nurses' and medical associations; and, above all else, prodding more funds from reluctant Treasury officials under fire from other, equally demanding, departments. There was daily a full plate of decision making for harassed ministry officials.

As indicated at the beginning of this chapter, however, the headline-grabbing major events in the decade were the switch to block funding for hospital and medical care under the EPF legislation in 1977 and the Canada Health Act in 1984. EPF had represented the most massive transfer of revenues (and therefore the substance of power) from the federal to the provincial governments in Canadian history. But to the medical profession and the provincial governments, the Canada Health Act appeared to be the reverse: an unwarranted, powerful and, for the provincial governments, politically hazardous federal intrusion into a field of provincial jurisdiction.

The issue appeared clear-cut: whether physicians should be permitted, at will, to extra-bill insured patients and whether provincial governments could authorize user fees to be charged to patients admitted to hospital inpatient or outpatient departments. The questions appeared simple, but they struck at the heart of the Medical Care Insurance Act, which stated:

> The plan [shall] provide for the furnishing of insured services upon uniform terms and conditions in accordance with a tariff of authorized payment established pursuant to the provincial law . . . on a basis that provides for reasonable compensation for insured services rendered by medical practitioners and *that does not impede or preclude, either directly or indirectly whether by charges made to insured persons or otherwise, reasonable access to insured services by insured persons.* (emphasis added)

As noted earlier, the profession-sponsored medical care prepayment plans had introduced the *service* contract to compete with the insurance companies' *indemnity* contracts. The service contract concept had three important elements: (1) the physician was required to sign a contract with the prepayment plan, agreeing to accept the plan's payment as payment in full; (2) because the plan was serving, in effect, as the physician's collection agency, it was agreed that the plan would deduct 10 percent from the authorized fees for overhead administration; (3) if the funds available from premiums revenue were insufficient to meet the 90 percent obligation, the plan was empowered to prorate the payment downward so that expenditures and revenues were in balance.

However, in every province having a profession-sponsored plan there were physicians who did not sign contracts and were thus nonparticipating (or, what under Medicare were called in two provinces, "opted out") physicians. These physicians set their own fees, and those of their patients who were plan subscribers were reimbursed at 90 percent of the amount provided in the operative fee schedule. The practice of extra-billing insured patients was thus established.

Under Medicare in Ontario, the proportion of physicians opting out averaged about 13.5 percent until 1978, when, with the end of income controls, it increased to 18 percent, only to fall back, after substantial fee increases, by 1983 to about 12 percent. But the Ministry of Health reported that only about 5 percent of all accounts were actually extra-billed. This meant that fewer than 5 percent (probably 2–3 percent) of patients contributed an additional estimated $50 million dollars to 12 percent of Ontario's physicians, with those billing the highest amounts to OHIP also extra-billing the largest amounts to patients. (Extra-billed fees were often substantial; my own ophthalmologist extra-billed 100 percent, thus nullifying the insurance protection. I know of a gynecologist who billed $750 for an operation for which the patient was reimbursed at the OHIP rate of $250.) In Nova Scotia, approximately 53 percent of doctors extra-billed; and in Alberta about 47 percent (Edmonton, 55 percent; Calgary, 62 percent), adding about $9 million to physicians' incomes. It was estimated by Health and Welfare Canada that the total of extra-billing charges approximated $100 million in 1983. The CMA argued that this added about 2 percent to the total cost of physicians' services. This aggregate figure is, of course, irrelevant. The central question is the impact of a specific extra charge on a specific patient or family.

While the practice of extra-billing had been criticized by consumer groups since the beginning of Medicare, the rapid surge in the number of doctors extra-billing following the ending of income controls in 1978 brought public discussion to fever pitch in the federal election of 1979. As we have seen, one of the first actions to be taken by Health Minister Crombie was to appoint the Hall Health Services Review. Before Hall could report, the Clark government was defeated, and during the ensuing election campaign the former health minister Monique Begin spearheaded the attack on extra-billing and user fees and vowed to end both practices on the Liberals' return to power.

Reinstated in the Health Ministry and supported by the 1980 Health Services Review judgment that extra-billing, if allowed to continue, would create an unacceptable two-tier system, Begin continued her criticism of the system and of the provinces that permitted it. There appears not to have been strong support in the cabinet, especially during the period of negotiations on the new Constitution, but the proposed policy was given substantial impetus, as we have seen, by the recommendations of the all-party parliamentary task force in August 1981.

The angry reactions of the provincial governments, and particularly by the ministers of health in British Columbia, Alberta, and Ontario, were matched only by the vehement outcries of spokesmen for the CMA and its provincial divisions. Massive publicity and lobbying campaigns were launched by all the medical associations, and Dr. Marc Baltzan of Saskatoon (whose father had been one of the two doctors on the RCHS that had recommended Medicare in 1964), during his term as president of the CMA, became almost as prominent a media figure as Mme. Begin herself.

Senior officials of Health and Welfare Canada had begun preparation of a position paper, at the request of the minister, shortly after her return to office. The first draft was discussed with provincial health ministers in Ottawa on May 26, 1982,[17] and a second draft with them in Vancouver on September 30, following which the provincial ministers issued a press release stating that the provincial governments would consider challenging the constitutional authority of the federal government to pass such legislation.[18] The battle lines were now drawn.

The confrontation escalated throughout 1983 as hyperbolic rhetoric flooded the news media. On the one side were the Liberal party and the government with their frontline spokesperson the minister of health. They were championed by the federal NDP, provincial Liberal and NDP parties, consumer and health coalitions, and senior citizens associations. On the other side were most of the provincial ministers of health and the national and provincial medical associations. Not since the issue of Medicare itself in the mid-1960s had there been such voluminous coverage in the media and such a torrent of editorials and letters to the editor.

What is surprising is that the affluent were not speaking out. A study by the Economic Council of Canada, using data collected during the census of 1976, revealed that the lowest 20 percent of income earners received two and a half times as many medical and hospital services as the top 20 percent. But the bottom 20 percent contributed 1 percent of the cost of the two plans, while the top 20 percent contributed 48 percent of the cost; indeed, the top 40 percent of income earners contributed 73.7 percent of the cost of the two programs, and the lower 60 percent contributed 26.3 percent, while receiving (in dollar terms) 72.4 percent of services.[19] Thus, when an affluent patient was extra-billed, he or she was, in effect, being taxed twice to subsidize low-income patients, who constitute the bulk of the practice of the average physician, many of whose patients would, in the absence of the government programs, be able to pay only part or none of the physician's fees.

On July 25 Monique Begin issued the long-anticipated White Paper, *Preserving Universal Medicare*.[20] Its main theme was that Medicare was threatened by "growing and spreading" direct charges to patients. In a surprisingly low-key discussion, the paper examined, in turn, hospital user charges, extra-billing, federal and provincial health spending, and premiums financing in British Columbia, Alberta, and Ontario, where uninsured persons might not be entitled to insured services. It commented on the existing Hospital and Medical Insurance legislation, pointing out their inadequacy in defining "reasonable access" and that the penalty to a province not meeting the federal conditions of withholding the total federal cash contribution was too blunt an instrument. It concluded: "We cannot preserve Medicare by charging the sick; we cannot preserve Medicare by judging who is poor and who is not; we can only preserve Medicare by ensuring its basic principles."

The reactions were not unexpected, including unqualified condemnation by some provincial governments—"electioneering," "blackmail," "a poor example of federal-provincial cooperation," "will seriously damage the health care system." President Marc Baltzan of the CMA said that:

> The proposals do not begin to address the major problems of Medicare [which are] underfunding and worn out facilities. . . . It is an obvious backdoor intrusion into an area of provincial jurisdiction. . . . Ottawa cannot directly legislate how health care programs are financed and administered, so Mme. Begin plans to use Ottawa's fiscal leverage—some would call it financial blackmail—to force provincial governments to operate provincial health care programs according to the dictates of the federal government.[21]

The national and provincial health coalitions and consumer associations praised the document.

On December 13, 1983, the Canada Health Act was introduced in the House of Commons and given first reading. The reactions of provincial governments, medical associations, and health coalitions duplicated those of early summer. Following the Christmas recess, Bill C-3 was given second reading on January 16, 1984, and debate continued on January 17 and 20. It was then referred to committee, which held extensive public hearings— where all the old arguments, pro and con, were rehashed and widely reported in the media—and reported back to the Commons on March 21. It was passed by both House and Senate and proclaimed law on April 17, its financial sanctions to become effective July 1, 1984, although its other provisions became effective April 28.[22]

The Canada Health Act consolidated the Hospital Insurance Act of 1957 and the Medical Care Insurance Act of 1966 and defined more precisely the conditions upon which federal payments would continue. The five conditions were restated to be public administration, comprehensiveness, universality, portability, and accessibility. Since all provincial programs were publicly administered, that condition need not concern us here. The condition of universality was altered by requiring that 100 percent of residents, rather than the 95 percent required under the Hospital Insurance Act, be entitled to insured services; this provision affects only the three provinces requiring payment of premiums as a condition for entitlement to insured services. The conditions with respect to comprehensiveness were, in the main, restatements of the earlier legislation, but those respecting portability of benefits were tightened up.

The condition of accessibility was expanded by prescribing, for the first time, the procedures for negotiating payments to providers of insured services. The relevant section of the act reads as follows:

12(1) In order to satisfy the criterion respecting accessibility, the health care insurance plan of a province:

(a) must provide for insured services on uniform terms and conditions and on a basis that does not impede or preclude, either directly or indirectly, whether by charges made to insured persons or otherwise, reasonable access to those services by insured persons;

(b) must provide for payment for insured health services in accordance with a tariff or system of payment authorized by the law of the province;

(c) must provide for reasonable compensation for all health services rendered by medical practitioners or dentists; and

(d) must provide for the payment of amounts to hospitals, including hospitals owned and operated by Canada, in respect of the cost of health services.

(2) In respect of any province in which extra-billing is not permitted, paragraph 12(1)(c) shall be deemed to be complied with if the province has chosen to enter into, and has entered into, an agreement with medical practitioners and dentists of the province that provides:

(a) for negotiations relating to compensation for insured health services between the province and provincial organizations that represent practising medical practitioners or dentists in the province;

(b) for the settlement of disputes relating to compensation through, at the option of the appropriate provincial organizations referred to in paragraph (a), conciliation or binding arbitration by a panel that is equally representative of the organization and the province and that has an independent chairman; and

(c) that a decision of a panel referred to in paragraph (b) may not be altered except by an Act of the legislature of the province.

The most significant new stipulations are two: a province must provide reasonable compensation for *all* medically necessary insured health services, and the provinces are not required to adopt binding arbitration but, if they do, the decision of the arbitration panel cannot be altered by the government but must be approved by the legislature where, it may be assumed, the award would be intensely debated. The first provision had been added as a result of lobbying by the Canadian Professional Association of Interns and Residents in the hope that the requirement of compensation for all services would preclude the restriction of billing numbers (as British Columbia was then doing) to control physician supply. The second was added as a result of pressures from the CMA when it failed to block the measure altogether. It should be noted that the reference to dentists' services applies only to dental surgery in hospitals.

The act also contained procedures for providing information to the minister and for the minister to follow in the event of a province failing to meet any of the criteria. It also provided for the withholding from the cash payment to a province an amount equal to the total amount of extra-billing and the amount of user charges authorized by the province. Such deductions were to be accounted for separately in the public accounts; if extra-billing or user charges were eliminated within three fiscal years, the total amount deducted would be paid to the province.

Although the Liberal government's advocacy of the policy to ban extra-billing and user charges had been formally announced in the White Paper in July 1983, and the NDP's criticism of the practice had been known for years, many commentators believed that the Liberals, responding to public opinion polls strongly critical of extra-billing, had introduced the bill as a potential issue in the upcoming elections in the hopes of embarrassing the Conservative party and its new leader, Brian Mulroney, presumably trapped by the objections to the measure by so many Conservative provincial governments. But the unanimous vote in the House of Commons came as no surprise, for, ignoring the provincial governments and many Conservative supporters in the medical profession, Mulroney had announced his party's support for the bill in December. Dramatically, he had stated in the House of Commons on December 9, "As far as the Conservative party is concerned, Medicare is a sacred trust which we will preserve."[23] Quite clearly, extra-billing and the integrity of Medicare had been defused as an election issue favorable to the Liberals and the NDP, and it seems reasonable to assume that this highly publicized new position contributed to the Conservatives' overwhelming victory in September 1984.

Provincial Responses to the Canada Health Act

As noted above, the objective of the Canada Health Act was clear: to change provincial governments' behavior and to achieve that goal by imposing a penalty, the withholding of a dollar of transfer payments for every dollar doctors extra-billed or that was collected by hospitals in the form of user charges. But before examining responses to the Canada Health Act, it will be helpful to recall the two episodes involving Saskatchewan and Quebec and to examine anew the case of British Columbia in 1981—three occasions in which the issue of extra-billing had been confronted prior to the Canada Health Act.

In Saskatchewan, it will be recalled, the issue whether a physician could charge an additional fee at the time of rendering service was second only to the issue of whether there should be a government-administered program at all. During the strike, mediated by Lord Taylor in July 1962, when it became clear that the government would likely win on the major question, the price exacted by the profession was acceptance by the government of the right to extra-bill, or what was designated in the Saskatoon Agreement as Mode 3 billing. (Extra-billing in Saskatchewan was moderate, totaling $1.4 million in 1984 and dropping to $665,000 in 1985, compared with about $9 million in Alberta.)

The issues of opting out and extra-billing were at the heart of the specialists' strike in Quebec in October 1970. Claude Castonguay, the minister of health, had proposed a compromise: 3 percent of practitioners in each specialty and 3 percent of general practitioners in each of Quebec's administrative regions would have the right to opt out. But the government, caught in the crossfire between the specialists, who said it was not enough, and the opposition parties and trade unions, who said it was too much, provided in the final version of the legislation for three categories: *les engagés*, who opt in and collect their fees in full from the Quebec Health Insurance Board; *les désengages*, who opt out but agree to charge no more than the authorized fees to their patients, who would then be reimbursed in full; and *les nonparticipants*, who do not opt in, charge their self-determined fees, and whose patients are not reimbursed. Still adamantly opposed to the legislation, the specialists went on strike, only to be ordered back to work on pain of stiff penalties in the midst of the crisis brought on by the Front de Libération du Quebec, who had kidnapped the British trade commissioner, James Cross, and the minister of labor, Pierre Laporte, whom they later killed.[24]

In 1987 a total of 15,707 doctors were in category 1; only 7 (5 general practitioners and 2 specialists) were in category 2; and 29 doctors (15 general practitioners and 14 specialists) were in category 3.[25]

Prior to the Canada Health Act, only one other provincial government—that of British Columbia—had dealt with the issue of extra-billing, or as some provincial medical associations, including that of British Columbia, preferred to call it, balance-billing. Until 1981, extra-billing had posed no serious problem in British Columbia. Both profession and public had long experience with the large network of prepayment plans prior to Medicare which permitted no extra-billing, and there was keen competition in the lower mainland in what was generally recognized as an overdoctored area. But in 1981, with the BCMP benefit fee schedule lagging behind inflation and with the capture of the executive and presidency of the BCMA by the right-wing Medical Reform Group, negotiations for a new fee schedule were marked by explosive rhetoric, threats, work stoppages, and extra-billing in several cities in the interior.

The conflict reached a climax during the May 17–19 annual meeting of the BCMA in the city of Penticton, exacerbated by the coincidence of a closely contested by-election in the Penticton constituency, where the NDP had focused on the issue of extra-billing. In his banquet address to the BCMA, the Honorable Jim Neilson, minister of health, announced that legislation would be introduced to end balance-billing and that it might also become necessary to ration billing numbers (i.e., the right to bill BCMP for services to insured patients) in order to limit the number of doctors practicing in the lower mainland.[26] The audience broke out in a cacophony of catcalls, hisses, shouts, and footstomping that would have alarmed the stewards at a meeting of stevedores. (I was there as an observer.) Despite the hostile reaction, the legislation prohibiting extra-billing was passed, proclaimed on July 7, and made retroactive to April 1, 1981.[27]

So, prior to the Canada Health Act, three provinces had already dealt with the issue of extra-billing; one had accepted it as a price to be paid for a larger objective, and two had prohibited the practice outright. Other provinces had been warned of the strength of the profession's opposition. How did those confronting the problem respond to the Canada Health Act?

Nova Scotia

Nova Scotia was the first province to act on extra-billing, beginning its negotiations with the medical society shortly after the passage of the Canada Health Act. It was the province in which government-profession relations were perhaps the best in Canada. When Medicare was introduced, the profession-sponsored prepayment plan, Maritime Medical Care, became the designated administrative agency, overseen by a Medical Care Commission, responsible to the minister of health. Fee negotiations had normally been favorable to the profession, whose 1,430 members were among the highest paid in the country. Doctors were not required to opt out and could therefore bill the patient, the Medicare plan, or both. Extra-billing followed the pattern of other provinces in which doctors receiving the highest incomes from Medicare also extra-billed the highest amounts.

The negotiations were confidential, and on June 1, 1984, the government introduced enabling legislation to end the practice. But it also introduced a new procedure for settling disputes over fee negotiations, namely, "final offer" arbitration in which each side presents its final offer to an arbitration board which has power to choose one or the other offer, but not to decide on a compromise.[28] The ban became effective on July 1, 1984, so that Nova Scotia lost no funds in transfer payments from the federal government. In December 1984 a one-year contract and in 1986 a three-year contract were negotiated without recourse to arbitration. The peaceful resolution of the issue in Nova Scotia must have appeared a benign omen to Health Minister Begin in Ottawa, but not all the provincial decisions were to be so tranquil.

Saskatchewan

There was no doubt that in Saskatchewan the issue of extra-billing, returned to the public agenda by the Canada Health Act, would have to be renegotiated; both the government and the Saskatchewan Medical Association (SMA) viewed the clause in the Saskatoon Agreement authorizing Mode 3 billing as a moral commitment.[29] After several meetings with Health Minister Graham Taylor, the SMA decided to tie the issue of extra-billing to the annual negotiations on fee levels. Finally, on May 2, 1985, the minister announced that agreement had been reached. The accord was called Saskatoon Agreement II and provided for the right of physicians to opt out and bill patients directly, provided they did not charge more than the official fee schedule, or if the physicians did extra-bill, the patient would not be reimbursed.[30] (This arrangement followed the Quebec model.)

Manitoba

Manitoba and Ontario were the only provinces to require physicians to opt out of Medicare and bill directly all of their patients if they decided to extra-bill any of them. Opting out, therefore, carried the risk of unpaid bills if patients who claimed they could not pay at the time of receiving the service did not remit their reimbursement check to the physician. Unlike Nova Scotia's and Alberta's physicians, they did not have the option of billing the patient, the plan, or both. Prior to January 1985 the issue of extra-billing had appeared relatively minor, since only 75 of over 1,700 physicians had opted out. However, with the passage of the Canada Health Act, requiring provincial governments to provide information on the extent of extra-billing, it was revealed that extra-billing by the opted-out doctors was substantial.[31]

Long dissatisfied with the lengthy negotiations over fee increases (many referred to them as the "annual turkey trot"), the MMA was the second provincial association to take seriously the proposal of the 1980 Health Services Review that, in return for an end to extra-billing, fee negotiations should be subject to conciliation and binding arbitration, and for about two years had been urging its adoption on a reluctant government. Now the MMA strongly urged the trade-off. It was not unanimously supported by the membership, however. About ninety members, most of them Winnipeg specialists, had formed the Association of Independent Physicians (AIP), parallel to the counterpart AIP organization in Ontario, and regularly and vociferously attacked such a ban as destructive of professional freedom.[32]

Following confidential negotiations, in January 1985 the government and the MMA's board of directors jointly announced an interim agreement that included conciliation and binding arbitration, an increase in fees, and agreement to amend the act to require the Manitoba Health Services Commission (MHSC) to deduct MMA membership dues from its payments to all doctors—another divisive issue in the MMA.[33] With the AIP threatening legal action against the MMA executive unless a mail vote was taken, a referendum was agreed upon, and on July 15 the MMA released the results: 86 percent had voted in favor. But when the ensuing legislation was passed, it contained two unusual clauses in the section on binding arbitration. The arbitration panel "shall review prevailing economic conditions in Manitoba," and the amount of funds to be transferred from the government to MHSC to pay medical fees was to be tied "to the ability of the Manitoba government to fund said medical pay out."[34] But the legislative attempt to restrict the range of the arbitration panel's discretion was to no purpose, for the first occasion on which arbitration was resorted to, the award was so much higher than the increases granted by the government to teachers, civil servants, and hospital workers that the government withdrew from the agreement.

Ontario

Of all the provincial medical associations, the OMA produced the most clamorous verbal attacks on, and the most highly organized resistance to, the Canada Health Act, and ended up with a twenty-five-day strike against the

Ontario Health Care Accessibility Act. But as dramatic as the strike was, the extraordinary political events that preceded the episode and made passage of the accessibility act possible were even more unprecedented and surprising. Those events were briefly outlined in chapter 1: the defeat of the long-lived Conservative dynasty on June 18, 1985, by a majority of Liberals and NDP members, following the signing of an accord by the two opposition parties. In return for a commitment by the NDP to support the Liberals for a minimum of two years, the Liberals agreed to introduce legislation outlined in their joint Agenda for Reform. The third item on the agenda was legislation to meet the terms of the Canada Health Act.

The strands holding the Damocles sword of a ban on extra-billing had begun to fray. The OMA had now to think of the previously unthinkable, for there had been a sea change in the political climate surrounding the issues of health care in Ontario.

The OMA's leaders were not the exclusive voice of the profession; there were two other associations (almost all of them OMA members) speaking from diametrically opposed positions: the AIP, most of them opted-out specialists, with a membership peak of about 1,500, later reported to have declined to about 800; and the Medical Reform Group of about 160, who supported the Canada Health Act and attempted to counteract the shrillness of the OMA and AIP attacks on any attempts to curtail physicians' billing practices.

Pitted against the powerful OMA, with its $2 million war chest, and the militant and vociferous AIP was a formidable array of disparate groups supporting the government's position. First, of course, were the Liberal and NDP parties, buoyed by their recent victory over the previously indestructible Conservatives. Next was the Coalition of Senior Citizens Organizations, representing approximately 400,000 members, still flexing its muscles after contributing to the defeat of the federal government's move to de-index pensions. The third group, the Ontario Health Coalition, sparked by the Ontario Federation of Labor, was even larger, claiming to represent over 3 million health care consumers, although there was obviously substantial duplication in the numbers.

Central to the campaigns of both sides in the dispute were the print and electronic media, which daily chronicled the actions and statements of all parties. The influence of Toronto's two leading dailies—the *Globe and Mail* and the *Toronto Star*, both of which assigned a covey of reporters as well as editorialists and devastating cartoonists to the story—was especially great, in that both editorially supported the government's ban and criticized the doctor's strategy.

The Health Care Accessibility Act (Bill 94) was introduced in the legislature on December 20, 1985. Second reading took place on February 11, 1986, with a recorded vote of 60 (Liberals and New Democrats) to 40 (Conservatives). It was then referred to the Committee on Social Development, which held public hearings. Although the OMA had had almost two years since the passage of the Canada Health Act to plan its responses to any anticipated Ontario action, it was not until January 18, 1986, that the OMA's 250-member general council held its first strategy meeting. The outcomes were substantial rhetoric but few decisions on early action.[35]

On March 17, representatives of the CMA appeared before the committee. President Dr. William Vail stressed the threat to professional freedom embedded in the proposed legislation and reported that the CMA had launched legal proceedings to have the Canada Health Act declared in violation of the Canadian Charter of Rights and Freedoms, and therefore unconstitutional, and urged that Ontario's legislation not be passed until a determination had been made by the courts.[36]

On March 18 the AIP presented its case before the committee. Vice-president Dr. William Goodman made the most excessive attack yet leveled against the legislation. His brief said, "In the extreme, this legislation leads to state doctors like the notorious Mengele of the Nazi concentration camps and like the state psychiatrists in Russian political prisons." Both Dr. Goodman and president Dr. Joan Charbonneau said that they would break the law if it were passed because they believed in the principle of a doctor's right to decide what to charge patients.[37]

On April 10, after two postponements, the OMA finally made its presentation.[38] President Dr. Earl Myers said that because of the gap of approximately 24 percent (it was actually closer to 40 percent) between the OMA's official fee schedule and the OHIP's benefit schedule, "this legislation requires physicians, on pain of significant penalty, to surrender a substantial portion of their fees through their professional career as a subsidy to a government social program." (This assertion ignores the taxpayers' subsidy of physicians' incomes through the payment of their negotiated fees on behalf of low-income and indigent patients.) Dr. Hugh Scully, chairman of the OMA's council, emphasized the safety-valve function of extra-billing, in that it provided a civilized means of registering dissatisfaction with the government-administered system. The OMA's brief ended with a proposed compromise offer from Dr. Myers: "Specifically, the OMA promises an end to extra-billing of (1) all senior citizens, (2) all patients receiving public financial assistance, and (3) any patients requiring emergency treatment." It was the first time that the OMA had admitted that there were problems in the system arising from extra-billing. The proposal had apparently already been discussed in secret meetings between the OMA and government representatives. It was rejected by the latter on the grounds that it would retain a two-tier system and not meet the requirements of universality and uniform terms and conditions of the Canada Health Act.

There were also spokespersons, of course, of the public interest and consumer groups. Their positions have already been noted and need not be repeated here.

On April 19 the council of the OMA held its second strategy meeting, authorizing, first, a mass rally on May 7 before the legislative building at Queen's Park in Toronto and, second, a withdrawal of services by all Ontario physicians at the discretion of the president.[39]

The Conservative party under its new leader, Larry Grossman, minister of health and provincial treasurer in the former Davis government, found itself—in terms of public opinion, as Grossman admitted—on the wrong side of the issue. With the decisions of the OMA council for overt actions, the Conservative caucus had now to deal with the specifics. On April 25 Phillip Gillies told reporters that the caucus had decided that doctors should not be permitted to strike over Bill 94 and that, if services were withdrawn, the Conservatives would support back-to-work legislation.[40]

The first demonstration of professional solidarity was a large rally before the legislative building at Queen's Park in Toronto on May 7. Approximately three thousand physicians from all over the province attended in their white coats and responded enthusiastically to condemnatory and threatening speeches by OMA officials and their legal counsel. The most significant stratagem was the broadening of the perceived threats. Denial of the right to extra-bill would result in the loss of a powerful bargaining tool in fee negotiations. But there were more: the threat of capping incomes as in Quebec, the possibility of proration (reducing the level of fee payments to less than 90 percent), utilization controls being set arbitrarily, and redistribution of personnel and the limiting of billing numbers as in British Columbia.[41] These potential threats to professional autonomy undoubtedly persuaded many that they were defending more than the rights of the 12 percent who extra-billed.

There was one other factor that induced many general practitioners to come on board, namely, that the members of the executive of the General Practitioner section of the OMA made it clear to the specialists that the support of the former was linked to the OMA's reducing the income gap between general practitioners and specialists. And this the specialists agreed to do.[42]

The ultimate weapon—a provincewide strike—began on June 12, with claims of support ranging from 55 to 70 percent. On the fifth day of the strike, June 16, a large "pep rally," attended by about 1,300 doctors, convened in the Royal York Hotel in Toronto. Following rousing speeches, about half of these members converged on Queen's Park and stormed the legislative building, pushing security guards and leaping over crowd-control barriers. The evening television news featured these scenes of white-coated protesters, which few viewers had ever thought possible of their physicians.[43] It was an image that would blur only with time.

The next escalation was the closing of ten (later, fourteen) emergency departments in Metro Toronto hospitals. Paramedics and ambulances stood by to transfer patients to emergency wards that were still open. On the same day, the newly elected president, Dr. Richard Railton, at a press conference following a special meeting of council, announced that the strike would be carried into a second week and did not rule out the possibility of closing intensive care units and entire hospitals as a protest strategy.[44] On June 25 doctors at York County Hospital decided that they would withdraw all services, even in life-threatening circumstances. This prompted a letter to all licensed doctors from the College of Physicians and Surgeons warning that essential services must be maintained to avoid misconduct charges by the college.[45]

On July 4 the length of the strike equaled that of the Saskatchewan College of Physicians and Surgeons in 1962—twenty-three days. But that same day, Dr. Railton called off the strike, saying that it would end on the following Monday—after twenty-five days. There would be a shift in strategy to rotating strikes "to keep the fight alive" (which did not happen). At a press conference, Railton said that he did not blame the media entirely for the OMA's failure "to reach the public," but, he said, "that has been part of the problem."[46] (Indeed, there had been a number of letters to the editors of both the *Toronto Star* and the *Globe and Mail* accusing the media of bias against the OMA's stance.)

The ending of the strike brought on the typical postpartum depression. It was estimated by OMA spokesmen that the average general practitioner had lost eight thousand dollars in billings, and some specialists acknowledged that they had lost as much as twenty to thirty thousand dollars. It is difficult to know how much credence to give these estimated losses. Later figures released by OHIP indicated that the average doctor billed OHIP for only "between eight and nine percent fewer services in June than in May, 1986." Said Dr. Railton, "The toll has been great as far as costs are concerned, but

we all headed into the strike knowing that it was going to cost us money...
most are suffering now from the emotional let-down of losing. After running
on adrenalin for three weeks, there has been a tremendous ethical and
psychological drain."[47]

On July 4 the OMA had launched its long-promised court challenge of the
constitutionality of the law. On July 6 it was announced that the case would be
expedited by pairing it with the challenge earlier filed by the CMA against the
Canada Health Act. Premier Peterson announced that his government would
do everything possible to expedite the case.[48]

There were two epilogues to the strike, pronounced by Dr. Railton. The
first was an interview in which he was extraordinarily forthcoming and frank.
Commenting on the psychological impact of the withdrawal of services on his
membership, he said

> The anger and frustrations of the strike broke up friendships, mar-
> riages, and partnerships. There has been a tremendous ethical and
> philosophical strain on all the doctors because, by nature, doctors are
> very caring people. They don't like to feel that they have stranded any
> patient.... But we found as the strike grew, that was the only way we
> were going to get our point across. It was a strain on doctors and col-
> leagues, especially in the smaller communities. The doctors' place in
> society has changed. After this strike, some people will be disillusioned
> and disappointed, especially those who have put doctors on an impos-
> sible pedestal. I think that doctors will later return to being a highly re-
> garded group in society, but may not be put on an unnaturally high
> pedestal—they shouldn't be there anyway.[49]

But in an article under his byline written for the *Toronto Star*, August 11,
1986, entitled "The Ontario Medical Association Looks Ahead," Dr.
Railton's tone was entirely different, as if the article had been written by
someone else. It claimed a remarkable degree of public support "in the face
of the unlimited resources available to the government and the obvious bias
of the news media coverage in Toronto."

> The OMA intends to streamline its communications in the hope that
> we will be able to make our case more effectively. Ontario's doctors are
> not prepared to allow their professional freedom to go down the drain
> simply because a minority government has passed what we consider to
> be bad legislation. We intend to keep the issues alive through public
> education, rotating sanctions and any other means at our disposal. To-
> day's physicians believe we have a solemn duty to preserve the profes-

sional freedom that has been handed down from generation to generation for 5,000 years [?]. It is unthinkable to us that our profession's traditions, honored through the ages without benefit of legislation [the Medical Profession Act?], could be struck down in a modern society that has enacted a Charter of Rights and Freedoms.

What he clearly ignored was the reminder by Justice Hall in the report of the RCHS, and repeated in the report of the Health Services Review: "When the state grants a monopoly to an exclusive group to render an indispensable service it automatically becomes involved in whether those services are available and on what terms and conditions." It was disappointing that the article was not, indeed, a "Look Ahead" but rather a repetition of the rhetoric and a promise of continuing actions that had done more to damage respect for Ontario's medical profession than any other event in its history.

But only three years later it is heartening to record that there appeared to be a change in orientation in the attitudes and policies of the OMA. Under the new president, Dr. Hugh Scully, the OMA participated in the Health Review Panel appointed by Premier Peterson and concurred in its positive recommendations. Complaints by patients of extra-billing have been few, and their aggregate charges, reimbursed by the Ministry of Health, relatively minor. One can only hope that a new era of cooperation has begun.

Alberta

It was in Alberta that the strongest last-ditch battle by doctors against any attempt to ban extra-billing was expected. Extra-billing was more prevalent in that province than in any other, with an average of 43 percent of all doctors doing so in 1983. Especially critical in public discussions of the issue was the revelation in March 1985, by the president of the College of Physicians and Surgeons, that in 1984 over eight hundred physicians, or 24 percent, had violated the college's guidelines in extra-billing patients on welfare or those being subsidized in their health insurance premiums. While he said that the college continued "to strongly support balance billing as a fundamental and inalienable right of physicians," he added that the failure of some doctors to adhere to the guidelines had caused the college "unending grief." It was not that Alberta's physicians fared badly. *Taxation Statistics 1986* reported that Alberta's doctors had the highest average incomes among all the provincial medical associations in Canada.

Despite widespread public opposition to the practice of extra-billing, the right of the profession to do so was as fervently defended by the government as by the Alberta Medical Association (AMA). On February 23, 1984, Health Minister David Russell had informed the House of Commons Committee on Health that Alberta was quite prepared to accept the penalties, which would have amounted to as much as $14 million in 1983. "The erosion of Medicare is a myth," he told the committee. "The real threat to Medicare lies in Health Minister Begin's attempts to pass a punitive and damaging Health Act that reflects the move away from co-operative federalism to an arbitrary unilateralism that is not in the interest of Canada."[50]

At the annual meeting of the AMA in October 1984, the outgoing president, Dr. Neil Gray, vowed that doctors would not voluntarily surrender the right to extra-bill. "If it's going to go," he said, "it's going to be taken away."[51] But in Alberta, "the times they were a-changing," as the drop in oil prices devastated the economy. Alberta budgeted in fiscal 1986–87 for a deficit of $2.5 billion, and if extra-billing were not banned by March 31, 1987, Alberta would lose nearly $36 million in payments from Ottawa. In addition, public opposition to the practice, spearheaded by the Friends of Medicare (the Alberta division of the National Health Coalition), was increasing. Moreover, extra-billing had declined as the Alberta economy went into shock, from an average of 43 percent of physicians to 23 percent.

The strike by Ontario's doctors apparently brought the issue to a head, and discussions between the AMA and the new health minister, Marvin Moore, began in mid-June. On July 31 the minister announced the terms of the agreement. In addition to the ban on extra-billing, provision was made for increases in certain items in the fee schedule and for the procedure of binding arbitration in the event of dispute over fee negotiations. It also provided for the so-called Quebec option: a physician could opt out of the plan and charge any fee as long as the patient accepted the fact that he or she would not be reimbursed.[52]

There remained now only New Brunswick, where extra-billing and hospital user fees amounted in 1985 to about $142,000. The government waited until the last moment to escape the penalties, announcing on March 21 that agreement had been reached with the medical society that extra-billing would end on March 31, 1987.[53]

With the actions by the five provinces discussed above, the main objectives of the Canada Health Act—the banning of extra-billing and hospital user fees—spearheaded by Begin and supported by millions of Canadians, had been achieved. But the costs of rounding off the ragged edges of "universal accessibility" had been high in terms of political and social conflict, and of the morale and public image of the medical profession, as the action struck at one of the major tenets of the profession's belief system. One can only hope that time, the great healer, will again work its miracles and that lowering the temperature of rhetoric on both sides will lead to a rapid restoration of normal and harmonious relations between two interdependent groups—the profession and the public, represented by its governments.

Part Three

Future Directions

Chapter Ten

The Continuing Agenda

Having examined the Canadian health system in part 1, and its evolution in part 2, it is now desirable to shift our perspective from what has been accomplished in the past to major problems and opportunities that will confront Canadians in the future. Five major areas have been selected: cost containment, the aging of the population, the impending surplus of physicians, the shifting emphasis from sickness care to wellness, and the possibilities of introducing innovations in the health services delivery system. Obviously, this list is not exhaustive. Other problems include the rapid expansion of high technology, the increasing costs of malpractice litigation, the difficulties inherent in fee negotiations and hospital budget setting, and the unknown impact of the AIDS epidemic on health care resources.

Cost Containment

As in every other industrially advanced nation, in Canada containing costs within the health care system will remain the number one concern for the foreseeable future. Even though Canada has been one of the nations most successful in containing health care costs in the past two decades, nevertheless, health expenditures now account for up to one-third of provincial budgets. Moreover, the pressures for increased spending appear inexorable: the aging of the population, the expanding physician supply, the disincentives for efficiency inherent in the fee-for-service method of paying physicians, lack of incentives for hospital efficiency, breakthroughs in medical technology, and the difficulties of introducing potential innovations in health care delivery because of the "uniform terms and conditions" requirements of the Canada Health Act.

Although our primary concerns are the two programs of hospital and medical care, it will be helpful to place those expenditures in the context of total public and private health spending. Table 5 presents data on total health expenditures for the years 1975, 1981, and 1987. Overall health expenditures increased from $12.27 billion in 1975 to $47.93 billion in 1987. The proportion allocated to hospitals declined from 44.4 percent in 1975 to 41.1 percent in 1981 and 39.2 percent in 1987. The proportion allocated to physicians' services declined from 15.7 percent in 1975 to 14.9 percent in 1981 but increased to 16.0 percent in 1985. Overhead administration costs of the prepayment system dropped from 1.7 percent of the total in 1975 to 1.5 percent in 1981 and to 1.2 percent in 1987, or 2.4 percent of the costs of the two health insurance programs. (Cf. the approximately 12.5 percent for similar costs in the United States.)

However, to make interyear comparisons more meaningful, the table also presents the expenditures in terms of deflated dollars (1981 = 100.0). Even when expressed in constant dollars, the increases from 1975 to 1987 are dramatic (in total, an increase of 83.3 percent), far exceeding the 12.3 percent increase in population over the same period. Per capita spending, in constant dollars, increased from $891.80 in 1975 to $1,045.88 in 1981 (an increase of 17.28 percent) and to $1,447.91 in 1987 (38.44 percent increase over 1981). Although the share of the total expended on hospitals declined from 44.4 percent to 39.2 percent, nevertheless total expenditures by hospitals increased 62.2 percent, and for all other institutions (mainly due to the increase in long-term care facilities), 93.6 percent. Expenditures on physicians' services in constant dollars increased 87.3 percent, owing in part to an increase of 21.6 percent in physician supply. Some other increases were even more extraordinary: home care, 373 percent over the twelve years; ambulance services, 247 percent; and drugs and appliances, 138 percent. This latter increase is due, in part, to the fact that all provinces have drug programs for various groups and also subsidize the purchase of prostheses and wheelchairs.

The gap between Canada and the United States in the percentage of the GNP allocated to the health system—8.9 and 10.6 percent, respectively, in 1987—is of special interest. Professor R. G. Evans of the University of British Columbia has analyzed the contributing factors. He finds that with respect to hospitals it is the difference in "service intensity," i.e., the volume of more and more expensive technology.[1] During the period 1971–82, the volume of servicing per capita received by Canadians from the hospital system rose 0.6 percent per year, while in the United States it rose 3.7 percent annually. Over the eleven years the difference cumulated to 6.4 percent versus 48.8 percent. With respect to physicians, the difference is accounted for almost entirely by the difference in fees, which, after extraordinary increases in 1969–71 (when Medicare was introduced in Canada), during the eleven years 1972–82 actually declined relative to the general price level 2 percent per year on average, while fees in the United States were outstripping inflation by 1.4 percent per year. This difference of 3.3 percent per year cumulated over the period as a whole to 39.8 percent.[2]

The main explanation for the lower costs in the hospital sector is, as we saw in chapter 2, that the three major functions relating to the system are administered by one agency—the Ministry of Health. These functions are (1) hospital planning, including the location, size, and equipment of hospitals and the programs they offer; (2) determining the annual percentage increase to be granted for hospitals' global budgets; and (3) making the payments. In the medical sector, fee increases are negotiated between the medical association and the Health Ministry, with the Treasury officials much involved, and some provinces having recourse to binding arbitration.

Although it seems likely that the ability to control the acquisition of new technology on an orderly basis will continue, there is less reason to be optimistic about medical expenditures. The extraordinarily high incomes generated by the introduction of Medicare established a new norm for physicians' "target incomes." When annual fee increases following 1970 failed to keep pace with the rates of inflation, major confrontations between provincial governments and medical associations occurred, especially in 1981 and 1982, leading to unprecedented fee increases that in general have brought physicians' incomes approaching their high levels of 1969–70. But the pressures are building again, and as Manitoba's recent experience suggests, even the mechanism of binding arbitration may not provide the necessary resolutions.

We thus have the seemingly irresistible force meeting the immovable object. But the confrontations of the past are something that neither the profession nor the public can tolerate. Perhaps changes in the delivery system, such as U.S.–style health maintenance organizations (HMOs), may make a greater contribution to profession and public alike, a topic to be considered below.

Table 5.
Total Canada Health Expenditures, 1975, 1981, and 1987.

Category	1975				1981				1987[a]					
	Millions $	% of total	% of GNP	Con-stant $[b]	Millions $[b]	% of total	% of GNP	% In-crease 1981/1975	Millions $	% of total	% of GNP	Con-stant $	% In-crease 1987/1981	% In-crease 1987/1975
Total expense	12271.3	100.0	7.26	20249.7	26698.0	100.0	7.75	31.8	47934.7	100.0	8.90	37129.9	39.1	83.3
Personal health care	10699.7	87.2	6.33	17656.3	23162.7	86.8	6.72	31.1	42136.1	87.9	7.81	32638.3	40.9	84.8
Institutional	6730.7	54.8	5.98	11106.7	14383.6	53.9	4.17	29.5	24347.2	51.2	4.60	19014.1	32.2	71.2
Hospitals	5443.0	44.4	5.22	8981.4	10983.0	41.1	3.19	22.3	18808.0	39.2	3.52	14569.2	32.6	62.2
Other institutions	1194.0	9.7	.71	1978.4	3031.0	11.4	.88	53.2	4945.6	10.3	.93	3830.9	26.4	93.6
Home care	37.4	.3	.02	61.7	163.6	.7	.05	165.1	377.5	.8	.07	292.4	78.7	373.9
Ambulances	56.2	.5	.03	92.7	186.0	.7	.05	100.6	415.3	.9	.06	321.7	73.0	247.0
Professional services	2655.5	21.6	1.57	4382.0	5806.0	21.7	1.68	14.2	10933.3	22.8	2.05	8468.9	45.9	93.2
Physicians	1924.4	15.7	1.14	3175.5	3983.2	14.9	1.14	25.4	7678.8	16.0	1.44	5947.9	49.3	87.3
Dentists	596.6	4.9	.35	984.5	1500.3	5.6	.44	52.4	2609.6	5.4	.49	2021.4	34.7	105.2
Chiropractors	66.5	.5	.04	109.8	173.2	.6	.05	57.7	336.7	.7	.07	276.3	59.5	151.6
Optometrists	34.3	.3	.02	54.6	72.4	.3	.02	32.6	141.8	.3	.05	109.8	51.6	101.0
Podiatrists	13.3	.1	.01	22.0	21.8	.1	.01	– .1	36.3	.1	.01	20.1	– .1	– 9.5
Private nurses	13.9	.1	.01	22.9	15.2	.1	.01	– 50.6	26.0	.1	.00	20.1	32.2	40.6
Physiotherapists	5.1	.0	.00	8.5	38.4	.1	.01	351.7	82.8	.2	.02	64.1	66.9	687.0

Drugs and appliances	1313.6	10.7	.78	2167.4	2973.1	11.1	.86	37.1	6655.5	13.9	1.25	5155.3	73.4	137.8
Prescribed	578.7	4.7	.34	954.9	1307.1	4.9	.38	36.9	2821.0	5.9	.55	2105.8	61.1	120.5
Nonprescribed	532.5	4.2	.30	845.7	1099.9	4.1	.32	30.0	2731.1	5.7	.51	2315.5	110.5	173.7
Eyeglasses	170.1	1.4	.10	280.7	431.0	1.6	.13	53.5	838.2	1.7	.16	649.2	50.6	131.2
Hearing aids	14.8	.1	.01	24.4	31.0	.1	.01	27.0	48.0	.1	.01	37.2	20.0	52.4
Other appliances	37.6	.3	.02	62.0	104.2	.4	.03	68.0	216.4	.5	.04	367.6	252.8	492.9
Other health expenses	1571.6	12.8	.93	2595.3	3535.3	13.2	1.03	36.2	5798.7	12.1	1.09	4491.6	27.0	73.0
Prepayment admin.	209.6	1.7	.12	345.9	407.4	1.5	.12	17.7	578.3	1.2	.11	447.9	9.9	29.4
Public health	515.8	5.0	.31	851.3	1117.3	4.2	.32	31.2	2130.8	4.4	.40	1650.5	47.7	93.8
Capital expense	412.4	4.2	.36	1010.5	1409.4	5.3	.41	39.4	2132.4	4.4	.40	1651.9	17.9	63.4
Health research	100.5	.8	.06	165.9	245.5	.9	.07	45.0	411.5	.9	.08	316.6	28.9	90.8
Miscellaneous	133.2	1.1	.08	210.9	355.6	1.3	.10	68.6	545.7	1.1	.10	422.7	18.8	100.4

Source: Health and Welfare Canada.

[a]Provisional.
[b]Deflated in accordance with the implicit deflator of the GNP (1981 = 100).

The Changing Demographic Profile

Central to the future needs for and the costs of health services in all Western nations are the rates of growth of the total population and the demographic shift of the age groups within it, particularly, in Canada as elsewhere, in the rapid "graying" of the population—the increasing proportion of the elderly.

This phenomenon of a rapidly aging population has prompted a flood of reports by Statistics Canada, Health and Welfare Canada, government commissions and task forces, and individual academics. In 1983–84, the CMA appointed and financed the Task Force on the Allocation of Health Resources, which commissioned Woods Gordon, a management consulting firm, to analyze the likely effects of an aging population on the health care system. Its report provides probably the most extensive projections now available on the magnitude of the problems Canada faces in providing essential services for the elderly.

The analysts dealt first with population projections. Their high, medium, and low projections are shown in table 6, indicating that Canada's population in 2021 is likely to range between 29.3 and 32.9 million persons. But the most striking data are the projections on the proportion of the elderly.

In the census of 1981 those sixty-five and over represented 9.7 percent of the total population. Even more significant for the health and social services systems, those eighty years and over totaled 451,000, or 19 percent of those sixty-five and over. That number is projected to double by 2021, constituting by then almost one-quarter of the elderly. Those seventy-five and over now receive approximately three times as many days of hospital care as those sixty-five to seventy-four.

The analysts then calculated the effect of these projected changes on utilization in each of five health services areas, assuming that no changes are made in the status quo health services delivery system. Those projections are shown in table 7.

They then calculated what these increases would mean in terms of increased resources, on the assumption that current resources were in balance with demand in 1981. See table 8.

These projections were then translated into dollar amounts based on 1981 average per diem operating costs and construction costs, expressed in 1981 dollars. See table 9. Continuation of the present system would require a return to the high level of hospital bed construction characteristic of the high-flying 1960s. Almost one thousand 300-bed nursing homes would need to be built.

Table 6.
Projected Canadian Population to 2021 and Proportion of the Population Aged 65 or Over

	Total Population 2021 (millions)[a]	Percentage change 1981–2021	Annual Percentage Increase	Proportion 65 or over[b] 2001	2021
High	32.9	35.2	0.76	12.8	17.5
Medium	31.3	28.6	0.63	13.0	18.2
Low	29.3	20.2	0.46	13.2	19.0

Source: Woods Gordon Report.

[a] 1981 = 24.3 million.
[b] 1981 = 9.7 percent.

Table 7.
Projected Percentage Increases in Health Services Use, 1981 to 2021

Health service area	1981–2001 20 years	Annual	1981–2021 40 years	Annual
General hospitals	48.8	2.01	89.1	1.61
Long-term facilities	68.3	2.04	118.8	1.98
Mental health facilities	38.3	1.63	68.0	1.31
Physician services	27.2	1.21	45.0	0.93
Home care nursing visits	62.6	2.46	117.8	1.97

Source: Woods Gordon Report.

Table 8.
Projected Percentage Increases in Health Service Demand because of Demographic Change

Health service area	Resource	1981–2001	1981–2021
General hospitals	Beds	44	84
Long-term facilities	Beds	63	110
Mental health facilities	Beds	11	35
Physician services	Physicians	28	47
Home care nursing visits	Nurses	64	121

Source: Woods Gordon Report.

The task force concluded, "If we continue to put old people into institutions at the rate we do now, the costs will not only be prohibitive, we will perpetuate the callous practice of warehousing the elderly. . . . The thrust in the re-direction of health care resources undeniably needs to be in the development of community resources to keep the elderly out of institutions for as long as possible, not only to reduce costs, but to enhance the quality of life."[3] At the direction of the task force, Woods Gordon then tested four scenarios on its projected model: (1) reduce institutionalization from the current level of 9.45 percent to 6.00 percent (the U.S. level) and provide the released patients with home care; (2) reduce utilization of mental health facilities to the low level already achieved by Saskatchewan; (3) reduce the average length of stay in general hospitals by one day for the nonelderly patients; and (4) introduce nurse practitioners into the primary health care system to offset some of the future need for more physicians. This last recommendation will be difficult to implement, given the oversupply of general practitioners and adherence to the fee-for-service system. Scenario 1 would reduce the need for the construction of 65,000 hospital beds and 150,000 long-term beds. Total financial savings are estimated in table 10. To achieve the goal of deinstitutionalization would require, over the period to 2021, a sevenfold expansion of home care services.

At the colloquium "Aging with Limited Health Resources," sponsored by the Economic Council of Canada in Winnipeg, Manitoba, in May 1986, there were a number of outstanding contributions, two of which are especially relevant here. The first was by Professor John Horne, a health economist at the University of Manitoba.[4] He made several adjustments to the Woods Gordon scenarios.

Horne calculated that Woods Gordon had overestimated the number of nursing home residents who could be transferred back to the community and raised the nursing home target from 6 percent to 7 percent. He believed that Woods Gordon had overestimated the costs of long-term patients in hospitals and, therefore, the savings to be gained in transferring them to nursing homes. He believed that a similar miscalculation had been made in estimating the savings in transferring patients from nursing homes to the community, since most would be discharged from less-intensive care (and therefore less expensive) facilities.

Using data from Manitoba's ten-year program of home care, he similarly concluded that Woods Gordon had underestimated the costs of that type of service.

He pointed out that the Woods Gordon target of reducing the average hospital length of stay of the nonelderly had already been achieved in a number of provinces; indeed, if all provinces were to reduce the length of stay

Table 9.

Projected Operating and Construction Cost Increases by 2021

Health service area	Annual operating costs ($ million)	Capital construction costs ($ million)
General hospitals	7,100	17,700
Long-term facilities	4,300	12,400
Mental health facilities	380	360
Physician services	1,900	—
Home care nursing visits	43	—
Total	13,723	30,460

Source: Woods Gordon Report.

Table 10.

Financial Savings of Three Scenarios (1981 dollars)

	Savings from Status Quo Scenarios (by 2021)	
Scenario[a]	Annual operating costs ($ million)	Capital construction costs ($ million)
1—Elderly	5,900	16,300
2—Mental Health	225	360
3—Hospital use	630	370
Total	6,755	20,360

Source: Woods Gordon Report.

[a]In the fourth scenario, 2,700 physicians are offset by 2,700 nurse practitioners.

to those levels, the savings would be $340 million higher than the Woods Gordon estimate. He also believed that nationwide recourse to day surgery, short-stay obstetrics, early discharge programs, pre-admission testing, self-care units, and statistical discharge prompting systems could reduce hospital days of care by 30 percent.

Horne then added a fifth scenario, involving increasing the operational efficiency of hospitals. Horne supported the feasibility of savings through increased efficiency by reference to the extensive 1969 *Task Force Reports on the Cost of Health Services in Canada*, which had indicated potential savings of 10–30 percent by use of work study techniques and other recommended measures.[5] To be on the cautious side, Horne estimated cost savings of 7 percent, which would total $680 million.

Scenario 6 involved eliminating some marginally effective medical services. As he said, "This scenario is added to the list in recognition of the

Table 11.
Financial Savings from Status Quo Projections of Annual Operating Costs in the Year 2021 (1981 dollars)

Scenario	Woods Gordon ($ million)	John Horne ($ million)
1—Elderly	5,900	2,300
2—Mental health	225	225
3—Hospital use	630	1,700
4—Nurse practitioners	—[a]	630
5—Hospital costs	—[b]	680
6—Medical care	—[b]	450
Total	6,755	5,985

Sources: Woods Gordon Report; Horne, "Financial Savings."

[a]Not calculated.
[b]Not scenarioed.

growing literature indicating that some services are either ineffective or, more commonly, are used at rates in excess of those compatible with marginal effectiveness."[6] He cited studies of surgical procedures in Manitoba, the frequency of well-baby examinations and routine diagnostic technologies such as chest X rays, electrocardiography, and endoscopy. "The problem is the paucity of good evaluative studies that most bedevils provincial governments who are bound by their own health insurance statutes to pay for any service deemed medically necessary by a physician."[7] He selected an arbitrary figure of 10 percent to illustrate how important it is to improve the quality of evaluative studies in this area. The projected financial benefit of scenario 6 is $450 million in 2021.

Professor Horne summarized the potential savings in his revision of the Woods Gordon scenarios. See table 11. These various projections alert us to the magnitude of the shifting patterns of health care demands that Canada can expect to encounter in the decades ahead, and the scenarios suggest policy choices that Canadians can make if the political will is there to make them.

The other significant contribution at the colloquium in Winnipeg was that of Professor Noralou Roos and colleagues, reporting on their longitudinal studies of medical and hospital utilization by the aged in Manitoba.[8] Among their studies they have focused on the wide variation in surgical procedures and hospital admission rates across small areas and across physicians' practices. Their conclusions are constructive refinements of the nature and extent of the problems and add a new perspective.

It is not "the elderly" and it is not even "the very elderly" who are high users of health care services. The great majority of elderly individuals are healthy and infrequently hospitalized. Only a small segment of this population produces the statistics of concern to health care planners.

Hospital stays of elderly patients, particularly the very elderly, are much less likely to be resource intensive [i.e., expensive] than are the hospital stays of younger individuals. Elderly patients' hospital days are more likely to be spent in low-cost small hospitals, rather than in high technology teaching hospitals, and in lengthy stays [which include substantial amounts of custodial care] than are those of younger individuals.

Dying is a much more important factor than aging *per se* in the high usage of hospitals. For the elderly, as for the non-elderly, a dramatic increase in utilization occurs in a relatively short period before death [one year or less].

The elderly population's use of health care resources is strongly influenced by factors other than "need." *The availability of hospital beds, how physicians practise medicine, and the increase in physician supply over the next several decades will undoubtedly influence hospital consumption more than will the aging of society.* (emphasis added)

The results of these and related studies on high hospital utilization and on the idiosyncratic patterns of physicians' practices, combined with the impending surplus of physicians, reinforce the case of the advocates of a rationalization of the health services delivery system, if the needs of Canada's aging population—indeed, of all Canadians—are to be met adequately and economically. Clearly, Woods Gordon's and Horne's scenarios point in the right directions. Their contributions and those of a host of related studies have illuminated the debate that will inform effective public policy decisions.

Physician Surplus

As noted earlier, three factors contributed to Canada's physician supply: the error by demographers in forecasting the Canadian population for the royal commission in 1964, which led to the expansion of existing medical schools and the creation of four new ones, the unanticipated increase in doctors immigrating to Canada, and the failure of the predicted exodus of doctors following the introduction of Medicare. The consequence, as we have seen, is a physician-population ratio of 1:491 in 1988. The WHO has

Table 12.

Physician Supply, Requirements, and Surplus (Shortage), 1980 and 2000

Category	Physician Supply 1980	2000	Physician Requirements 1980	2000	Surplus (Shortage) 2000
General Practice	19,219	31,488	18,535	26,618	4,870
Medical Specialties	9,368	14,978	9,322	12,483	2,495
Surgical Specialties	6,506	7,225	6,286	8,219	(994)
Laboratory Specialties	2,574	3,282	2,696	3,621	(339)

Source: Health and Welfare Canada.

set an optimal target ratio of 1:650, lending credence to the perceptions of several provincial health ministries of a surplus in a number of metropolitan centers. The concern of provincial governments is the escalating volume of medical services provided by physicians—an average annual increase of approximately 2 percent—and their attendant costs. Canada is not alone, however. A report by the Graduate Education Medical Advisory Council projected a surplus of 70,000 physicians in the United States in 1990 and a surplus of 120,000 by 2000.[9]

Several provincial studies of medical manpower have been published, but since it is basically a national problem, the Conference of Deputy Ministers of Health established the Federal-Provincial Committee on Health Manpower in 1982. Its report was released in 1985.[10] It divided physician manpower into four categories: general practice, medical specialties, surgical specialties, and laboratory specialties, including nuclear medicine. Physician requirements were established, taking into account the increasing population (age-sex adjusted for a more elderly mix) and an increasing proportion of female physicians. (On average, female physicians provide fewer services.) See table 12.

To reduce the surplus, the Advisory Committee proposed a series of options that governments could consider, while emphasizing the short time available because of the numbers of students, interns and residents already in the pipeline. The committee noted four areas in which policy options are available.

Physicians from abroad. Each year an average of about 380 landed immigrant physicians enter Canada. Of these about 138 are "selected," or designated as filling a position that cannot be filled by a qualified Canadian, and the remaining 242 are sponsored relatives or refugee physicians. About 55 Canadian graduates of foreign medical schools per year return to Canada, and a further 183 foreign medical school graduates practice in Canada on temporary visas. The committee recommended that the number of selected immigrants be reduced from about 140 to 50 per year, that foreign medical graduates (including Canadian citizens) be reduced to 115 per year, and that the number practicing on temporary visas be reduced by 50 percent.

Postgraduate training positions. The committee recommended that the output from Canadian postgraduate training into the pool of general practitioners be reduced by encouraging trainees to proceed to surgical and laboratory specialties and that in addition there be a 20 percent reduction in output from Canadian postgraduate training of general practitioners and medical specialties. Even with such adjustments, the committee foresees a continuing surplus by the year 2000.

Medical school enrollment. The committee recommended that by 1986 the annual output from postgraduate training of general practitioners be reduced by 125 per year and that this number be reduced by an additional 20 percent in output from Canadian postgraduate training in medical specialties by 1994.

Distribution payments to physicians. In this area the committee recommended that effective measures be adopted to ensure that physicians establish their practice only in areas of demonstrated need for medical services. Their position is, in effect, the British Columbia policy of restricting billing numbers, discussed below.

These are drastic solutions with politically unattractive consequences: reducing opportunities for young people to pursue a medical career and reductions in medical training staffs, in internships, and especially, in residencies, which would place more responsibility on busy specialists. But the alternatives are also unattractive, since each physician adds $150,000–$250,000 annually to the provincial medical care bill for income, overhead, diagnostic tests, hospital admissions, prescriptions, and the like.

Only one province, British Columbia, has attacked head on the problems of physician oversupply and maldistribution, although several provinces have programs and incentives to attract physicians to rural and northern areas. In 1979 a committee, including members of the British Columbia College of Physicians and Surgeons and the BCMA, recommended "that in certain areas restrictions concerning the number of physicians billing the Medical Services Plan be considered as a means to temper the supply and maldistribution of physician manpower."[11] No action was taken.

In 1982 a second representative committee recommended that billing numbers be restricted. In 1984 the Provincial Medical Manpower Committee was created, including representatives of the BCMA, the College of Physicians and Surgeons, the British Columbia Health Association (mainly, hospitals), the Professional Association of Interns and Residents, and the Faculty of Medicine at the University of British Columbia. The committee issued a report, "Guidelines for Medical Manpower Plans," for use by local, hospital-based manpower committees and by regional manpower committees based on regional hospital districts.

Without legislative authorization the policy to limit billing numbers (i.e., the right to bill the BCMP for insured services) was introduced in September 1983. Approximately one-third fewer billing numbers were issued in the ensuing two years.[12]

On January 16, 1985, Dr. Mia Raza, a general practitioner, whose husband (a specialist) had settled in Kamloops, launched a suit in the Supreme Court of British Columbia challenging the British Columbia Medical Services Commission's decision to deny her a billing number. On March 21 the court ruled in her favor.

On May 5, 1985, the legislature passed the Medical Services Amendment Act, authorizing the commission to restrict billing numbers. On January 5, 1986, in another court challenge, the British Columbia Supreme Court ruled that the law did not violate the Charter of Rights and Freedoms and was therefore constitutional. Justice Lysyk compared doctors to other workers, saying, "In the public sector no one suggests that any level of government is obliged to hire civil servants or contractually retain the services of others beyond its perceived needs."[13]

But that was not the end. The decision was appealed in the British Columbia Court of Appeal, which overruled the supreme court and ordered the BCMP Commission to issue billing numbers to all applicants, despite the government's request that no numbers be issued, pending its appeal to the Supreme Court of Canada.[14] In August 1988 and the first week of September, over two thousand new numbers were issued, which deeply concerned the government about the additional costs that would occur.[15] Accordingly, the government appealed the decision to the Supreme Court of Canada, which in December 1988 refused permission to appeal the decision.[16] The implications for a rational medical manpower policy are serious indeed.

Shifting Emphasis from Sickness Care to Wellness

The enactment of the Hospital Insurance and Medical Care Insurance Acts in 1957 and 1966 represented the apex, in Canada, of the public's acceptance of the underlying foundation of modern medical practice—the biomedical disease model. As Dr. Norman White has defined it, the biomedical disease model "is a concept of sickness in which a strict linear causal sequence is followed from *cause* to *lesion* to *symptom* (or etiology to pathology to outcome)."[17] People were to be taxed to remove the financial barriers to access to their medical doctors and their hospital-based armamentarium of high technology. The two parliamentary decisions were the most widely supported social measures ever passed in Canada. The expectation was that after an initial rise in costs (to meet previously unmet needs), expenditures, like morbidity, would decrease. But despite the many extraordinary successes of modern medicine, ubiquitous faith in the biomedical disease model has begun to decline as costs and morbidity continue to grow. Doubling the proportion of the GNP allocated to the treatment system has not achieved a commensurate improvement in health status of the general population. To quote Dr. White again, "Despite increasing investment in ever-more sophisticated delivery systems and technologies, our general health status is not improving as we believe it should."[18]

The last two decades have witnessed wide-ranging searches for alternative approaches. A major new thrust occurred in 1974 with the publication of *A New Perspective on the Health of Canadians*, issued by the minister of health, the Honorable Marc Lalonde, based on research by H. L. Laframboise, director general of the Long Range Health Planning Branch, Health and Welfare Canada. Dr. Trevor Hancock, a public health specialist, has written: "The Lalonde report was the first modern government document in the Western world to acknowledge that our emphasis upon a biomedical health care system is wrong, and that we need to look beyond the traditional health care (sick care) system if we wish to improve the health of the public. The Lalonde report was followed by similar reports in Britain, Sweden, and the U.S.A."[19]

The Lalonde Report's main contribution was the outlining of a conceptual framework for the analysis and evaluation of the health field. It divided the field into four elements: human biology, environment, life-style, and health care organization. Based on extensive analyses of the causes of morbidity and mortality and of expenditures on facilities, professional education, and treatment services, the report concluded that Canadians had placed too much trust in the biomedical disease model, thereby overextending their health services organization to the neglect of biological research, environmental cleanup, and life-threatening life-styles.

The report has had an important, if not major, impact on attitudes and on the perspective from which the health care system is assessed. Although one cannot attribute recent advances directly to the report, there have been major legislative enactments at all levels of government, tightening up antipollution controls on industry directed especially to improving water quality and reducing acid rain. The inability to achieve a treaty with the United States on acid rain (it is estimated that 50 percent of acid rain falling on Canadian lakes, forests, and people originates in the United States) has been the Canadian government's most serious foreign policy failure, although under President Bush's administration there appears some reason for optimism. There has been a nationwide movement to regulate and curb smoking in public transportation, including airlines, and in public buildings and the workplace. (With a federal tax increase of $4.00 per carton of cigarettes in the April 1989 budget, the cost of a package of twenty-five cigarettes in most provinces is now over $4.00—indeed, in New Brunswick, as much as $6.25, or US$5.25.) And environmental issues were at the forefront in the national elections in 1988.

The move away from the biomedical disease model has received substantial support from the WHO. Its strategy for attaining the goal of "Health for all by the year 2000" is based upon the recognition that "Health does not exist in isolation. It is influenced by a complex of environmental, social and economic factors ultimately related to each other. . . . Action taken outside the health sector can have effects much greater than those obtained within it."[20]

"Healthy public policy," as the new approach is called, has been embedded more recently in the larger concept of health promotion. At a major international conference organized by the WHO and Health and Welfare Canada in November 1986, the *WHO Ottawa Charter for Health Promotion* was adopted. In it, health promotion is defined as "the process of enabling people to increase control over, and improve, their health." Five main approaches were proposed: building healthy public policy, creating environments supportive of health, strengthening community action, developing personal skills, and reorienting health services.

Health promotion has now been incorporated in federal government policy. In a document entitled *Achieving Health for All: A Framework for Health Promotion*, Health and Welfare Canada outlined a strategy that "complements and strengthens the existing system of health care."[21] The study outlined three *challenges*: (1) reducing inequities, in view of the fact that health status is directly related to economic status; (2) increasing the prevention effort, mainly by changing life-styles; and (3) enhancing people's capacity to cope with chronic conditions, disabilities, and mental health problems.

To meet these challenges, the document then proposed a set of health promotion *mechanisms*: (1) self-care, or the decisions and actions individuals take in the interest of their own health; (2) mutual aid, or the actions people take to help each other; and (3) healthy environment, or the creation of conditions and surroundings conducive to health.

These mechanisms, in turn, lead to three major *strategies* for health promotion: (1) fostering public participation to channel the energy, skills, and creativity of community members into the national effort to achieve health; (2) strengthening community health services which provide a natural focal point for coordinating services such as assessment, home care, respite care, counseling, and the valuable services of volunteers; and (3) coordinating healthy public policy. "All policies which have a direct bearing on health need to be coordinated. The list is long and includes, among others, income security, employment, education, housing, business, agriculture, transportation, justice, and technology." In conclusion, "The mutually reinforcing strategies taken together with the mechanisms, comprise the basic elements of the Health Promotion Framework. It is important to state that one strategy or mechanism on its own will be of little significance. Only by putting these pieces together, and setting priorities, can health promotion carry meaning and come alive. We believe the approach we propose allows us to respond effectively and ethically to current and future health concerns."

The federal initiatives have been matched by complementary actions among the provinces. In Ontario, for example, three separate task forces reported in 1987. The first, chaired by Dr. John Evans, later president of the Rockefeller Foundation, issued a report entitled *Toward a Shared Direction for Health in Ontario.*[22] The panel, which included representatives of the professions, the public, and the government, was obviously impressed by the concept of healthy public policy, for its main recommendation called for the "integration of government policy for health as the shared responsibility of many different Ministries whose programs and policies in the areas of occupational and environmental health, social welfare, housing, manpower training and research have a fundamental impact on the health of Ontario's population over and above the formal health care system." To achieve the necessary coordination the panel recommended the establishment of a "Premier's Council on Health Strategy," saying:

Such a prestigious agency would demonstrate the highest level of commitment to explore new ways of approaching health and health care. ... The Premier's participation would also demonstrate the commitment of the government to a concept of health which goes beyond the formal management of the health care system by the Ministry of Health. It would acknowledge that the health of Ontario's residents is influenced significantly by the broader social, economic and environmental policies and priorities of government as a whole.

The premier's council was created in 1988. Its membership includes the premier, the ministers of seven departments, and fifteen other distinguished citizens, including health professionals.

The second panel, chaired by Dr. Robert Spasoff, was called the Panel on Health Goals for Ontario and it complemented the Evans Report by citing a large number of specific goals for the province.[23] The third panel, chaired by a former Olympic athlete, Steve Podborski, issued its report, *Health Promotion Matters in Ontario*, after examining health promotion activities and potential in nine Ontario communities.[24] The panel's perception of a "bottom-up" rather than a "top-down" health system anticipates new roles for the Ministry of Health and new local partnerships on health promotion issues.

The concepts of wellness, health promotion, and healthy public policies are now well understood by all governments in Canada, but implementing them will be difficult. The Health and Welfare document *Achieving Health for All* observed, "Adjusting the present health care system in such a way as to assign more responsibility to community-based services means allocating a greater share of resources to such services." And there is the rub. Most of the needed resources must be allocated by provincial governments which, in the current vernacular, find themselves between a rock and a hard place. On the one hand is the decrease in transfer payments from the federal government under EPF; on the other hand is the inescapable financial commitment to an overbuilt hospital system and the rapidly increasing supply of physicians. It should be emphasized that what the advocates of healthy public policy are proposing is not an abandonment of our current treatment system—that would be folly—but a shift in emphasis made possible, in fact, by the availability and the quality of the treatment system that Canada has built.

Innovations in the Delivery System

There is one other major subject on the continuing agenda, made necessary by both the desire for improved quality of care and the demands of cost containment. The Canadian medical profession and Canadian governments can no longer ignore the revolution in the organization and delivery of health services in the United States that gained momentum in the 1980s and is forecast to accelerate in the decades ahead—namely, the burgeoning development of HMOs and of preferred providers organizations or, as they are sometimes called, independent practice associations. The generic term used to encompass the various types is alternative delivery systems.

The Canadian public medical care insurance system adopted the patterns of medical services delivery pioneered by the prepayment plans that the medical profession sponsored—mainly solo practice and fee-for-service payments. It is a wasteful and unnecessarily expensive system, with built-in incentives for overservicing and unnecessary surgery and hospitalization.

Although there are many group practices in Canada, there is only one HMO based on the U.S. model—the Group Health Clinic in Sault Ste. Marie, Ontario. Launched by the United Steel Workers union before Medicare, its subscribers now compose about one-half of the Sault's population. It receives its funds from the OHIP on a modified capitation plan called capitation-negation. Like HMOs, it receives a monthly capitation payment for each member on its roster, but if a member receives services outside the clinic which the clinic could provide, the clinic loses that month's capitation payment on behalf of that member.[25] There are two other comprehensive prepayment group practice clinics in Canada, both in Saskatchewan—the Prince Albert Community Health Center and the Saskatoon Community Health Center, but they are not paid by the capitation method.

In addition to the Sault Ste. Marie clinic, there are twenty-four other HSOs in Ontario, resembling HMOs in that they are paid by the capitation method, but they essentially provide only primary care. Total enrollment in Ontario HSOs in 1988 was just over 200,000. On average, Ontario HSOs use 16 percent fewer days of hospital care and the Sault's clinic 22 percent fewer than the population generally. They are eligible to receive an ambulatory care incentive payment in respect of this reduced utilization. There are also, in Ontario, thirteen community health centers (CHCs) with a total membership of 43,000. All are community sponsored, and their purpose is to provide primary care services in underserved, low-income communities. They are paid by OHIP on the basis of the programs they offer, rather than by the capitation method of the HSOs.[26]

But it is in Quebec that the most dramatic measures were taken to alter the system of providing primary care. The proposals were made in the first volume of the report of the Castonguay Royal Commission on Health and Social Welfare in 1967. With the election of the Liberals in 1970, Castonguay became the minister of health and began to introduce measures based on his own recommendations. Of chief interest here was the proposal to introduce local community service centers (CLSCs), where doctors, nurses, social workers and community organizers working together were to try to develop the new (social) medicine and be responsible for all the social and health needs of the community. Some seventy CLSCs were created, but the Quebec Federation of General Practitioners encouraged the creation of over four hundred private, traditional polyclinics in which physicians retained control. The results thus fell far short of the idealistic goals.[27]

In 1971 the Conference of Health Ministers (federal and provincial) requested a full investigation of CHCs under the direction of Dr. John Hastings of the University of Toronto. That report strongly recommended the development of payment systems other than the present form of fee-for-service, the creation by the provinces of CHCs, and their funding through global or block budgets.[28] The Hastings Report elicited much discussion but little action by the provinces.

In 1982 a second commission was appointed, this time by the new minister of health in Ontario, Larry Grossman. The chairman of the task force was Dr. J. Fraser Mustard, former dean of medicine at McMaster University.[29] It, too, endorsed CHCs and HSOs, and the minister stated that the ministry would support their development. As we have seen, not much happened.

But there are now welcome signs that the Ontario Ministry of Health is moving forward. Speaking to the Ontario Hospital Association in April 1989, the Liberal minister of health, Elinor Caplan, announced that the government would launch approximately six projects a year over the next three years. These would take the form of nonprofit corporations to be known as Comprehensive Health Organizations and would provide medical and other health services, including hospital care, and be paid by the Ministry on a capitation basis. Enrollment would be voluntary. She also announced that the OMA was cooperating fully with the ministry and that inquiries had come in from over thirty interested communities.

It has been posited that there are two times when change is possible. One is when there is a budget feast; then change can be bought. The other is when there is a budget famine, when change becomes inevitable. Perhaps, in this era of financial restraint, improvements in our health services delivery system—as good as we believe it be—can be made. Vision, political will, and cooperation among all the participants are the basic requirements.

Chapter Eleven

Conclusion

In the summer of 1974 a week-long symposium of the Sun Valley Forum on National Health was held in Sun Valley, Idaho, attended by thirty-nine participants, including seven Canadians. Its agenda was the Canadian health insurance system. The proceedings were published under the title *National Health Insurance: Can We Learn From Canada?*[1] The concluding section, "Implications for the United States," consisted of two parts: the first, a chapter written by Professor Theodore Marmor, addressed the question, Can We Learn from Canada? The second part was the symposium report "Implications for the United States," drafted by the rapporteur Richard Berman, which had been circulated for approval to the participants from the United States. The conclusions drawn from the Sun Valley Forum's examination of the Canadian health care system as of 1974 provide a logical and convenient point of departure for these final remarks.

In his introduction, Andreopoulos considered health care in various countries. Based on three criteria—the ratio of health professions to the total population, the extent of prepaid coverage, and the ratio of treatment facilities to the population—he concluded that "in hospital and medical insurance coverage Canada equals the best of the five countries [Australia, Denmark, Sweden, the United Kingdom, and the United States] chosen for comparison."[2]

These were welcome remarks, of course, but two following paragraphs were at odds with the facts.

The Canadian health plans took no steps to control the type, quantity, and quality of hospital services, and made no attempt to determine the number and types of doctors that would be needed to care for the population. Consequently Canada today [1974] has too many specialists and not enough primary doctors.

Because in Canada hospital insurance was started first, doctors were given an incentive to hospitalize patients whether they needed it or not. Every town and city was encouraged to build hospitals and to gain economically and socially from funds supplied by federal and provincial treasuries. With federal construction funds available and 50 percent of hospital costs guaranteed under hospital insurance, Canadian communities built more acute and general hospitals than they needed.[3]

These observations are largely incorrect. The Saskatchewan experience, where the HSPC was established two years before the hospital insurance program was launched, will be examined first. HSPC early appointed a medical doctor, a graduate of the University of Toronto program in hospital administration, as director of its Hospitals Division, which by 1948 had several nurse, technician, and accountant consultants to provide assistance and supervise standards. The province was divided into twelve health regions, each with a designated regional hospital. Regions were divided into districts, each with a designated district hospital. Other, usually small, hospitals were designated community hospitals. The entire system was based on the tertiary hospitals in the cities of Regina and Saskatoon. Bed-population ratios for each level of function and providing for referrals of patients requiring secondary or tertiary care were built into the formulas and strictly adhered to.[4] There was no encouragement to build "for economic and social reasons." It should be noted that the path-breaking 1944 Michigan Hospital Survey Report provided important guidelines.

In 1948, as part of its National Health Grants Program, the federal government provided matching grants of $1,000 per active treatment bed and $1,500 per long-term bed. But even with provincial matching contributions, local communities were still required to raise substantial funds.

The National Health Grants Program also included a nonmatching Health Survey Grant to enable provinces to assess their resources, calculate their needs for health professions personnel and hospital facilities, and plan for the introduction of health insurance. All provinces participated, and through regular meetings of provincial health survey directors with senior health officials in Ottawa, national resources and needs were known for the first time.[5]

In addition, when the national Hospital Insurance Act and its accompanying detailed regulations was passed in 1957, the concerns for rational planning and quality standards were clear: each provincial government must establish a hospitals planning division (several provinces already had one); it must license, inspect, and supervise hospitals and maintain adequate standards. And in the federal-provincial agreements which provinces must sign, the government was required to indicate explicitly how these requirements would be met. As an example of provincial responses, the Ontario Hospital Services Commission Act of 1956 set forth as the first responsibility of the commission, "To ensure the development throughout Ontario of a *balanced and integrated* system of hospitals and related health facilities."[6]

With the establishment of the commission, I was appointed consultant and director of research and immediately launched a massive hospital planning exercise. Fortunately, the annual returns of hospitals to the Ontario Department of Health contained the names and residence addresses of all patients, so that in developing a regionalized system based on the teaching hospitals associated with the five medical schools, the utilization rates and referral patterns of every community were known. Because of the lead time required to bring a hospital on-line and in view of the rapid population increases and expansion of suburban communities, close liaison was maintained with the research division of the Department of Municipal Affairs and with the planning departments of Ontario Hydro and Bell Telephone Company so that future hospital needs based on detailed population projections could be anticipated well in advance. The "Ontario Master Plan of Hospital Facilities" was completed in 1958 and presented to the Ontario Hospital Association at its annual meeting in November 1958. The whole process was directed "to having the right hospital facilities in the right place at the right time" and largely prevented duplication of facilities, technology, and programs. It has been recognized over the past two decades that, as a result of changing health needs, changing modes of treatment, improved transportation (including networks of ambulances and air-ambulances), and other factors, the original target of 5 beds per 1,000 was too high, and most provinces have taken steps to reduce their ratio of beds to population.

So, contrary to Andreopoulos's observations, all Canadian health ministries, prior to the introduction of their programs and continuing thereafter, had planning agencies in place to ensure a "balanced and integrated" regionalized hospitals system, with due emphasis on quality.

There is also reason to doubt the accuracy of the statement that Canada has "too many specialists and not enough primary physicians." In fact, the statement is somewhat confusing. In 1974 there were, of course, places where primary physicians were needed; there still are, even though overall, as noted in chapter 10, there is now a surplus. If the statement means that there are too many specialists in relation to the number of general practitioners, it should be noted that in the postwar period in Canada, in contrast to the United States, the numbers of specialists and general practitioners have been almost equal. As table 12 indicates, in 1980 there were 19,219 general practitioners and 18,448 specialists. In 1986 there were 24,770 general practitioners and 22,802 specialists.

Quality

On the issue of quality control, apart from the legal responsibilities of the health ministries to maintain standards, a number of activities are undertaken by the hospitals themselves, or their associations, to monitor and upgrade quality. Most, if not all, hospitals have quality assurance programs in place, as do many nursing homes. In addition, most of the provincial hospital associations mount large in-service training programs. And, of course, there is the Canadian Council on Health Facilities Accreditation. Until 1952 hospital accreditation in Canada and in the United States was under the aegis of the Joint Commission on Accreditation of Hospitals. In that year the CHA, the CMA, and the Canadian Nurses Association established the independent Canadian Council on Hospital Accreditation, which inspects and accredits public hospitals and many psychiatric hospitals owned by provincial governments. In 1987, as a result of the numbers of nursing homes and ambulatory care centers seeking accreditation, the name was changed to Canadian Council on Health Facilities Accreditation. The number of accredited hospitals increased from 254 in 1954 to 632 in 1987 and accounted for 91.7 percent of all beds, surely an indication of improving quality. It should be noted that the membership dues of hospitals in their respective associations, as well as the costs of the accreditation surveys, are accepted as operating costs by the health ministries and are therefore paid by the public.

One other reference in Andreopoulos's introduction needs correction. The phrase "with federal construction grants available" should read "with federal and provincial construction grants available." And the balance of the sentence, reading "and 50 percent of hospital costs guaranteed," should read "and with 100 percent of hospitals' approved budgets guaranteed."

Professor Marmor grouped his comments in three categories: costs, access, and quality. I follow his outline here.

Costs

Hospitals

From 1975 to 1985 annual hospital expenditures increased from $5.560 billion to $15.912 billion, or from 3.34 to 3.45 percent of the GNP. Nevertheless, this represented a significant shift in funding, as the hospitals' share of total health spending fell from 45.8 to 40.6 percent. This shift resulted from a number of factors. First was the deliberate decision on the part of several health ministries to reduce the number of active treatment beds. In addition, many hospitals close some beds in the summer months to accommodate staff vacations. And in the last two or three years, some beds have been closed temporarily in intensive care units because of the shortage of highly qualified nurses. Another, more positive factor has been the extension of insured benefits to include nursing home and home care services, made possible, in part, by the introduction of the new Extended Care Grant by the federal government in 1977.

Physicians

As already noted, costs of physicians' services increased from $1.92 billion in 1975 to $6.25 billion in 1985, representing an increase from 15.7 percent of total health expenditures to 16.0 percent, as well as an increase from 1.14 percent of the GNP to 1.35 percent (about one-quarter of the rate of increase in the United States).

As Marmor indicated at the Sun Valley forum, "Disputes over physician incomes . . . have been among the most conspicuous of the postenactment politics of health care."[7] But obviously, such widely publicized disputes are inevitable when, as in Canada, the share of national income to be allocated to a profession is decided between the professional association and the government. As a recent article in the *New England Journal of Medicine* put it:

> In the United States the battles [for income increases] are fought in a myriad of private struggles between physicians and their employers, or their hospitals (or their competitors). . . . The general pattern is obscured. In Canada, by contrast, the struggle over shares of income between physicians and the rest of society is played out as large-scale public theater, with all the rhetorical threats and flourishes that political clashes require. . . . That system serves to focus and channel such conflicts and to bring them into the headlines, but it has also afforded Canadian physicians a greater degree of professional autonomy.[8]

Apart from lower fee schedules for medical services in Canada (although average net incomes are comparable), there are two other reasons for the lower per capita expenditures on physicians. One is the lower administrative costs in the doctor's office, since there is no need "for documentation by a multiplicity of insurers, as well as coping with the determination of eligibility, direct billing of patients and collections."[9] All resident patients are eligible, and all physicians' billings are sent to one provincial agency on standardized forms. In several provinces large clinics submit their accounts by computer, and in British Columbia all billings are now computerized.

The second reason is the much lower costs of malpractice insurance in Canada. In 1912 the CMA established the nonprofit Canadian Medical Protective Association, to which most doctors belong. Until recently all members were insured at a flat rate, but there are now six categories. The 1988 rates ranged from $950 for general practitioners who practice no obstetrics, surgery, or anesthesia, to $2,100 for general practitioners who do practice any one of these specialty services, to $6,600 for general surgeons, and to $9,800 for obstetricians and cardiovascular, orthopedic and neurosurgeons. The number of suits has remained stable: 906 in 1985, 895 in 1986, and 915 in 1987. But the awards in 1987 increased by 35 percent over 1986 to a total of $24.1 million.

Of course, the nonprofit administration accounts for only a small part of the difference in the malpractice experience of Canada and the United States. More important are three other factors: (1) Canadians appear in general to be a less litigious people than their southern neighbors; (2) lawyers are not retained on a contingency fee basis; and (3) hearings are held before a judge and not a judge and jury.

Access

Professor Marmor's concerns with respect to access were with the effects of national health insurance on utilization, especially in relation to income. There were available at the time of the Sun Valley conference three studies of the effect of the introduction of Medicare on utilization of medical and hospital services: the before and after studies of McDonald et al. and Enterline et al. of the impact on a selected sample of households in Montreal, and the studies by Beck in Saskatchewan.[10] As Marmor observed, "The [Quebec] studies shows not only an increase in the use of physicians by income groups under $5,000, but a decline in physician visits for income groups over $9,000" (p. 292). Beck found similar results: "Only the three lowest classes (i.e., no income, $1–$1,499 and $1,500–$2,499) displayed a general increase in contacts with hospitals over time. The remaining classes show a slight tendency to have less contact with hospitals over time."

In 1975 the Economic Council of Canada conducted a major survey, already referred to in chapter 9. That survey indicated that those in the lowest income quintile received two and one half times as many health services (measured in dollar terms) as those in the highest quintile. A more recent study was based on data accumulated during the Canada Health Survey in 1978–79.[11] Initially it was to have been a continuous monthly survey, but it was unfortunately canceled in a budget-slashing foray by the federal government in 1979.

Two types of questionnaires were administered to twelve thousand households. The first was an interviewer-administered questionnaire seeking information concerning family income, sociodemographic characteristics of each individual, and the health status of each family member. The second questionnaire, which was self-administered, included data on the individual's medical history, use of tobacco or alcohol, as well as the respondent's experience as a passenger or driver of a motor vehicle. In brief, the most significant findings were as follows:

The number of disability days, the number of current health problems, the respondent's medical history, and the number of accidents are among the most important and significant determinants of the use or nonuse of inpatient hospital care.

The results confirm the contention that the use or nonuse of inpatient hospital care by potential beneficiaries of the national health insurance program is independent of their economic status.

The findings are consistent with the contention that employed respondents incur higher opportunity costs when health services are used than non-participants in the labor force and that these costs reduce the propensity of the individual to use inpatient care.

The discriminant analysis suggests that an increasing supply of physicians significantly reduces the probability of the individual experiencing an episode of hospitalization during the year. Thus, these results are not only consistent with other studies but also with the contention that an improvement in the supply of physicians increases the number of patient-provider contacts which results in the early detection and outpatient treatment of conditions that would eventually require hospitalization during later and more severe conditions.

The size of the respondent's area of residence exhibited a negative and significant relationship with the use or nonuse of inpatient care. As a consequence, these results support the contention that, relative to smaller communities, the greater availability of alternate sources of care such as chronic and convalescent hospitals, nursing home and home care programs, in major cities and the other urban centers reduces the likelihood of the individual using inpatient care.

The results indicate that the family income of the respondent failed to contribute significantly to the discrimination of users from nonusers. . . . Hence, these results are consistent with the proposition that the use or nonuse of services by individuals insured by the Medicare program is determined more by their health needs than by their family income.

Although the issue was not directly addressed in the survey, these conclusions suggest that there is a minimum of patient-initiated overuse of medical services.

In his two seminal works on systems analysis, David Easton defined the functions of government as being "predominantly oriented toward the authoritative allocation of values in a society."[12] Since competing values were at the heart of the conflicts that characterized the introduction of health insurance in Canada, it is worthwhile to remind ourselves just what some of those new values were. Among the most important are the following:

1. That health services be available to all Canadians on equal terms and conditions. Obviously, this is a value easier to legislate than to accomplish, given the still-prevailing, though less inequitable, maldistribution of physicians. But at least there is no longer a direct financial barrier to access to essential services.
2. That the indignities of the means test, with its accompanying harassment by municipal relief inspectors demanding reimbursement, no longer be imposed on the "medically indigent."
3. That the costs of health services for the indigent be assumed by the senior levels of government and not by municipal governments, where the heaviest burdens were likely to occur in municipalities least able to pay. The two programs thus ended three and one half centuries of Elizabethan Poor-Law tradition.
4. That the costs of health services no longer be borne primarily by the sick and the minority able to obtain voluntary insurance but by all income earners, roughly in accordance with their ability to pay.
5. That the "Robin Hood" function of equalizing health care costs to patients, performed in the past by physicians through the "sliding scale of fees" principle, be accomplished through the tax system.

6. That the programs be administered by public agencies accountable to legislatures and electors.

There are undoubtedly other values implicit in the programs, but these emerge as the most significant and represent a paradigmatic shift in Canadians' belief systems, influenced greatly by their collective experiences in the depression and two world wars.

As one reflects on the long political process that brought the two programs into being and recalls Graham Allison's observation that government policy-making is characterized by "compromise, coalition, competition and confusion among government officials,"[13] it remains remarkable how rational were the outputs of the political bargaining on health insurance. For the legislative acts were well-conceived means to predetermined ends and had a high degree of inner logic and consistency. As suggested in chapter 1, part of the explanation must lie in the fact that there are far fewer leverage points in the Canadian than in the American political system: one minister is responsible, and only one committee of Parliament, the cabinet, is ultimately responsible.

In thinking about the policy process, one is also impressed by the contribution to government policy decisions of dedicated and committed political leaders. Ian Mackenzie, Tommy Douglas, Paul Martin, Leslie Frost, Woodrow Lloyd, Walter Gordon, Judy LaMarsh, Lester Pearson, Monique Begin, and others used their positions of authority, influence, and power to make choices about alternative futures for Canada. They were assisted by similarly committed leaders like Stanley Knowles, not in positions of authority, but in the opposition, where they could inform, needle, prod, and criticize; or like Justice Hall, chairman of the RCHS, which reinforced the conviction that a national program was essential and that it should be publicly financed and administered. For several of them, the personal costs were high, but the values for which they fought were idealistic, humane, and compassionate, reducing risk and fear and expanding confidence, hope, and freedom.

Appendixes

Appendix A

Federal Social Security Programs

The federal government of Canada funds the seven social security programs described below. (In addition, provincial and territorial governments provide a variety of their own health and welfare programs that are not cost-shared by the federal government. For an example, see Appendix D.)

Old Age Security, Guaranteed Income Supplement, and Spouse's Allowance

Persons sixty-five or over may qualify for either a full pension or a partial pension, depending on their years of residence in Canada after reaching age eighteen. In 1989 the Old Age Security (OAS) pension was $330 per month, indexed to the Consumer Price Index (CPI).

An OAS pensioner with little or no income apart from OAS may, upon application, receive the Guaranteed Income Supplement, based on the pensioner's income in the preceding year. The maximum for a single person in 1989 was $392 monthly, also indexed. A married couple, both of whom are pensioners, may receive up to a maximum of $255.76 a month each.

The spouse of an OAS pensioner may be eligible for a spouse's allowance if that spouse is between sixty and sixty-five years of age. The amount of the allowance is subject to an income test on the basis of the couple's combined yearly income. The maximum spouse's monthly allowance in 1989 was $586, also indexed. No contributions are required for these allowances; they are paid out of the federal government's Consolidated Revenue Fund.

Canada Pension Plan and Quebec Pension Plan

The CPP covers all employees in nine provinces and the two territories. The Quebec Pension Plan (QPP) covers employees in Quebec. Employees pay 1.9 percent of contributory earnings, excluding the first $2,500 of earnings. The maximum earnings on which contributions can be made is $25,900. These contributions are matched by the employer. Self-employed persons contribute 3.8 percent on the same earnings range. Contributions are deductible for income tax purposes. Benefits are taxable. Benefits are increased annually to reflect increases in the CPI. The maximum monthly benefit in 1989 was $556.89. The CPP also provides disability and survivor's benefits. Contributions and benefits under the QPP are identical.

Family Allowances

A monthly FA is paid on behalf of a dependent child under the age of eighteen to a parent (usually the mother) who is a resident of Canada. Benefits are escalated annually by the excess of inflation over 3 percent. Provinces may, by agreement with the federal government, vary the monthly federal FA payable within that province, provided that (1) the allowance is based only on the age of the child, the number of children in the family, or both; (2) no monthly allowance is less than 60 percent of the current federal rate; and (3) total payments in a province with its own rates are, as far as is practicable, when averaged over four consecutive years, the same as if the federal rate had been in effect. Only Alberta and Quebec have entered into such agreements. Quebec also adds a provincial supplemental allowance. The 1989 monthly FA rate was $32.74 per child. Payments are made from the federal government's Consolidated Revenue Fund.

Canada Assistance Plan

Under agreements with the provinces and territories, the federal government shares 50 percent of the costs incurred by provinces and municipalities in providing:

assistance to persons in need;

welfare services to persons who are in need or likely to become in need unless such services are provided; and

work activity projects which are designed to improve the employability of persons who have unusual difficulty in finding or retaining jobs or in undertaking job training.

"Assistance" includes aid to persons in need for:

basic requirements, i.e., food, shelter, clothing, fuel, utilities, household appliances, and personal requirements;

items incidental to carrying on a trade or other employment (e.g., permits, tools, or other equipment) and items necessary for the safety, well-being, or rehabilitation of a person in need (e.g., essential repairs or alterations to property, items required by disabled persons);

certain welfare services (e.g., day care) purchased by, or at the request of, a provincially approved agency;

care in homes for special care (e.g., homes for the aged, nursing homes, child care facilities, and hostels for battered women and children). Since April 1, 1977, the major portion of federal costs related to long-term residential care for adults has been subsumed under the Extended Health Care Services Program of the Federal-Provincial Fiscal Arrangements and Federal Post-Secondary Education and Health Contributions Act (see chapter 9); and

certain health care costs (e.g., drugs, dental care) if they are not covered under universal health care programs of the provinces.

"Welfare services" mean services having as their object the lessening, removal, or prevention of the causes and effects of poverty, child neglect, or dependence on public assistance and include:

day care services for children;

homemaker, home support, and similar services to support individuals and families in emergency situations or as an aid to independent living in the community for the elderly and the disabled;

casework, counseling, assessment and referral services (includes services for children who are in need of protection because of abuse or neglect and preventive services to children in their own home); adoption services;

rehabilitation services, including services to the chronically unemployed (e.g., life skills training, retraining and job-placement services) and services to meet the special needs of persons at risk of being socially isolated, with particular emphasis on the aged and mentally disabled;

community development services designed to encourage and assist members of deprived communities to participate in improving the social and economic conditions of their community;

consulting, research, and evaluation services with respect to welfare programs; and

administrative services relating to the delivery of assistance and welfare services programs.

New Horizons Program

The primary goal of the program is to alleviate loneliness by making available contributions to groups of older, retired persons to plan and organize community-based activities of their own choice and design. Programs must be nonprofit in nature. Funds are not available for salaries to project directors or participants or for travel.

Projects funded since 1972 may be grouped into the following categories of activities:

sports, fitness and recreation,
social integration,
arts and crafts,
historical,
service oriented,
media/information,
performing arts and entertainment,
educational,
organizational, and
research.

Vocational Rehabilitation of Disabled Persons Program

Under agreements with all provinces and territories except Quebec,[1] the federal government contributes 50 percent of costs incurred by the provinces and territories in providing a comprehensive program for the vocational rehabilitation of physically and mentally disabled persons. Eligible clients are physically or mentally disabled persons who are considered capable of attaining a level of functioning which would enable them to pursue a substantially gainful occupation.

Services to individuals under a comprehensive vocational rehabilitation program include:

assessment;
counseling;
restorative services;
provision of prostheses, wheelchairs, technical aids, and other devices;
vocational training and employment placement;
provision of books, tools, and other equipment required during the
    course of the vocational rehabilitation process; and
provision of maintenance allowances on an individual needs basis.

Unemployment Insurance

About 95 percent of all workers in Canada are protected by unemployment insurance (UI). To be insurable, workers must be employed by the same employer for at least fifteen hours a week or must make at least $106 a week. Neither the self-employed nor workers over sixty-five can insure their earnings.

To receive regular benefits a person must have worked in insurable employment for at least ten to fourteen weeks (the "qualifying period"). The number of weeks needed depends on the unemployment rate in the region where the claimant lives. Everyone on regular benefits must be able to work and be looking for another job. Claimants on regular UI who are taking training courses are the one exception. As well as regular benefits, UI pays special benefits to people who cannot work because they are sick, injured, quarantined, pregnant, or adopting a child.

Employers deduct workers' premiums from their pay and turn them over to the UI Account, along with their own contribution. In 1989 workers paid $1.95 for every $100 of insurable earnings; employers paid $2.73.

Appendix B

A Public Opinion Survey of National Health Programs in the United States, Britain and Canada, 1988

In late 1988, the editors of *Health Management Quarterly* requested Louis Harris Associates, in conjunction with the Harvard School of Public Health, to undertake a survey of public opinion in the United States, Canada, and Great Britain to ascertain the views of adults on the performance and desirability of their nation's health care systems. Tables 13–15 and the other information below are reproduced with the permission of the editor of *Health Management Quarterly*.

Table 13.
Three Health Systems: Comparative Facts

Facts	United States (mixed private and public)	Canada (government insurance)	Great Britain (national health service)
Population (000)	240,856	25,625	56,458
Per capita health spending	$1,926	$1,370	$711
Health as % of GNP	11.1%	8.5%	6.2%
Life expectancy	74.7	76.5	74.8
Infant mortality (per 1,000)	10.6	7.9	9.4

Table 14.
Three Nations Rate Their Own Health System

Evaluation	United States (%)	Canada (%)	Great Britain (%)
System requires fundamental change or complete rebuilding	89	42	69
System works "pretty well"—needs only minor changes	10	56	27
Not sure	1	2	4

Table 15.
Preference for an Alternative System

Country	Own system vs. American (%/%)	Own system vs. Canadian (%/%)	Own system vs. British (%/%)
United States	—	37/61	68/29
Canada	95/3	—	91/ 5
Great Britain	80/12	59/28	—

The following figures indicate the percentage of Americans in different categories who would prefer the Canadian system of health care.

Insurance	61
No insurance	62
Executives	67
White-collar workers	59
Unskilled labor	60
Low income	58
Middle income	68
Upper income	56
Did get needed care	58
Did not get needed care	80
Satisfied with care	57
Dissatisfied with care	83

Citizens of the respective countries responded as follows to the three questions below (figures show percentages):

1. Which of the following statements comes closest to expressing your overall view of the health care system in your country?

	United States	Canada	Great Britain
On the whole, the health care system works pretty well, and only minor changes are necessary.	10	56	27
There are some good things in our system, but fundamental changes are needed to make it work better.	60	38	52
Our health care system has so much wrong with it that we need to rebuild it completely.	29	5	17
Not sure.	1	1	4

2. If the government were to spend more money on only one of the following, which one would you want the money spent on?

	United States	Canada	Great Britain
Defense	9	3	1
Education	34	29	12
Health care	24	28	56
Housing	12	16	8
Social security	20	21	21
None/not sure	1	3	2

3. Overall, how do you feel about the health care services that you and your family have used in the last year?

	United States	Canada	Great Britain
Very satisfied	35	67	39
Somewhat satisfied	45	27	37
Somewhat dissatisfied	11	4	11
Very dissatisfied	7	1	4
Not sure	2	1	9

Appendix C

A Chronology of Comparative Events Relating to Health Insurance in the United States and Canada, 1910–1987

Chronology

Canada

1914–19	Beginnings of municipal doctor and municipal hospital plans in Saskatchewan
1919	Adoption of health insurance plank in national Liberal party platform British Columbia government appoints commission of inquiry into health services
1928–34	Three committees of inquiry in Alberta
1929	British Columbia government appoints second royal commission; program recommended in 1932 report
1935	Alberta Health Insurance Act passed but never proclaimed British Columbia Health Insurance Act passed Canada Employment and Social Insurance Act passed
1936	Employment and Social Insurance Act ruled unconstitutional
1937	British Columbia health insurance program aborted

1940	Report of the Royal Commission on Dominion-Provincial Relations
1942	Federal health minister appoints Interdepartmental Committee on Health Insurance; submits report on health insurance for Canada
1943–44	House of Commons Special Committee on Social Security
1944	Saskatchewan Health Services Act
1945–46	Dominion-Provincial Conference on Post-War Reconstruction; federal government health insurance proposals presented; proposals rejected by provinces
1947	Saskatchewan Hospital Services Plan
1948	National Health Grants Program (public health, mental health, tuberculosis, etc., and hospital construction)
1949	British Columbia Hospital Insurance Service
	Alberta-subsidized municipal hospital services program
	Newfoundland cottage hospital system
1958	National hospital insurance program
1962	Saskatchewan Medical Care Insurance program
1964	Report of the Royal Commission on Health Services
1968	National medical care insurance program
1974	Lalonde Report, *A New Perspective on the Health of Canadians*
1977	Established Programs Financing Act; block funding replaces 50–50 cost sharing
1980	Report of the Health Services Review
1981	Parliamentary task force report on fiscal federalism paves way for Canada Health Act
1984	Canada Health Act
1987	All provinces in compliance with Canada Health Act; no user fees in hospitals; no extra-billing by doctors

United States

1910–15	American Association for Labor Legislation (AALL) achieves workmen's compensation laws in thirty states
1912	AALL forms Social Insurance Committee, advocating medical care insurance and including three leading members of the American Medical Association
1916–18	Health insurance bills introduced in sixteen state legislatures; none is passed
1920	American Medical Association passes resolution declaring its

opposition to "compulsory contributory insurance against illness"

1922   Sheppard-Towner Act, providing grants-in-aid to states for maternal and child health programs

1928–32   Committee on the Costs of Medical Care publishes twenty-eight reports on health issues; final report recommends group practice and that the costs be covered on a prepayment basis through the use of insurance, taxation, or both.

1934   Committee on Economic Security appointed by President F. D. Roosevelt

1935   Social Security Act (health insurance excluded for fear of endangering act as a whole)

1937   Formation of Blue Cross Hospital Service Plan Commission; continuing expansion of Blue Shield plans and of commercial insurance coverage

1938   National Health Conference, Washington, D.C.

1939–47   Succession of congressional bills: Wagner, 1939; Capper, 1941; Eliot, 1942; Wagner-Murray-Dingell, 1943 and 1945; Taft, 1947

Health insurance supported by President Truman

1945   Governor Earl Warren introduces health insurance bill in California legislature; Warren Bill is opposed by CMA and defeated

1948   National Health Assembly, Washington, D.C. Oscar R. Ewing, federal security administrator, issues report, *The Nation's Health: A Ten Year Program*

1949–64   Various bills introduced in Congress: Flanders-Ives Bill, King-Anderson Bill, Forand Bill, and Kerr-Mills Act; all opposed by American Medical Association

1965   King-Anderson Bill (H.R. 1 and S. 1) reintroduced

President L. B. Johnson signs Medicare bill in presence of President Truman in Independence, Missouri

1972   Amendments to Social Security Act establish professional standards review organizations

1973   Health Maintenance Organizations Act

1974   Health Planning and Resources Development Act

1977   President Carter's hospital cost containment bill

1983   Congress adopts prospective payment system for hospitals

1984   Congress adds Child Health Assurance Program to Medicaid

Appendix D

Provincially Funded Health Programs

In addition to the two major programs of hospital care and medical care insurance, funded jointly by the federal and provincial governments, all provinces fund additional programs, the basic one being a broad range of traditional public health services, to which municipal governments also contribute. Programs vary from province to province. The following listing is based on Ontario, where the population registered for the health insurance programs totaled 9,420,000 in fiscal year 1988–89.

Supplements to Medicare

Ambulance Services and Travel Grants

During the year a total of 4,554 patients were transferred by the province's air ambulance fleet; another 10,378 patients were carried on chartered and scheduled airlines. Land ambulances responded to 1,137,257 calls. A total of 58,600 northern health travel grants, amounting to $9.4 million, were issued to people needing specialized medical and hospital services outside their communities.

Ontario Drug Benefit Program

Free prescription drugs are available to all senior citizens, people on social assistance, home care patients, and residents of extended care facilities and homes for special care. Total cost in 1988–89: $684 million.

Assistive Devices

This program pays 75 percent of the costs of such assistive devices as wheelchairs, prostheses, artificial eyes, and hearing aids. For the very needy, several voluntary agencies pay the balance.

Nursing Homes

In contrast to hospitals, almost all of which are operated on a not-for-profit basis, most of the 339 nursing homes are proprietary. Nursing home care is an insured service but patients must pay part of the costs. Since most patients receive Old Age Security, they are permitted to retain a substantial part of the pension for personal spending. In 1988–89 operating funds from the Ministry of Health to nursing homes amounted to $395.1 million.

Psychiatric Hospitals

Psychiatric care is also an insured hospital service.

Insured Professional Services Benefits

Medical	$3,539,867,569
Dental (mainly children and the elderly)	7,266,654
Optometric	67,577,073
Chiropractic	74,584,882
Osteopathic	250,047
Chiropody	5,968,610
Physiotherapy	25,716,925

Source: Ontario Ministry of Health, *Annual Report 1988–89.*

Notes

Preface

1. Andreopoulos, *National Health Insurance: Can We Learn from Canada?*, p. 2.
2. Ibid., p. 231.

Chapter One

1. The objection to senators as cabinet ministers is that senators cannot be admitted to the House of Commons and therefore cannot appear during the daily question period to respond to questions about the activities of their departments.
2. On rare occasions the prime minister may appoint an outsider, but the appointee must be elected in a by-election within three months, which means finding a safe constituency seat, perhaps by appointing an incumbent member to an administrative agency or a judgeship.
3. There was an active Social Credit movement in California during the mid-thirties, led by Luther Whiteman and based in San Francisco. When he found that Social Credit could not compete with the Townsend movement, he joined Townsend. For further details, see my M.A. thesis, "The Social Credit Party of Alberta."
4. It should be noted that, in contrast to the U.S. Constitution, in Canada the "residual powers" are allocated to the federal government.
5. Shortly after the November 1988 elections, a newly elected Conservative M.P. died. The ensuing by-election saw a member of the Alberta Reform party elected who had a strong commitment to Senate reform.
6. Smiley, *Canada in Question: Federalism in the Seventies*, p. 63.

Chapter Two

1. Canada, Interdepartmental Advisory Committee on Health Insurance, *Report*.
2. Canada, Royal Commission on Dominion-Provincial Relations, *Report*, pp. 42 and 36.

3. Canada, Dominion-Provincial Conference on Post-War Reconstruction, *Plenary Conference Discussions*.

4. In his budget address on May 17, 1989, Ontario treasurer Robert Nixon announced that OHIP premiums would be abolished on December 31 and replaced by a payroll tax commencing January 1, 1990. See Ontario Legislature, *Debates*, May 17, 1989.

5. Canada Health Act, S.C. 1984, C.6.

6. Federal-Provincial Conference, 1965, *Proceedings*, p. 17.

7. This act was named in 1986 as the Federal-Provincial Fiscal Arrangements and Federal Post-Secondary Education and Health Contributions Act, 1977.

8. Readers may be interested in the results of a public-opinion poll conducted by Louis Harris and Associates in 1988 comparing public attitudes toward the health care systems in the United States, Canada, and Great Britain. See appendix B.

Chapter Three

1. Beveridge, *Social Insurance and Allied Services*; Canada, (Heagerty) Advisory Committee on Health Insurance, *Report*; Marsh, *Report on Social Security for Canada*.

2. Kelly, Arthur D., "Early Prepayment Plans."

3. Ibid.

4. The main source for this section is chapter 10, "The Evolution of Health Insurance in Canada," of the *Report of the Royal Commission on Health Services* (Ottawa: Queen's Printer, 1964). As consultant to the commission, I drafted that chapter, basing the period to 1949 on my Ph.D. dissertation, "The Saskatchewan Hospital Services Plan." A more detailed review of this early period is now available in C. D. Naylor, *Private Practice, Public Payment*.

5. Naylor, *Private Practice, Public Payment*, p. 41.

6. Rorem, *The Municipal Doctor System in Rural Saskatchewan*.

7. Saskatchewan, Saskatchewan Health Survey Committee, *Report*.

8. Taylor, "Saskatchewan Hospital Services Plan."

9. Ibid.

10. Munroe, "Health Insurance and the Medical Profession," *Canadian Medical Association Journal*, 1112–14.

11. Blackader, "Presidential Address," *Canadian Medical Association Journal* 7 (July 1917): 585–89.

12. Hastings, "The National Importance of Health Insurance."

13. "In Brief," *Canadian Medical Association Journal* 7 (May 1917): 448–49.

14. Taylor, "Saskatchewan Hospital Services Plan," p. 15.

15. *Victoria Daily Colonist*, November 10, 1919.

16. *Globe and Mail*, August 9, 1919.

17. *Victoria Daily Times*, January 20, 1920.

18. British Columbia, Royal Commission on Health Insurance, *Report*.

19. Canadian Medical Association, *Report of the Committee on Economics*.

20. Public Archives of British Columbia files.

21. British Columbia College Council, "Brief to Health Insurance Committee," *Canadian Medical Association Journal* 34 (February 1936): 206.

22. *Victoria Daily Times*, April 2, 1936.

23. Ibid., January 9, 1937.
24. Taylor, "Saskatchewan Hospital Services Plan."
25. Employment and Social Insurance Act, S.C. 1935, C.1.
26. *Attorney General for Canada* v. *Attorney General for Ontario* (1937) A.C. 326.
27. Canada, Royal Commission on Dominion-Provincial Relations, *Report.*

Chapter Four

1. Ian Mackenzie to Mackenzie King, December 27, 1939, King Papers.
2. Canada Advisory Committee on Health Insurance, *Report*, pp. xi–xxii.
3. Order-in-Council P.C. 836, February 5, 1942.
4. Beveridge, *Social Insurance and Allied Services.*
5. Marsh, *Report on Social Security for Canada.*
6. Canada, Interdepartmental Advisory Committee on Health Insurance, *Report.*
7. Ian Mackenzie to Mackenzie King, January 8, 1943, King Papers.
8. Canada, Department of Finance, Economic Advisory Committee, *Report on Health Insurance Proposals*, January 20, 1943.
9. Ian Mackenzie to Mackenzie King, January 20, 1943, King Papers.
10. Canada, House of Commons, Special Committee on Social Security, *Minutes of Proceedings and Evidence, 1943.* The verbatim *Proceedings* were issued daily while the committee was in session and will not be further cited.
11. Canadian Medical Association, Special Meeting of General Council, *Transactions*, January 18–19, 1943, mimeographed.
12. Ibid.
13. House of Commons, Special Committee on Social Security, 1943, *Proceedings*, p. 141.
14. Ibid., p. 366.
15. House of Commons, Special Committee on Social Security, *Report* (No. 82), July 23, 1944.
16. Ian Mackenzie to Mackenzie King, reporting on the meeting, August 19, 1943, King Papers.
17. House of Commons, Special Committee on Social Security, *Final Report*, July 28, 1944.
18. Claxton Papers, June 13, 1944.
19. Dominion-Provincial Conference, 1945, *Plenary Conference Discussions*, p. 7.
20. Ibid., p. 59.
21. Ibid., pp. 90–91.
22. Ibid., p. 119.
23. Mackenzie King Diary, May 3, 1946, King Papers.

Chapter Five

1. Agnew, *Group Hospitalization Plans in Canada.*
2. Shillington, *Road to Medicare in Canada.*
3. Joint Committee of the Canadian Insurance Industry, *Financing Health Services in Canada.*

Chapter Six

1. Saskatchewan, Health Services Survey Commission, *Report of the Commissioner*, October 4, 1944.

2. Statutes of Saskatchewan, 1944 (2d sess.), The Health Services Act, C.51.

3. For a discussion of this and other early social assistance health services programs in Canada, see Taylor, "Social Assistance Medical Care Programs in Canada."

4. T. C. Douglas, Address to the Saskatchewan Hospital Association, November 6, 1945, Douglas Papers.

5. *Regina Leader Post*, January 2, 1947.

6. Saskatchewan Hospital Services Plan, *Annual Reports, 1947–1951*.

7. Personal interviews with the minister of health, the Honorable George Pearson, and with senior BCHIS officials in 1947, 1948, and 1949.

8. *Vancouver Sun*, February–March 1951.

9. British Columbia Hospital Insurance Service, *Annual Report, 1951*.

10. Personal interviews with L. F. Detwiller.

11. *Vancouver Sun*, April 2, 1954.

12. Taylor, *Financial Aspects of Health Insurance*.

13. Ibid.

14. Canada, Dominion Bureau of Statistics, *Hospital Statistics, 1954*.

15. Canada, House of Commons, *Debates*, May 14, 1948, p. 3933.

16. The amount for public health research would increase over five years to $500,000.

17. Canada, House of Commons, *Debates*, May 14, 1948, p. 3933.

18. Taylor, "Government Planning."

19. Ibid., pp. 501–10.

20. L. G. Bernard, quoted in Thompson, *Louis St. Laurent*, p. 241.

21. Ibid., p. 242.

22. The main source for references to elections, including dates, results, and political party platforms, is Carrigan, *Canadian Party Platforms, 1867–1968*, and will not be further cited.

23. *Toronto Star*, July 13, 1949.

24. Canadian Medical Association, *Statement of Policy, 1949*.

25. Taylor, *Confidential Report on Health Insurance for the Government of Ontario, 1954*, mimeographed.

26. Ontario Legislature, *Debates*, March 23, 1955, p. 1144.

27. Federal-Provincial Preliminary Conference, 1955, *Proceedings*, p. 126.

28. Federal-Provincial Conference, 1955, *Proceedings*, p. 21.

29. Meeting of Federal and Provincial Ministers of Health and Finance, *Proceedings* (January 27–30, 1956).

30. House of Commons, *Debates*, January 30, 1956.

31. *Globe and Mail*, April 4, 1957.

32. Canadian Council on Health Facilities Accreditation, *Annual Report, 1987*.

Chapter Seven

1. Premier T. C. Douglas to Dr. J. L. Brown. This letter contained eleven "general principles [and] came to be regarded by the College as a virtual Magna Charta, setting forth its rights and the Government's commitment to them," Douglas Papers.

2. Howden, M.D., "The Swift Current Program."

3. Kelly, "The Swift Current Experiment," pp. 406–11.

4. For a review of the effectiveness of the political activities of the organized medical profession, see Taylor, "The Role of the Medical Profession." The article is also available in the Bobbs-Merrill Social Science reprint series.

5. McConnell, *Private Government and American Democracy*. See also Merriam, *Public and Private Government*; Gilb, "Professional Associations as Governments"; Lancaster, "The Legal Status of 'Private' Organizations"; and Lakoff, *Private Government*.

6. Registrar George W. Peacock to Premier T. C. Douglas, April 28, 1959, Douglas Papers.

7. T. C. Douglas to George W. Peacock, May 1, 1959, Douglas Papers.

8. Saskatchewan College of Physicians and Surgeons, "Resolutions," *Saskatchewan Medical Quarterly* 25 (4) (December 1959): 281–82.

9. Copy of radio address, Douglas Papers.

10. Council of the College of Physicians and Surgeons of Saskatchewan, *Statement of Policy*, March 2, 1960.

11. Ontario Medical Association, *Report to Council*, 1959.

12. G. W. Peacock to Health Minister J. Walter Erb, January 18, 1960, Douglas Papers.

13. *Regina Leader Post*, April 26, 1960.

14. *Toronto Star*, June 10, 1960.

15. *Interim Report of the Advisory Planning Committee on Medical Care* (September 25, 1961).

16. Statutes of Saskatchewan, 1962 (2d sess.), The Saskatchewan Medical Care Insurance Act, C.1.

17. See Badgley and Wolfe, *Doctors' Strike*, p. 40.

18. *Regina Leader Post*, January 6, 1962.

19. D. Tansley to George Peacock, February 8, 1962, Lloyd Papers.

20. H. D. Dalgleish to W. G. Davies, February 22, 1962. The term "civil conscription" had been used by the Australian High Court in declaring the Australian medical care program unconstitutional, but law professor E. A. Tollefson maintains that this argument is unfounded in the Canadian constitution. See Tollefson, *Bitter Medicine*.

21. W. D. Davies to H. D. Dalgleish, March 2, 1962, Lloyd Papers.

22. H. D. Dalgleish to W. G. Davies, March 16, 1962, Lloyd Papers.

23. W. G. Davies to H. D. Dalgleish, March 22, 1962, Lloyd Papers.

24. Statement of Premier Lloyd to meeting with college council, March 28, 1962, Lloyd Papers.

25. Council of the College, "Memorandum," April 4, 1962, Lloyd Papers.

26. *Regina Leader Post*, April 11, 1962.

27. Woodrow S. Lloyd, "Statement to the Saskatchewan Legislature," April 12, 1962, Lloyd Papers.

28. *Regina Leader Post*, May 3, 1962.
29. "Statement of Premier W. S. Lloyd to College of Physicians and Surgeons, June 22, 1962," Lloyd Papers.
30. *Regina Leader Post*, June 23, 1962.
31. Ibid., July 4, 1962.
32. Ibid., May 30, 1962.
33. *Ottawa Journal*, June 15, 1962.
34. *Toronto Star*, June 19, 1962.
35. *Regina Leader Post*, June 19, 1962.
36. *Winnipeg Tribune*, June 18, 1962.
37. *Canadian Medical Association Journal* 87 (July 21, 1962): 142–43.
38. *Globe and Mail*, June 15, 1962.
39. *Saskatoon Star Phoenix*, June 20, 1962.
40. "Notes of Meeting between Cabinet and the Council of the College of Physicians and Surgeons," June 22, 1962, handwritten notes taken by the premier's administrative assistant, Lloyd Papers.
41. *Regina Leader Post*, June 23, 1962.
42. *Canadian Press*, July 1, 1962.
43. *Canadian Forum*, July 9, 1962.
44. *Regina Leader Post*, June 3, 1962.
45. *Toronto Star*, July 4, 1962.
46. *Canadian Press*, July 9, 1962.
47. Badgley and Wolfe, *Doctors' Strike*, p. 65.
48. *Regina Leader Post*, July 20, 1962.
49. This section is based on personal interviews.
50. This section is based on a report by Lord Taylor entitled "Saskatchewan Adventure." It is a remarkable document on his role as mediator, expanded from a seventeen-page memorandum (now in the Lloyd Papers) he dictated just before leaving Regina in 1962.
51. *Regina Leader Post*, July 17, 1962.
52. Ibid., July 18, 1962.
53. *Saskatoon Star Phoenix*, July 18, 1962.
54. *Regina Leader Post*, July 18, 1962.
55. Ibid.
56. A. D. Kelly, "Saskatchewan Solomon," *Canadian Medical Association Journal* 87 (August 25, 1962): 416–17.
57. Ibid.
58. *Regina Leader Post*, July 23, 1962.
59. "Saskatoon Agreement," *Regina Leader Post*, July 23, 1962.
60. W. W. Wigle, "Saskatchewan Before, During, and After," *Canadian Medical Association Journal* 87 (September 8, 1962): 574–75.

Chapter Eight

1. National Liberal Federation, *Study Conference on National Problems*.
2. Report of Committee on Economics in *Transactions* of the Ninety-fourth Annual

Meeting of the Canadian Medical Association, June 19–21, 1960, p. 29.

3. Canada, House of Commons, *Debates*, December 21, 1960, pp. 1023–24.

4. Shillington, *The Road to Medicare*, p. 139.

5. Ontario Legislature, *Debates*, April 25, 1963, pp. 2766–83.

6. Royal Commission on Health Services, *Report*, vol. 1.

7. Excerpts from an editorial in the *Canadian Medical Association Journal* 86 (January 14, 1961): 116–17.

8. Canadian Medical Association, *Transactions of a Special Meeting of the General Council*, January 29–30, 1965.

9. LaMarsh, *A Bird in a Gilded Cage*.

10. Simeon, *Federal-Provincial Diplomacy*.

11. Personal interviews.

12. Personal interviews.

13. Denis Smith, *Gentle Patriot*, p. 215.

14. Ibid., p. 216.

15. House of Commons, *Debates*, April 5, 1965.

16. Canadian Medical Association, General Council, *Transactions*, 1965, p. 14.

17. Federal-Provincial Conference, 1965, *Proceedings*, p. 15.

18. Ibid., p. 16.

19. Ibid., pp. 29–30.

20. Ibid.

21. Ibid., pp. 29–74.

22. *Toronto Star*, February 10, 1966.

23. *Globe and Mail*, November 9, 1965.

24. Ibid., November 12, 1965.

25. Personal interviews.

26. *Toronto Telegram*, August 6, 1966.

27. *Globe and Mail*, September 8, 1966.

28. House of Commons, *Debates*, October 19, 1966.

29. *Montreal Gazette*, October 17, 1970.

Chapter Nine

1. Soderstrom, "Federal-Provincial Cost-Sharing."

2. Federal-Provincial Fiscal Arrangements Act, S.C. 1972, C.13.

3. House of Commons, *Debates*, June 23, 1975, p. 7026.

4. *Globe and Mail*, October 7, 1975.

5. Conference of Federal and Provincial First Ministers, *Proceedings*, June 14, 1976.

6. The Federal-Provincial Fiscal Arrangements and Established Programs Financing Act thus embraced three distinct elements: (1) the equalization concept; (2) federal sharing of the costs of hospital insurance, medical care insurance, and postsecondary education; and (3) continuation of the Revenue Guarantee. The concept of "established programs" had surfaced in 1965. In its demands for greater autonomy, Quebec had railed against the conditions embodied in the Hospital Insurance Act and demanded that the funds to which it was entitled should be transferred as "unconditional" income-tax points. This concession was agreed to by the federal

Liberal government on the assumption that the program was so "established" and popularly supported that federal standards would be maintained. The right to "contract out" of the shared-cost program was embodied in the Established Programs (Interim Arrangements) Act, 1965. Only Quebec exercised the option.

7. Interview with the Honorable David Crombie, September 13, 1986.

8. Hall, *Canada's National-Provincial Health Program for the 1980s*, p. 6.

9. Ibid., p. 27.

10. "Backbenchers" is the term applied to government party supporters who do not hold cabinet or parliamentary secretary offices.

11. Canada, Parliamentary Task Force on Federal-Provincial Relations, *Fiscal Federalism in Canada*, p. 115.

12. Ibid., p. 113.

13. Ibid., p. 114.

14. Canada, Department of Finance, *Amendments to the Federal-Provincial Fiscal Arrangements Act (Bill C-96), An Explanation* (Ottawa: The Department, 1986).

15. Canadian Medical Association, Task Force on the Allocation of Health Care Resources, *Health: A Need for Redirection.*

16. Ibid., p. 112.

17. *Globe and Mail*, May 27, 1982.

18. Ibid., September 30, 1982.

19. Boulet and Henderson, *Distributional and Redistributional Aspects of Government Health Insurance in Canada.*

20. Canada, *Preserving Universal Medicare.*

21. *Globe and Mail*, July 26, 1983.

22. Canada Health Act, S.C. 1984, C.6.

23. House of Commons, *Debates*, December 9, 1983, p. 44.

24. For a description of this most dramatic episode in the evolution of health insurance in Canada, see chapter 7 of Taylor, *Health Insurance and Canadian Public Policy.*

25. Quebec Health Insurance Board, *Annual Report, 1987.*

26. *Vancouver Sun*, May 19, 1983.

27. Ibid., July 8, 1981.

28. Statutes of Nova Scotia, 1984, C.50.

29. In the mid-1960s steps had been taken to separate the political functions of the College of Physicians and Surgeons, described in chapter 7, through the establishment of an independent Saskatchewan Medical Association.

30. Statutes of Saskatchewan, 1985, C.85.

31. *Medical Post*, June 26, 1984.

32. Ibid., January 8, 1985.

33. Ibid., January 22, 1985.

34. Manitoba Legislature, *Debates*, July 1985.

35. *Globe and Mail*, January 19, 1986.

36. *Medical Post*, March 25, 1986.

37. *Toronto Star*, March 19, 1986.

38. Ibid., April 11, 1986.

39. Ibid., April 20, 1986.

40. Ibid., April 26, 1986.

41. Ibid., May 8, 1986.
42. Ibid., March 5, 1986.
43. Ibid., June 17, 1986.
44. Ibid., June 18, 1986.
45. Ibid., June 26, 1986.
46. Ibid., July 5, 1986.
47. Ibid., July 6, 1986.
48. Ibid., July 5, 1986.
49. Ibid., July 7, 1986.
50. Ibid., February 24, 1984.
51. *Medical Post*, October 16, 1984.
52. *Edmonton Journal*, August 1, 1986.
53. *Toronto Star*, March 22, 1987.

Chapter Ten

1. Evans, "Illusions of Necessity." See also Alan Detsky et al., "The Effectiveness of a Regulatory Strategy in Containing Costs."
2. Evans, "Illusions of Necessity."
3. Canadian Medical Association, Task Force on the Allocation of Health Resources, *Investigation of the Impact of Demographic Change on the Health Care System in Canada* (Woods Gordon Report), p. 18.
4. Horne, "Financial Savings."
5. *Report of the Committee on the Costs of Health Services.*
6. Horne, "Financial Savings," p. 12.
7. Ibid.
8. Roos and Shapiro, "Aging with Limited Resources."
9. Ginzberg, *From Physician Shortage to Patient Shortage*, p. 3.
10. *Report of the Federal-Provincial Advisory Committee on Health Manpower.*
11. Black, *Report of the Joint Committee on Medical Manpower.*
12. Personal communication from the deputy minister of health.
13. *Globe and Mail*, January 6, 1986.
14. *P. S. Wilson and C. L. Mavson v. Medical Services Commission and Attorney General of British Columbia*, British Columbia Court of Appeal, Vancouver, April 5, 1988.
15. *Medical Post*, September 6, 1988.
16. Ibid., December 14, 1988. Critical of this judicial intervention in the legislative process, Professor Allan Hutchinson of York University's Osgoode Hall Law School said: "By intervening in the budgetary process of health care provision in such a partial way, the unelected judges blow their already tenuous cover. They not only invade the political terrain, but they usurp the function of our elected representatives in that area. Surely it is not the judges' business to second-guess legislators on the difficult choices in regulating health care costs" (*Toronto Star*, December 30, 1988).
17. White, "Future Models in the Health Field," p. 1.
18. Ibid., p. 2.
19. Hancock, "Beyond Health Care," p. 9.
20. Mahler, "Health 2000," p. 6.

21. Canada, *Achieving Health for All*.
22. Evans, *Toward a Shared Direction for Health in Ontario*.
23. Spasoff, *Health Goals for Ontario*.
24. Podborski, *Health Promotion Matters in Ontario*.
25. Lomas, *First and Foremost in Community Health Centres*. There is some confusion in Canada in the terminology used to describe these various types of organizations. Under new legislation, the Sault-Ste-Marie clinic will become a Comprehensive Health Organization.
26. Ontario Ministry of Health, *Annual Report, 1988*.
27. Renaud, "Reform or Illusion?"
28. *Report on the Community Health Center Project*.
29. *Report of the Task Force to Review Primary Health Care in Ontario*.

Chapter Eleven

1. Andreopoulos, *National Health Insurance: Can We Learn from Canada?*
2. Ibid., p. 3.
3. Ibid.
4. *Report of the Saskatchewan Health Survey Committee*. Regionalized planning began in 1945 and culminated in volume 2 of the *Report*, entitled *The Master Plan for Hospitals in Saskatchewan*. I served as research director and editor for the survey committee from 1948 to 1951.
5. Taylor, "Government Planning."
6. Statutes of Ontario, 1956, C.31.
7. Andreopoulos, *National Health Insurance: Can We Learn from Canada?*, p. 238.
8. Evans et al., "Controlling Health Expenditures—the Canadian Reality," p. 576.
9. Ibid., p. 573.
10. McDonald et al., "Physicians' Services in Montreal before Universal Health Insurance"; Enterline et al., "The Distribution of Medical Services"; Beck, "Economic Class and Access to Physician Services."
11. Manga, Broyles, and Angus, "The Use of Hospital and Physician Services."
12. Easton, *A Systems Analysis of Political Life*, and Easton, *A Framework for Political Analysis*, p. 5.
13. Allison, "Conceptual Models and the Cuban Missile Crisis," p. 708.

Appendix A

1. Although Quebec does not participate in the VRDP program, a significant portion of the costs borne by the province in providing goods and services to disabled persons is shared by the federal government under the CAP.

Bibliography

Ottawa, Canada
  National Archives
    Brooke Claxton Papers.
    Mackenzie King Diary.
    Mackenzie King Papers.
Regina, Saskatchewan
  Saskatchewan Archives
    Tommy Douglas Papers.
    Woodrow Lloyd Papers.

Books and Articles

Agnew, G. Harvey. *Group Hospitalization Plans in Canada.* Toronto: Canadian Medical Association, 1934.

Allison, Graham T. "Conceptual Models and the Cuban Missile Crisis." *American Political Science Review* 63 (3) (September 1969): 669–718.

Andreopoulos, Spyros. *National Health Insurance: Can We Learn from Canada?* New York: Wiley, 1975.

Badgley, F. R., and Samuel Wolfe. *Doctors' Strike.* Toronto: Macmillan, 1967.

Beck, R. G. "Economic Class and Access to Physician Services under Public Medical Care Insurance." *International Journal of Health Services* 3 (3) (1973): 341–55.

Begin, Monique. *Medicare: Canada's Right to Health.* Montreal: Optimum Publishing Co., 1987.

Beveridge, Sir William. *Social Insurance and Allied Services.* London and New York: Macmillan, 1942.

Blackader, A. D. "Presidential Address." *Canadian Medical Association Journal* 7 (July 1917): 585–89.

Blishen, Bernard. *Doctors and Doctrines.* Toronto: University of Toronto Press, 1969.

Boan, J. A., ed. *Proceedings of the Second Canadian Conference on Health Economics.* Regina: University of Regina, 1983.

Canadian Council on Health Facilities Accreditation. *Annual Reports.* Ottawa: The Council, 1954–87.

Canadian Medical Association. *Report of the Committee on Economics.* Toronto: The Association, 1934.

Canadian Medical Association. Ninety-fourth Annual Meeting. *Transactions.* June 19–21, 1960. Ottawa: The Association.

Canadian Medical Association. Special Meeting of General Council. *Transactions.* January 18–19, 1943. Mimeographed.

Canadian Medical Association. Special Meeting of General Council. *Transactions.* January 29–30, 1965. Ottawa: The Association.

Canadian Medical Association. Task Force on the Allocation of Health Care Resources. *Health: A Need for Redirection.* Ottawa: The Association, 1984.

Coburn, David, et al., eds. *Health and Canadian Society.* Toronto: Fitzhenry and Whiteside, 1987.

Deber, Raisa, and Eugene Vayda. "The Environment of Health Policy Implementation: The Ontario Example." In *Oxford Textbook of Public Health*, edited by G. Knox, 3:441–61. London: Oxford University Press, 1985.

Easton, David. *A Framework for Political Analysis.* Englewood Heights, N.J.: Prentice-Hall, 1965.

———. *A Systems Analysis of Political Life.* New York: Wiley, 1965.

Enterline, P. E., V. Salter, A. D. McDonald, and J. C. McDonald. "The Distribution of Medical Services before and after 'Free' Medical Care—the Quebec Experience." *New England Journal of Medicine* 289 (May 31, 1973): 1152–55.

Evans, R. G. "Illusions of Necessity: Evading Responsibility for Choice in Health Care." *Journal of Health Politics, Policy, and Law* 10 (3) (Fall 1985): 439–68.

Evans, R. G., et al., "Controlling Health Expenditures—the Canadian Reality." *New England Journal of Medicine* 320 (March 2, 1989): 571–77.

Evans, R. G., and Greg Stoddard, eds. *Medicare at Maturity.* Calgary: University of Calgary Press, 1986. Based on Proceedings of a Conference on Canadian Health Policy at Banff, Alberta, in 1984 which was modeled on the Sun Valley Forum of 1974 and attended by both American and Canadian participants.

Gilb, Corrine. "Professional Associations as Governments." In *Hidden Hierarchies.* New York: Harper and Row, 1966.

Ginzberg, Eli. *From Physician Shortage to Patient Shortage.* London and Boulder: Westview Press, 1986.

Gordon, Walter. *A Political Memoir.* Toronto: McClelland and Stewart, 1977.

Hancock, Trevor. "Beyond Health Care: From Public Health Policy to Healthy Public Policy." *Canadian Journal of Public Health* 76 (supplement 1) (May–June 1985): 9–11.

Hastings, Charles. "The National Importance of Health Insurance." *Canadian Journal of Public Health* 8 (November 1917): 308–9.

Heiber, S., and Raisa Deber. "Banning Extra-billing in Canada: Just What the Doctors Didn't Order." *Canadian Public Policy* 13 (January 1987): 62–74.

Horne, John N. "Financial Savings from a More Radical Approach to Alternative Delivery Methods by the Year 2021." *Colloquium on Aging with Limited Resources.* Ottawa: Economic Council of Canada, 1986.

Howden, C. P. "The Swift Current Experiment." *Saskatchewan Medical Quarterly* 13 (4) (December 1949).

Iglehart, J. "Health Policy Reports: Canada's Health Care System." *New England Journal of Medicine* 315 (3) (July 17, 1986): 202–8; 315 (12) (September 18, 1986): 778–84; 315 (25) (December 18, 1986): 1623–28.

Joint Committee of the Canadian Insurance Industry. *Financing Health Services in Canada.* Toronto: The Committee, 1954.

Kelly, Arthur D. "Early Prepayment Plans." *Bulletin of the History of Medicine* 28 (6) (November–December 1954).

———. "Saskatchewan Solomon." *Canadian Medical Association Journal* 87 (8) (August 25, 1962): 416–17.

———. "The Swift Current Experiment." *Canadian Medical Association Journal* 60 (3) (March 1948): 406–11.

Lakoff, Sandford. *Private Government.* London: Scott, Foresman and Co., 1973.

LaMarsh, Judy. *A Bird in a Gilded Cage.* Toronto: McClelland and Stewart, 1968.

Lancaster, Lane. "The Legal Status of 'Private' Associations Exercising Governmental Powers." *Southwest Social Science Quarterly* 15 (1935): 325–36.

Lindblom, Charles. *The Policy-Making Process.* Englewood Cliffs, N.J.: Prentice-Hall, 1968.

Lipset, S. M. *Agrarian Socialism.* Berkeley: University of California Press, 1950.

Lomas, Jonathan. *First and Foremost in Community Health Centers: The Center in Sault Ste. Marie.* Toronto: University of Toronto Press, 1985.

McConnell, Grant. *Private Government and American Democracy.* New York: Alfred A. Knopf, 1946.

McDonald, A. D., J. C. McDonald, N. Steinmetz, P. E. Enterline, and V. Salter. "Physicians' Services in Montreal before Universal Health Insurance." *Medical Care* 11 (1973): 269–80.

McHenry, Dean. *The Third Force in Canada.* Toronto and New York: Oxford University Press, 1950.

Mahler, H. "Health 2000: The Meaning of 'Health for All' by the Year 2000." *World Health Forum* 2 (1) (1981): 5–22.

Manga, Pran, R. W. Broyles, and D. Angus. "The Use of Hospital and Physician Services under a National Health Insurance Program: An Examination of the Canada Health Survey." 1981. Mimeographed.

Merriam, Charles E. *Public and Private Government.* New Haven: Yale University Press, 1944.

Mohamed, A. M. "Keep Our Doctors Committees in the Saskatchewan Medicare Controversy." M.A. thesis, University of Saskatchewan, Saskatoon, 1964.

Mott, Frederick D. "Hospital Services in Saskatchewan." *American Journal of Public Health* 37 (December 1947): 1539–44.

Mott, F. D., and Milton Roemer. *Rural Health and Medical Care.* New York: McGraw-Hill, 1945.

Munroe, A. R. "Health Insurance and the Medical Profession." *Canadian Medical Association Journal* 4 (December 1914): 1112–14.

National Liberal Federation. *Study Conference on National Problems.* Kingston, Ontario, September 1960. Mimeographed.

Naylor, C. D. *Private Practice, Public Payment: Canadian Medicine and Politics, 1911–1966.* Montreal: McGill-Queen's University Press, 1987.

Pickersgill, J. W., and Donald Forster. *The Mackenzie King Record, 1945–46.* Toronto: University of Toronto Press, 1970.

Roos, Noralou, and B. H. Shapiro. "Aging with Limited Resources: What Should We Be Worried About?" In *Colloquium on Aging with Limited Resources.* Ottawa: Economic Council of Canada, 1985.

Rorem, C. Rufus. *The Municipal Doctor System in Saskatchewan.* Publication no. 11 of the Committee on the Costs of Medical Care. Chicago: University of Chicago Press, 1931.

Rosenfeld, Leonard S. "Province-wide Hospitalization in Saskatchewan." *Public Affairs* 10 (June 1947): 157–63.

Shillington, C. Howard. *The Road to Medicare in Canada.* Toronto: Del Graphic, 1972.

Sigerist, Henry E. "Medical Care for All the People." *Canadian Journal of Public Health* 35 (July 1944): 253–67.

Simeon, Richard. *Federal-Provincial Diplomacy.* Toronto: University of Toronto Press, 1972.

Smiley, Donald V. *Canada in Question: Federalism in the Seventies.* Toronto: McGraw-Hill Ryerson, 1975.

———. *Conditional Grants and Canadian Federalism.* Toronto: Canadian Tax Foundation, 1963.

Smith, Denis. *Gentle Patriot: A Political Biography of Walter Gordon.* Edmonton: Hurtig, 1975.

Soderstrom, Lee. *The Canadian Health Care System.* London: Croom Helm, 1978.

"Symposium on Health Insurance." *Canadian Journal of Public Health* 8 (November 1917): 308–19.

Taylor, Malcolm G. *Administration of Health Insurance in Canada.* Toronto: Oxford University Press, 1956.

———. "Confidential Report on Health Insurance for the Government of Ontario." 1954. Mimeographed.

———. *The Financial Aspects of Health Insurance.* Toronto: Canadian Tax Foundation, 1958.

———. "Government Planning: The Provincial Health Survey Reports." *Canadian Medical Association Journal* 70 (February 1954): 204–9.

———. *Health Insurance and Canadian Public Policy.* Montreal: McGill-Queen's University Press, 1988.

———. "Program Design and Evaluation: The Ontario Hospital Services Plan." *Canadian Journal of Public Health* 50 (4) (April 1959): 136–43.

———. "Provincial Social Assistance Medical Care Plans in Canada." *American Journal of Public Health* 44 (June 1954): 750–59.

———. "The Role of the Medical Profession in the Formulation and Execution of Public Policy." *Canadian Journal of Economics and Political Science* 25 (February 1960): 108–27.

———. "The Saskatchewan Hospital Services Plan." Ph.D. dissertation, University of California, Berkeley, 1949.

Taylor, Malcolm G., Michael Stevenson, and Paul Williams. *Medical Perspectives on Canadian Medicare.* Toronto: York University, Institute for Social Research, 1984.

Taylor, Lord Stephen. "Saskatchewan Adventure." *Canadian Medical Association Journal* 110 (6) (March 1974): 725–30.

Thomas, Lewis. *The Youngest Science: Notes of a Medical Watcher.* New York: Viking Press, 1983.

Thompson, Dale. *Louis St. Laurent, Canadian.* Toronto: Macmillan, 1967.

Tollefson, E. A. *Bitter Medicine.* Saskatoon: Modern Press, 1964.

Van Loon, R. J. "From Shared Cost to Block Funding and Beyond: The Politics of Health Insurance in Canada." *Journal of Health Politics, Policy, and Law* 3 (April 1978): 454–78.

White, Norman F. "Future Models in the Health Field." Paper presented at the First Global Conference on the Future, Toronto, July 24, 1980.

Government Documents and Reports

Boulet, J., and B. Henderson. *Distributional and Redistributional Aspects of Government Health Insurance Programs in Canada.* Ottawa: Economic Council of Canada, 1979.

British Columbia. *Report of the Joint Committee on Medical Manpower.* Victoria: Ministry of Health, 1979.

British Columbia. Royal Commission on Health Insurance. *Report.* Victoria: King's Printer, 1932.

Canada. *Achieving Health for All: A Framework for Health Promotion.* Ottawa: Health and Welfare Canada, 1986.

Canada. *Preserving Universal Medicare: A Government of Canada Position Paper.* Ottawa: Department of Supply and Services, 1983.

Canada. *Report on Social Security for Canada* (Marsh Report). Ottawa: King's Printer, 1942.

Canada. *Report on the Community Health Center Project* (Hastings Report). Ottawa: Health and Welfare Canada, 1972.

Canada. Committee on the Costs of Health Services. *Report.* Ottawa: Health and Welfare Canada, 1969.

Canada. Dominion-Provincial Conference on Post-War Reconstruction. *Plenary Conference Discussions.* Ottawa: King's Printer, 1945–46.

Canada. Economic Advisory Committee. *Report on Health Insurance Proposals* (Clark Report). Ottawa: Department of Finance, 1943.

Canada. Federal-Provincial Advisory Committee on Health Manpower. *Report.* Ottawa: Health and Welfare Canada, 1985.

Canada. Health Services Review. *Canada's National-Provincial Health Program for the 1980s* (second Hall Report). Ottawa: Health and Welfare Canada, 1980.

Canada. House of Commons. Special Committee on Social Security. *Final Report.* July 23, 1944.

Canada. House of Commons. Special Committee on Social Security. *Minutes of Proceedings and Evidence.* Ottawa: King's Printer, 1943–44.

Canada. Interdepartmental Advisory Committee on Health Insurance. *Report* (Heagerty Report). Ottawa: King's Printer, 1942.

Canada. Parliamentary Task Force on Federal-Provincial Relations. *Fiscal Federalism in Canada.* Ottawa: Department of Supply and Services, 1981.

Canada. Royal Commission on Dominion-Provincial Relations. *Report.* Ottawa: King's Printer, 1940.

Canada. Royal Commission on Health Services. *Report* (Hall Report). Ottawa: Queen's Printer, 1964 (vol. 1); 1965 (vol. 2).

Conference of Federal and Provincial First Ministers, 1976. *Proceedings*. Ottawa: Department of Supply and Services, 1976.

Federal-Provincial Conference, October 1955. *Proceedings*. Ottawa: Queen's Printer, 1955.

Federal-Provincial Conference, 1965. *Proceedings*. Ottawa: Queen's Printer, 1965.

Federal-Provincial Preliminary Conference, April 1955. *Proceedings*. Ottawa: Queen's Printer, 1955.

Ontario. *Health Goals for Ontario* (Spasoff Report). Toronto: Ministry of Health, 1987.

Ontario. *Health Promotion Matters in Ontario* (Podborski Report). Toronto: Ministry of Health, 1987.

Ontario. *Toward a Shared Direction for Health in Ontario* (Evans Report). Toronto: Ministry of Health, 1987.

Ontario. Ministry of Health. *Annual Report*. 1988.

Quebec. Health Insurance Board. *Annual Report*. 1987.

Saskatchewan. Health Services Survey Commission. *Report of the Commissioner* (Sigerist Report). Regina: King's Printer, 1944.

Saskatchewan. Health Survey Committee. *Report*. Regina: King's Printer, 1951.

Index